Penguin Books
Money Made Us

Donald Horne is one of Australia's best known social critics. In the last twenty years he has done a lot of editing, including the Sydney *Observer, Quadrant* and the *Bulletin* (twice); he is now Senior Lecturer in Australian Politics at the University of New South Wales and a contributing editor to *Newsweek International.* He has contributed his own informed brand of analysis and interpretation to many magazines and newspapers, both foreign and Australian. Since writing *The Lucky Country* (a phrase which has passed into common usage, but not always with the author's intended ironies) he has written *The Permit, The Education of Young Donald, God is an Englishman, The Next Australia, But What If There Are No Pelicans? The Australian People* and *Death of The Lucky Country.* He is married with two children, and lives in Sydney.

DONALD HORNE

Money Made Us

PENGUIN BOOKS

Penguin Books Ltd,
Harmondsworth, Middlesex, England
Penguin Books Inc.,
7110 Ambassador Road, Baltimore, Maryland 21207, U.S.A.
Penguin Books Australia Ltd,
Ringwood, Victoria, Australia
Penguin Books Canada Ltd,
41 Steelcase Road West, Markham, Ontario, Canada
Penguin Books (N.Z.) Ltd,
182-190 Wairau Road, Auckland 10, New Zealand

First published in Penguin Books 1976

Made and printed in Australia at
The Dominion Press, Blackburn, Victoria

CIP

National Library of Australia
Cataloguing in Publication data

Horne, Donald Richmond, 1921-
Money Made Us

Index
ISBN 0 14 004302 0

1. Australia - Economic conditions. I. Title

330.994

Contents

Preface

I had intended writing a book that would have examined, from different perspectives, Australian systems of honour, political rhetoric, cults, styles of life, élite arts, popular entertainments, heroes, myths, monuments, other culture-forms, to see what they showed of how Australians imagined the world. The first chapter was to have taken the economic perspective, the second the imperial perspective. After writing 60,000 words of the first chapter, I decided I was writing not a first chapter but a book. I hope to write another book covering part of the rest of the original plan.

The original book was intended to be as much about its approach as about its content. The approach had two suppositions. The first was that to examine Australians' systems of honour, rhetoric, life-styles, cults, entertainments etc. was to examine how Australians defined the world and what mattered in it. The second supposition was that these fields can be examined from different perspectives (economic etc.), as light can be examined from different kinds of prisms. (I don't wish to be held too closely to this figure of speech.)

This concern with approach has remained, even though one chapter has become a book. In fact, the chapter became the book because I couldn't stop playing with the prism. I haven't written about my approach, as I had intended. That would probably take another book. But it is demonstrated.

This is one reason why I have not been interested in organizing the book around one big point. It accounts for demonstration pieces such as the chapter on water in Australians' imaginations, and also for a diffidence about hammering for long at points as they come up. Some of the people who have read the book and liked it have made the criticism that it should have concentrated more on one particular aspect or another, leaving out some of the other stuff. But then they go on to say they liked the other stuff.

I have left it as a series of experiments in ways in which, from the economic perspective, one might look at Australian views of existence as manifest in various culture-forms. Readers may use them as they wish.

One has to accept that there are almost always ambiguities as to what a book is 'really about', and that some of its most stimulating ideas may be only briefly cast up, perhaps in throwaway lines. However explicit an author is, his readers may still argue about what he is really doing. In trying to avoid this, one may merely strip off what are a book's best parts.

Thanks

My wife Myfanwy, as always, helped me at all stages. Conal Condren, Tim Curnow, Richard Kennedy, Ann McCallum, Douglas McCallum, Elaine Thompson and Bob Thompson all made very useful suggestions. Sarah Brenan was an extremely competent editor. Thanks also to Susie Roth, Libi Nugent, Eryl Brady and Chryss Grindrod for the typing; and to Angus and Robertson for permission to quote James McAuley's poem 'Tabletalk' from his *Collected Poems 1936-1970*.

The way in which the world is imagined determines at any particular moment what men will do.

WALTER LIPPMANN
Public Opinion

If men define situations as real, they are real in their consequences.

W. I. THOMAS,
The Child in America

The tradition of all the dead generations weighs like a nightmare on the brain of the living.

KARL MARX,
The Eighteenth Brumaire of Louis Bonaparte

CHAPTER ONE

Australian Shock

Three silver emblems had been attached to my uncle's coffin: the cross of Christ, the badge of the Australian Imperial Force and the insignia of the Freemasons. After the clergyman began the cremation service with a simplified reading from the Church of England prayer book, a Mason in full regalia stood up and spoke of the Great Architect of the Universe, and of our capacity to remove our faults and bring about the brotherhood of man. He placed a lambskin, symbol of innocence, on the coffin, then a sprig of rosemary, emblem of immortality. An officer of the Returned Soldiers' League, wearing his medals, spoke of a warrior's valiant heart and tranquil virtues and held up a paper poppy, symbol of the blood of Flanders' fields. Other 'returned men' of the Great War, also wearing medals, walked to the coffin and put their paper poppies on top of the Australian flag that lay on it; they stood in a semicircle, old men mourning an old man, right hands over their left breasts, while from a tape recorder the bugle sounded the Last Post and then the Reveille. Their leader recited Lawrence Binyon's lines: at the going down of the sun and in the morning we would remember them. The button was pressed. Along the rollers and through the curtains went my uncle's body, with its Christian, Masonic and Imperial insignia, its flowers, flag, lambskin, paper poppies and sprig of rosemary.

I went to my uncle's funeral while I was planning this book and when it was over it occurred to me that we might have been farewelling not only him, but all old men with their medals and sprigs of rosemary: we seem to be at the end of the days of the Returned Soldiers' League Freemason ascendancy, with its British loyalties, its badges and secret signs, its rituals, conspiracies and magic phrases, so important for so long in Australian politics and business.

Another funeral, another way of dying like an Australian: the funeral of Frank Packer, Knight of the British Empire. Outside St Andrew's Cathedral in Sydney the old millionaire's two riderless Mercedes mourned him. Inside, his body was carried down the aisle, followed by celebrities from the Age of Menzies; the occasion recalled generations of rich, uncultured Australians, great sportsmen, patrons of the turf, members of jockey clubs, diners at governors' tables, honoured by English monarchs for the service they rendered the public by making themselves rich. When I left Packer's funeral it occurred to me we might have been farewelling not only Packer and Knights of the British Empire, but the forms of capitalism which had treated him so well: by the time of his death people were suggesting the end of an economic era.

The 1970s may be producing that great transformation scene, that has been regularly prophesied since the 1830s and often prematurely proclaimed, in which things having been turned upside down will come out looking so different that finally, for better or worse, most people will not doubt that Australia is a nation, just like any other. Watersheds have been announced several times in my lifetime, but each turned out to be just another boulder in the creek. This time matters will probably be settled. Part of Australia's dynamic has been its imperial imagination, and for years this imperial imagination has had no more realities to feed on: if standards developed by a white outpost of the British Empire are maintained, they could destroy Australia.

But in addition to this shock – which has been obvious to more and more people – there is another form of challenge to Australia's habits that is so recent that it is difficult to define it so melodramatically. But the challenge itself seems clear enough: in ways that will be discussed in this book, Australia is one of the most 'economic' nations in the world – almost from the start its 'economy' has been one of its main declared purposes for existing and it is characteristic that its political rhetoric should be to a large extent expressed in economic terms – yet the Australian economy, like the economies of Australia's rich trading partners, is no longer working properly. The whole idea of ever-upward curves of 'economic development', one of the main 'purposes' of Australia, is being questioned. The questioning began in the early 1960s, following overseas fashion, on grounds of morality ('the affluent society'); then in the late 1960s in terms of practicability ('the environment crisis'); now in the mid-1970s on the grounds that the whole show may collapse. (Or to put it more moderately, that it may never again be possible to maintain low inflation, high 'growth', and full employment all at the one time.)

This book is connected with the shocks to Australia's economic imagination. It is about Australia's economic culture – the whole complex of fashions and habits connected with goods and services that are bought and sold. I intend to write a companion book which will be connected with the first shock; it will be about Australia's imperial culture. When whole cultures are threatened and those who manifested them are reacting to new, strange circumstances, it is a good time to write books about them. Perhaps these two books later will be a souvenir of how things were once seen in Australia.

One of the reasons why the politics of the last 15 years or so can seem so bizarre, and so many of the politicians such buffoons may lie in the way habitual views of what it is to be an Australian have been so regularly challenged by external events. This is what I mean by my chapter title 'Australian Shock'. With such disturbances in Australian cultural patterns, people are not sure about what is right, or of how to behave. This crisis in values and identity won't go away. Australian politics over this period has been partly about redefinition of what Australia is and how Australians should behave.

The sense of absurdity was made greater because of the Liberal and Country Parties' twenty-three years in office. In his Garran Memorial Oration of November, 1973, Gough Whitlam said on this long rule: 'In the United States one would have to go back to the Republican hegemony of twenty-four years – from the election of Lincoln to the election of Cleveland. In Britain itself, from which we take both our Parliamentary system and our civil service tradition one has to go back to 1807 – to the Tories under Liverpool, Canning and Wellington from 1807 to 1832 to find a comparable period of unbroken rule by a single Party.'

Staying in office for a long time may not mean anything in particular. In Menzies's case it did, since the parties in office were determined to preserve many of the Australian habits that we now see as most likely to disappear.

As I turn over the newspaper clippings, voices again call out their loyalty . . . Menzies, addressing Queen Elizabeth in Parliament House: 'I did but see her passing by, and yet I love her till I die.' . . . Holt, at the White House: 'I hope there will be a corner of your mind and heart which takes cheer from the fact that you have an admiring friend, a staunch friend that will be all the way with L.B.J.' . . . Gorton, at the White House, Australianizing Holt's message: 'We'll go a Waltzing Matilda with you.' . . . Bill McMahon, on his pilgrimage: 'I take as my text a few familiar words – that there comes a time in the life of a man in the flood of time that taken at the flood leads on to fortune.' . . . And all of their voices raised in praise of a 'national development' that was often a waste of resources and of a 'free enterprise' that didn't exist.

Just because Menzies lasted for a long time, an idea of normality grew up that was illusory. Menzies's long survival was freakish. It didn't represent an Australian consensus. There was an absolute majority of votes against him in 1954; and in 1961, if the electoral system had been slightly less favourable to his party he would also have been defeated. If Labor had won either of those elections things would now have been different. Even with a Liberal leader other than Menzies things might have *seemed* different. There were great changes in his sixteen years of continuous rule, but many of those in which people took most satisfaction were the very kinds of changes that least interested Menzies or which he despised. Part of the irony of this period was that some of those fields in which many Australians felt most like congratulating themselves on their achievement were those for which Menzies was least likely to give them praise.

Take an unexpected example. There is a good case for saying that the 1950s, the great Menzies decade, was that period of break-through for the arts, at least in poetry, in painting, in the novel, in drama, and in certain forms of general intellectual life that a couple of generations had been waiting for. But Menzies didn't quote A. D. Hope or Judith Wright or James McAuley; he didn't open a Nolan show or an Olsen show; he didn't go to *The Summer of the Seventeenth Doll* or praise *The Tree of Man*; he didn't subscribe to *Nation* or the *Observer*. He couldn't do so. He professed to hate all modern art. The very word 'intellectual' was one at which he regularly lifted an eyebrow. He seemed to prefer an Australia that didn't do too much thinking for itself. Yet a different prime minister, by associating with some of this new activity, might have dramatized the fact that Australia was less philistine than it seemed. If he had backed rhetoric with policy, by setting up the Commonwealth Cultural Council and the National Theatre that had already been planned in 1949 we might have been spared that belittling comparison of Australia with Canada that, for half a generation, followed the setting up of the Canada Council in 1957. It began to seem a measure of Australia's desperation that it had to look to the Canada of John Diefenbaker to learn how to behave.

Even when Menzies's successors announced new priorities they still acted like men of the past. In his sense of priorities John Gorton could be represented as someone who came out of the desert to act as the prophet of Gough Whitlam, but in his personal style Gorton could seem the most unfashionable of them all. There he was, in lifesaver's costume and cap, going out in a Bondi surf-boat with the boys – a Bronzed Anzac! The point comes out sharply with McMahon. There is a case for saying that, after Whitlam's prophet John Gorton had, partly by accident, partly by design, smashed up much of what was left from the Menzies era, the apparently decrepit McMahon government proved the greatest reform ministry the Liberals had provided in their twenty-three years. It lightened censorship. It de-colonized Papua New Guinea. It suddenly recognized the importance of 'the environment'. It took initiatives on Bangla Desh independent of U.S. policy, and protested against the French nuclear tests. It continued liberalizing the immigration programme and foreshadowed sweeping new laws on monopolies and trading practices. It phased out the means test and ordered a poverty inquiry. It announced urban planning initiatives and guidelines on foreign investment. But McMahon seemed at times to forget these were his government's policies. He swung from one expediency to another. He couldn't act like a man who knew who he was.

To show how important the themes of *the economic* and *the imperial* have been in ideas defining 'Australia' I will now go back over a decisive period in Australian nation-building. By 'nation-building' I don't mean discovering rivers or building power lines, but the only true nation-building: the ways people see themselves as a nation. Nations exist in the mind, and the nation created by some of the early rhetoricians of the new Australian nation was a nation of imperial loyalty and worship of 'development'. This was a point missed by Whitlam when he was asked in 1973 who were Australia's great men. He chose Alfred Deakin and John Curtin – because 'they gave an identity and purpose to the nation in new circumstances – federation and war.' I wish this were true. But there is a good case for saying that the two greatest identity-crystallizers of Australia were two other and quite different men, W. M. Hughes and S. M. Bruce, and the identities that they crystallized – of a loyal and 'developmental' Australia – were the kinds of images of Australia that Whitlam wanted to destroy.

Before I demonstrate the point, some reminders of John Curtin and Alfred Deakin . . . Curtin: an Irish policeman's son, a Catholic who turned rationalist and changed his faith to socialism in its age of innocence; anti-militarist in the First World War; union newspaper editor and drunk; then politician, teetotaller, Prime Minister of Australia; sensitive, oratory-visioned, cautious, hot-tempered, patient, shrewd, humanitarian, fretful; dying in office irritated by attacks from the press and his own party. Deakin: a Melbourne accountant's son, politely educated, drenched in the ideals of nineteenth century liberalism; most notable reformer and orator in the colony of Victoria, then one of the most progressive nations in the world; three times Prime Minister of Australia; admitting to his diary his preference for intellectual success over the excitements of politics; forced into coalition with his political enemies; then turned into a vegetable as his memory prematurely disintegrated.

What Curtin and his Labor government gave to Australians at the time of the Japanese threat was the belief that Labor was capable of governing. So far, governments have collapsed in Australia when faced by world crises, and Labor's political opponents, although imperialists and militarists, had collapsed when confronted by war. But it would be too much to say, as Whitlam did, that John Curtin gave identity and purpose to Australia. During the war against Japan the atmosphere in Australia was often dispirited. Because of a fractured national consciousness, loyalty to Australia could seem disloyalty to the

British Empire. It was hard to know what Australia was supposed to be loyal to.

It is just as doubtful that Alfred Deakin provided a strong sense of national identity although he gets more marks for trying, at least on national 'purpose'. He tried to give some sense to the new federation of which he was three times Prime Minister; it is now fashionable to describe him as one of the few Australian statesmen who did. But he had a dull audience. The Australian colonies had come together as a nation, so peacefully, rationally and diffidently, after such long formalities going back so many years, that having joined together they seemed almost to forget their reasons. Compared with the bustle of some colonial governments in the 1890s there was no hurry to do anything much. Only 56.68 per cent of the electors voted in the first Federal election, 50.27 per cent in the second, 51.48 in the third. Voting in South Australia went as low as 40.37 per cent; in Western Australia it was down to 30.41 per cent. In this period of enervation Deakin produced his best phrases. Despite differences in labels, for the first ten years all three political parties, as they took their turns at office, moving in and out of each others' embraces, had a go at putting into action the policies that Deakin was best at describing. There were two Deakins: Deakin the politician, clever manipulator and place seeker, was just another of the political trimmers who drew on the national policies of Deakin the noble orator and inventor of national purposes.

But Deakin's oratory was more important in suggesting what politicians might do than in telling Australians what they might be. It was a rational oratory of *policies,* of bright ideas. Australia was not a nation, but a municipality that was building up a reputation for go-ahead programmes. The first prime minister to try some nation-making was not Deakin, a man of private intellectual doubts and of such remarkable subtlety that throughout his years of office he wrote anonymously for the London *Morning Post,* commenting frankly on Australian politicians – opponents, allies and himself; it was Billy Hughes, tougher-grained (but also subtle, as men who build their reputations on blood sometimes are), Great War Prime Minister, competent butcher, orator of death. The next Prime Minister to build ideas of Australia not fully challenged until Whitlam became prime minister was the man who took Hughes's job from him, the rich Anglophile Stanley Melbourne Bruce,

Cambridge-educated scion of a Melbourne softgoods business. Hughes and Bruce developed the great oratorical themes of Empire and War, the threat of Bolshevism and the dominance of economic man that, together with spasmodic returns to themes of social welfare, provided the prevailing senses of drama and purpose in Australian political life.

To give an idea of the development of these prevailing dramas (which are still familiar to us), here is a quick look at the election campaigns of the first thirty years of Federation, the period in which Deakin, then Hughes, then Bruce dominated national oratory.*

In Deakin's programme there was a humane sense of priorities. He spoke of a policy of progress for a nation with equal laws and opportunities for all, healthy lives, honest toil, fair wages, fair hours, fair prices, fair conditions of employment, abolition of antagonism and prejudice. So great would be Australian progress that the civilized nations would follow Australia's economic and political leads; Australia would show a way to the rest of the world.† Important for this civilized growth were a well-planned manufacturing industry, fostered by a scientific, carefully adjusted programme of protection and based on the indisputable knowledge of capable independent experts, who as well as aiding manufacturing growth would assist the further development of agriculture and even throw light on the dark mysteries of unemployment.

For Hughes the earth was drenched in blood and there brooded over it the noble and patriotic spirit of self sacrifice. The eyes of the world were upon Australia: it was on trial in a time of supreme crisis and supreme duty. Even when the fiery furnace was cold and war won, the rhetoric of war still showed the light: in the 1919 election and even in the 1922 election audiences were still reminded of the long hours of terrible trial when the blood of the British race was spilt. But then there was a new theme: having in the bleakest hours of war preserved the bonds of Empire against the Hun, in the

* I have used in the following paragraphs a technique that will be found in a number of other places in the book: to compress patterns of political rhetoric down to a basic vocabulary that gives a simple view of what the world is, and what matters in it.

† The motif of showing the way to the rest of the world is common to the political rhetoric of most countries, even the most insignificant.

dark, troublous years that followed Hughes was saving the Empire from the poisonous doctrines of Bolshevism, as spread by parts of the Australian labour movement.

However it was mainly Bruce who fought the orator's battle for the Empire against the Bolshevism of parts of the labour movement: braving the effects of the stream of propaganda that came from Moscow, he was Briton enough to defend stable government and the Empire against revolution and chaos. As late as the 1928 election, ten years after the earth was drenched with British blood, he said: 'The principal question must be where the parties stand with regard to the Empire.'

While Deakin was an apostle of economic development, it was economic development on a human scale: one of its main objectives, prompted by a sense of fairness, was human happiness. Hughes placed more emphasis on national pride: if only it would develop its resources Australia was capable of almost indefinite expansion, to become one of the greatest manufacturing nations in the world. For a start, with his programme for building railways, roads, irrigation works and for the biggest immigration policy Australia had ever known, Hughes would have doubled Australia's population in twenty years. As old welfare programmes faded, Bruce took up this theme even more strenuously: where Deakin spoke of fairness, he spoke more of natural resources; where Deakin talked about wages, hours, prices, Bruce talked about roads, bridges, hydro-electricity, water conservation, developmental railways, afforestation, butter factories, this great continent, our great destiny. The main impulse behind Bruce's version of economic development was neither human happiness nor national pride, but fear: surrounded by coloured aliens, Australia's whole future depended on developing and populating this great continent of ours with a white race.

Now to correct Whitlam's historical judgement further: Deakin would have agreed with what Bruce said about the white race. Deakin was Australia's most successful racist orator. The first matter about which the new federation declared its enthusiasm was the White Australia policy. And it was because Deakin spoke of fairness for ordinary Australians much more often than Bruce did that as a racist he was probably more influential than Bruce. His skill in oratory helped him make White Australia, economic development, fair shares and Imperial loyalty all part of the one parcel. He was able to sell White Australia as part of a comprehensive secular faith that had something for everybody. Or to put it the other way: he was uniquely able to express the aspirations of the Australian people.

I might as well jump on another grave and say that the true heir of Bruce's policy of economic development, including the desire to make Australia more populous to stop the Asiatics from coming, was the Labor government of Curtin's successor, Ben Chifley. To be fair, this government was also the true heir of Deakin's humane concern for ordinary persons. And to be fair again, it was this humane concern that should continue to light up Deakin's name; his racism was a background darkness then shared by almost all his fellow countrymen.

As you see, the simple picture of Australians as a white race, or as a 'British race', and the simple picture of Australia as a continent whose principal *raison d'être* is to have the resources ripped out of it and its future charted in ever-upward curves of 'economic development' provide two of the most compelling motifs in Australian political oratory. From this point of view, the great Australian dramas have been the dramas of empire and the dramas of economic exploitation.

The Australia conjured up by much of its politicians' oratory can be defined in one simple picture: it has been a white man's resource-ripping nation.

I should now try to give some idea of what I have in mind when I speak of 'Australia's economic culture':

Economic: Some goods and services are bought and sold; these are seen as part of the economic system. Other goods and services are not bought and sold; these are not seen as part of the economic system. If a woman, defined as a housewife, produces a cake or cleans the house, this, by our convention, is not an economic act; but if the same woman, defined as a worker in a cleaning firm, cleans a house, this, by our convention, *is* an economic act. In the way we live now, value can be determined by buying and selling.

Culture: Two questions – *Why do people want to stay the same?* and *Why do people want to change?* – more or less set the perspectives by which anthropologists examine those human habits that can be described collectively. They also set the perspectives of this book, but I prefer the word 'fashion' to 'habit', because sooner or later all habits, like fashions, change: some pass fleetingly, dissolving like wisps of cloud, but even those that stay will, however slowly, change their shape.*

There is, of course, no *the* economic culture in Australia, no one system of fashions connected with providing the kinds of goods and services that are bought and sold. But even to talk about a number of economic cultures within Australia can be misleading. 'Culture' is an abstraction. In themselves, cultures don't exist. To describe a 'culture' is not to give an exact account of what everybody does; it is a list of collective habits, a list which should be useful for looking at particular situations and trying to describe them. So the subject of the book might be restated as 'fashions in cultural forms in Australia to do with the provision of the kinds of goods and services that are bought and sold'. But this seems such a hideous way of putting it that I'll just go back to 'Australia's economic culture'.

When speaking of 'cultural forms', I have in mind not only the most obvious ones – techniques, the ways Australians go about providing those goods and services that are bought and sold – but also the great baggage train of other fashions that have been part of the march of economic progress in Australia. It is important to acknowledge that economic matters don't end with dollars and cents. They are expressed in tens of thousands of cultural forms. Christmas shopping can be seen as an impelling mass festival; a postage stamp can be a stained glass window; a wheat silo a village church; a political speech a form of prayer; a national park a cathedral; and a belief in irrigation schemes a fanatical religion. Economic change can produce great community dramas with new character types. An economic cult can have its rites, rituals and secret signs.

This book is about fashions in such cultural forms. It is not

* I may have overdone the substitution of 'fashion' for 'habit'. At any particular time one can see, close up, a difference between fashions that change for the sake of change and habits that are hard to break. I shall leave 'fashion', to emphasize that in the long run, seen from a distance, 'habits' can also be seen as 'fashion', but over a longer time span.

meant to be comprehensive. In such subjects comprehensiveness isn't possible. It doesn't attempt to measure significance. Such measurement also isn't possible. It is concerned simply with some aspects of these processes. The approach used varies from one chapter to the next.

The aim is to throw light on the meanings and values associated with economic processes in Australia, and to do this by presenting many of the associated fashions in cultural forms. Because *the economic* matters so much to us, to do this, in quite a large measure, is to describe a number of the different ways one can be an Australian.

But talking of 'fashions' in such terms doesn't necessarily mean that Australians will go on adapting to external events as if 'Australia' was a single identity like a plant or an animal, adapting for survival. Some fashions seem to have a self-generating character that grows from ambiguity and whimsy, as much as, or more than, from adaptations to reality – and fashion can become quite unadaptable. People get used to fashions. They cling to them for their own sake, whatever the external events. They even go down with them. They may prefer self-destruction to change. This is one reason why humans are not 'reasonable' and why so many plans, including political plans, end in irony or fiasco. Humans have an almost infinite ability for not 'facing facts' and for pleasing themselves by perpetuating crises of value and identity.

When nations change it is in a context of stubborn past obsessions about what life is and what is important in it. In extremity, as individuals, we can die rather than give up the idea of what we are, although usually there is some form of compromise, however degrading. What a person 'is' can be sufficiently ambivalent for people to stay alive, no matter how great their humiliation. One of the main reasons we can become so unhappy is that even when our sense of identity – our 'pride' – is frustrated we would sooner go on living than kill ourselves. But on a scale more complex than the matter of individuals making decisions about themselves, compromises may not happen: on questions of collective consciousness (as in seeing ourselves as a 'nation') the momentum of old fashions may simply do us in.

More usually, nations 'decline'. Shocked by changed circumstances, they still try to go on as they did before. They hold on to views of reality that exile them from the dynamics of an epoch. In December 1974, the month when Britain announced the withdrawal of the last of its troops from Malaysia and Singapore and there were forecasts that it would soon move from third place to fourth place as a buyer of Australian exports, R. G. Menzies celebrated his eightieth birthday by writing two articles for the *Sydney Morning Herald* offering extracts from the rhetoric that had seen him through his sixteen years' prime ministership, including a reaffirmation that to Australia, Britian was still 'a great and powerful friend'. Such a retreat from the Australian shock is a kind of insanity.

When old, affronted views are maintained as stiffly as this, they are not the same as when life was in them: they have turned into a self-conscious 'backlash'. They no longer come naturally. They are not conservative but high camp, contrived self-concern, as fashion revivals are, or as Nazism was. Sometimes this makes a revival farcical, as with Premier Bjelke-Petersen's attempt to make Elizabeth II Queen of Queensland. Sometimes it heralds special danger.

CHAPTER TWO

The Looters and 'The Producers'

It became part of Europe's view of the world that the rest of it was there to be plundered for Europe's benefit. Even when this crude view was refined, countries outside Europe could still seem mere *sources of supply* as if the rest of the world were Europe's back yard, with pantries, gardens, wells, heaps of fuel, storehouses to provide raw materials to keep Europe going. Even people in these other countries sometimes saw them in this limited and subordinate way, as places you got something out of – minerals, fuels, foods, fibres – which you then sent off to Europe. And they were proud of it. Their sense of importance and success was related to the size and value of their exports. It was as if only exports finally mattered: shake life free of its accessories and you beheld the ultimate reality, the reason for everything else – the Export. This is one of the simple pictures some Australians have had of themselves: they defined Australia as a resources-exporting country. Producing exports could seem Australia's main 'purpose'.

The impulse to see Australia in this way is so important that it is worth several paragraphs to put it in context. In the sixteenth century there began those changes that would later lead to a view of the whole world as a storehouse for Europe. The East Indies provided the Portuguese, and then the Dutch, with spices. Mexico and Peru provided gold and silver for Spain, Brazil supplied diamonds and gold to Portugal. Russian fur traders came across Siberia and into Alaska, French fur traders spread out from the Great Lakes, and British fur traders travelled up the American west coast scouring North Asia and North America for furred animal pelts for Europe. At about the time of Australia's settlement the southern oceans were hunted over to produce whales, whose blubber could be boiled down to make soap or lamp oil for Europeans, and whose bones could be used as stiffening in

Europeans' umbrellas and corsets or used to make buggy whips or fishing rods. Africa was to supply black human beings to be sold to the plantation owners of the West Indies and eastern America, and the function of the West Indies was to grow sugar, tobacco, rice, indigo, cotton and sell it to Europe.

During the industrial revolution, flocks of sheep moved into virgin pastures in Australia, New Zealand, southern Africa, North America and Argentina because Europe's textile factories and carpet factories needed wool. There were other countries which served Europe's purposes by mining and exporting copper, nitrates, nickel, tin or by setting up plantations of rubber trees, cocoa, tea, coffee, coconuts. European settlers would survey a new region, clear its vegetation, arrange plants in straight rows, build houses, set up labour lines and turn the region into an engine for producing exports. With the growth of railways, new wheat farms spread across Siberia, across the centre and west of North America, across the South American pampas, across Australia and South Africa, transfiguring landscapes and producing new towns, new political pressures, new social types. When refrigeration was invented, a new purpose of some new lands was to turn grass into exportable beef and mutton. With the invention of the internal combustion engine the 'oil producers' were created, territories whose only interest lay in their pipes and derricks and docks. They were noted more for what went out of them than for what they were. The very word 'raw materials' suggested simplicity, honesty, prime importance.

Along with the idea of the primacy of the export of raw materials went two other supporting ideas: progress was not possible without a continuing flow of investment money from foreigners and regular supplies of bulk labour. The first substantial foreign investment was Spanish, in the gold and silver mines in Mexico in the second half of the sixteenth century, but the most significant European investors were the British, who spread their money to exporting countries all over the world, not only within their Empire. British investment was essential to the industrialization of the United States and, at the height of British power, Brazil and Argentina, the two largest South American nations, were economically part of the British Empire; the concern of the oligarchies who controlled them was to keep in with the British. In Argentina, British money pushed railway tracks across the pampas, throwing up small, bleak railway villages and changing Buenos Aires into a major railway centre and port. The result was the extermination of the pampas Indians, the lavish enrichment of the *estancieros,* the creation of the new class of impoverished *peons,* and a flood of European immigrants. In a couple of decades Argentina had been rearranged. It had become an effective raw material supplier. Its 'purpose' was to send wheat to British flour mills, mutton and beef to British wholesalers, wool to French and Belgian carpet factories.

Bulk labour came in various forms. In the West Indies and eastern America it was African slaves; in North America, Siberia and Australia it was convicts; in South America, Africa, Queensland, South-east Asia and the Pacific Islands, indentured labour. Across the steppes of Siberia, the prairies of North America, the pampas of South America, the veldt of Africa and the grasslands of Australia it also came in the form of migrants – producer fodder, ticketed and shipped out as bulk goods in the world's greatest planned movements of peoples.

In the first struggling, unorganized attempts at economic exploitation, labour could also be supplied by wild fringe men, anarchists by ordinary standards, even madmen: the frontiersman, the Cossack, the *gaucho,* the *bandiera.* Among them were the early nineteenth-century sealers who lived on islands near Tasmania or camped on beaches along the southern Australian coast and on Kangaroo Island: mostly ex-convicts or runaway convicts, clothed in animal hides, living with stolen Aboriginal women, trading sealskins (which went to London or Canton) for rum and tobacco – 'a complete set of pirates . . . amongst themselves they robbed each other, the weak being obliged to give way to the stronger', according to the law of the musket and the cutlass. Along with Sydney traders who swapped beads, blankets, axes and muskets for pork, sandalwood or *bêche-de-mer* in the cannibal islands of the South Pacific, the sealers were the first of the Australian exporters.

They clubbed seals so successfully that they destroyed their source of supply. Whalers took over and until 1833 whale products were the main Australian export. Camped on beaches here and there along 5,000 kilometres of southern Australian coast, from Twofold Bay to Swan River, bay-whaling teams (a score or so men, with a couple of boats and a boiling-down plant) waited for female whales to come into bays to calve. As soon as a female appeared they would row out, and try to harpoon it, tow it to the beach, slice it up, boil it down: the beaches were littered with whale bones. The system worked so well that there were no bay whales left: the bay whalers had produced an effective programme for exterminating bay whales. Over much the same period pairs of woodcutters ('mates') were getting to work on the red cedar of the New South Wales coast, working up the rivers, rafting the branded logs down to vessels that would take them to Sydney, from where some of the timber was so successfully exported that red cedar became almost extinct.

These early Australian exporters were plunderers: their technology was that of the club, the harpoon and the axe; their ecological programme was one of total annihilation. Something of the same sense of a quick hunt for booty marked the next two export rushes. The first was the rush to grow wool. When Yorkshire mills increased demand and the cost of ship freights went down, so that it was cheaper to ship wool to Britain from Australia than from Germany, the rush to run sheep had some of the characteristics of a gold rush. In the seaports, gamblers 'put their money into four legs' – they bought sheep as a bet. They added carts, supplies and human labour to the sheep and walked their investment over the Great Dividing Range and across the grasslands until they found some unoccupied land to use as a sheep run. By the 1840s sheep and cattle runs were spread over a huge crescent in the south-east, 2,000 kilometres in its inner curve, 600 kilometres at its widest. Sheep ate the kangaroo grass, converting it into the curly hair whose resilience and intergripping scales made it so good for spinning; fleeces were piled once a year on to bullock carts and sent to the ports. In his slab hut, with its mud and manure floor, bark roof, sapling furniture tied with greenhide, possum or dingo skin rugs, the squatter might dream of his sheep doubling again and again and his gambler's stake being multiplied ten or twenty times. He would be able to sell out and sail back to Britain or set himself up in the colony like a gentleman.

By the middle of the century one of the greatest debates in the eastern colonies, where wool was now the main export (in South Australia they talked about copper and wheat), was whether they were intended to be 'one great sheepwalk'. Eastern Australia seemed to have become a single-export economy of the crudest kind, with squatters dominating it in the crudest kind of manner. It was at this time that the cult of the *export* and the *exporter* developed that was to continue so strongly for so long. With the gold rushes the squatters had to share the glamour of export with the mining companies; in the 1850s and 1860s, gold replaced wool as the principal export.

At first the gullies and flats of the goldfields looked amateurish and individualistic enough for the 'digger', the little man with no money, to strike it lucky. On earth stripped to its gravel sat strange wooden engines; sails faced the wind to ventilate the shafts below. Horses plodded, turning cumbersome wooden crushing mills and puddling machines, or working wooden cranes. But when the easy gold ran out, it took money to drop shafts into the deeper reefs of quartz and the diggers had to work for wages: gold mining became an organized export industry. When Bendigo was the greatest quartz-mining town in the world, shaft-heads and mullock heaps stood up right in the centre of the town, amongst its most imposing buildings. Throughout the town there were the rumbles and dust of a thousand 'stampers' in the crushing batteries; creeks ran grey with muck; smoke billowed yellow from roasted ore. Goldmining was serious, organized, industrial, capitalist. Miners died from factory accidents and industrial diseases.

To demonstrate Bendigo's seriousness, large public buildings rose up in the Italian Renaissance style, with clock towers, fluted pillars, polished granite columns; they were matched in importance by the classical facades of the banks. With these buildings running along its 'mall', Bendigo became grand and showy in the manner of a new British provincial city, expansively imperial. Yet there was still a recognition in one corner that it was a city not of thrift and hard work but of luck: on the Gold Monument, within sprinting distance of the stock exchange, a statue of a digger panned for gold but behind him was the goddess of fortune.

However, the luck was going out of exports. With new breeds and new techniques there began to develop a greater sense of care and intelligence about wool-growing: squatters were somewhat more deserving of the high prestige they demanded than when they were merely lucky land-grabbers. With increased demand from Europe the number of sheep went up from sixteen million in 1861 to ninety million in 1891 (and then crashed in a drought). Exports of copper, lead, zinc, gold, silver, tin and coal counterbalanced the pre-eminence of wool as an export and with schools of mining, faculties of engineering and a certain amount of Australian metallurgical research, mining exports also began to look less a matter of luck. Again, it was due to changes in technology that wheat, beef and butter became honoured exports. These developments towards greater seriousness made the export cult more credible than when exports depended on the luck of loot. From being beachcombers and desperadoes, land-grabbers or stake-claimers, exporters had come to represent the essential part of the nation.

As benefactors concerned with simple, basic matters, exporters were the principals of what for decades were called 'the natural industries', a phrase that emphasized the inherent goodness and primacy of those who dealt with raw materials, compared with 'the artificial industries', which were seen as unhealthy parasitic growths, swelling the cancer of the cities and threatening the health of the nation. Exporters derived great honour from being seen as the guardians of Australia's 'natural resources', whose primacy and goodness provided the magic of Australia's existence. But the mysteries of this cult demanded that as well as being guardians of natural resources, they should also be exploiters. Rhetoric demanded continuing praise for natural resources; it also demanded continuing plans to use them. 'Our greatest Australian asset is the land', said the Melbourne *Argus* in the first Federal election. 'We have millions and tens of millions of acres lying unproductive. Our ambition should be to turn every acre to account.' It was like a fertility cult in which one must praise the goddess by constantly making her pregnant. 'We have illimitable resources,' said Deakin during the 1903 election. 'They are only waiting for stimulation.'

As well as 'natural', another key word was 'producer'. By the 1850s exporters were already being described as 'the producers', 'a class of infinitely more value than the commercial'. 'Let the producing interest be destroyed and the entire fabric of society must crumble in ruins', said one of the speakers in the debate on a new constitution for New South Wales in 1853. They went on being 'the producers' until the 1920s, when the word 'primary' was added.

'Primary producer' was also a term of great honour, especially since it came to be associated exclusively with farmers. Before then 'the producers' had included the mining industry ('a noble and splendid industry', whose mining and smelting towns employed an eighth of the male workforce). At the celebrations of Federation in Sydney in 1901 there was a triumphal arch dedicated to minerals as well as triumphal arches for wool and wheat. 'Minefield and farm' were dignified words often used together, and briefly after the Great War there was Australia Unlimited talk, of searches for new mineral deposits ('Australia has almost every metal required') and for the Australian oil fields that were believed to be hiding somewhere. There was a season of enthusiasm for the idea that there was greater purity in exporting *processed* metals than metals 'in their rawest state', and for a while words like 'smelting' and 'refinery' acquired hope and gravity. But in the 1920s the great mining days seemed finished. Mineral searches declined; more than 100,000 people left the mining towns; Australian mining engineers tried their luck in Malaya, Thailand, New Guinea, Fiji. Farmers began to enjoy more unchallenged esteem than ever before: 'primary producer' came to mean only the farmer, and the honour of the two titles of farmer and exporter became one. This was only part of a more general infantile reversion from which Australians did not begin to recover until somewhere in the 1960s. Merino sheep were of such importance that they even dominated the first Australian airmail postage stamp in 1929, and as late as 1969 a special issue of postage stamps on the primary industries commemorated only farm products. There was no mention of mining.

The era of 'the primary producers', stretching from the mid-1920s to the mid-1960s, with key words such as 'orderly', 'sound', 'proper development' was the age of public works, subsidies, bounties, tax concessions, slogans, commodity pools, orderly marketing schemes. It was a period of export-at-any-cost. Exports seemed so important that to raise questions of economic rationality could seem seditious. And there tended to be no distinction between subsidizing exports and subsidizing farmers. In the 1930s the slogan 'Grow More Wheat' and the devaluation of the Australian pound to help the farmers were two of the first responses to the Depression, and restoring 'the great export trades' seemed essential to again acquiring the love of the Bank of England. To help farmers cut costs the government created one of the highest unemployment rates in the world.

In the primary producers' Australia, the main reason for troubling to construct roads and railways was so that primary products might be conveyed to the sea ports, where there were sales yards, abattoirs, auction rooms, silos, wool stores, freezing works, docks and financial houses attending to the needs of primary producers. In a purely capitalist and materialist definition of Australia, values were assessed by book-keeping: money was the measure of what really mattered. There was no aristocracy with fancy ways to impede production, no intractable peasantry to withstand the impulses of progress; the land itself was simply a transferable asset, part of the plant. There was such a heavy concentration on 'the plant' (the land, the animals, the machines) and such a low use of men that Australian primary industries were among the most efficient in the world.

But in the sense of rugged individualists taking all the risks, Australia was not so capitalist. To varying degrees, primary industries were aided by government research, government agricultural colleges and extension schemes, government pest control, government sponsorship of cheap land and credit, government imports of immigrant labour, government assistance with cheap rail freights and bulk handling, government construction of irrigation systems and many other public works, government marketing programmes, government import protection, and straight money transfers as direct government subsidies. 'Industrialized' seems a better word than 'capitalist' – Australia was being run as an industrialized export business.

That was the impression given by some of the rhetoric, but since they were human beings the people running it didn't always keep up a calculating and rational approach of profit or loss. There were many petulant expressions of inefficient self-interest, and several obsessive aspirations towards ideas of goodness that were the opposite of the idea of a cool allocation of resources on grounds of efficiency. Later in this book I will discuss some of these strong, whimsical traditions (which are as much part of Australian moral life as its economic life). For the moment, here is just one episode: The 'trade diversion policy' of 1936, an example of the Britain-worship that was until recently part of the cult of the export. The trade diversion policy was prompted by a desire to keep Australia as a market for British textiles and motor cars by restricting the import of textiles from Japan and motor cars from the United States. Japan was Australia's second best customer for wool and its third best customer for wheat, and the balance of payments with the U.S. was more in Australia's favour than its balance of payments with Britain, but at a time when one of Australia's political slogans was 'Tune in to Britain', policy could see keeping in with the British as the only important economic consideration. Once Australia announced its restrictions the Japanese retaliated by banning the purchase of Australian wool and wheat. When reason prevailed over loyalty and Australia gave in, the Japanese started buying from Australia again, but at a smaller rate. They increased their research into synthetic substitutes for wool.

Trade could be seen as *British*: exporters were not only the backbone of the Australian economy, they were Empire patriots. In the late nineteenth century, when the excitements of the new imperialism were beginning to inflame Australians' self-importance, Britain took up three quarters of Australia's exports (and provided most of its overseas investment capital and nearly three quarters of its imports). In the twentieth century the proportions dropped a bit, even though Britain was still dominant, but the Empire Preference Scheme of 1932 made trade seem even more British. Producers in client industries, such as the dairy farmers, put their foodstuffs on British breakfast tables at prices lower than in Australia, but the combination of the sacredness of *the export* with the sacredness of British breakfast tables seemed to make this legitimate. The excuse for the trade diversion policy was that 'difficult-selling commodities' (such as price-subsidized butter) were 'absorbed' by Britain but that Britain might stop buying cheap butter from Australia if Australia bought cheap textiles from Japan instead of expensive textiles from Britain. That Japan might stop buying Australian wool and wheat wasn't taken into account. It was only in the early 1960s that the Britishness of trade, with all the honour that brought, was seen to fade.

By then, exports were seen as one of the ways Australia was coming of age. After the Second World War, and partly as a result of it, there was even more help for primary industries, but there were now also 'incentive schemes' for the export of manufactured goods. Because Nugget shoe polish sold well in other countries, the firm that manufactured it became a Trade Department hero. When 'Export Awards' were given to manufacturers, some of the multinational companies that won them included reference to the award in their advertising, suggesting that theirs was the real stuff, by international standards. The word 'export' became part of the brand name of goods that were mainly for sale in Australia. 'Export quality' suggested that world outside Australia where all good things went, and from which (as in 'specially imported') all good things came.

However, for most city-living Australians (that is, most Australians), by the mid-1950s the concern with exports as community drama, apart from a creeping barrage of tired phrases, was becoming manifest mainly in a recurrent 'export crisis'. The balance of payments would swing the wrong way, import restrictions would be announced, credit would be tightened, taxes would go up. Despite the preference for exports on postage stamps, wool seemed threatened by synthetics, wheat by gluts, and meat, dairy goods and fruit by the European Common Market. An 'export crisis' came to seem a typical Australian economic problem.*

Australia lacks the kind of bad paintings that commemorate famous battles with broad, exciting sweeps over huge canvases. By the time it got around to war, battles had become part of general movements that were beyond understanding and in which only bits of detail made sense. But there is at least one Australian battle scene that matches in spuriousness the most famous European paintings

* The idea of the 'export crisis' was, by that time, even more important in Britain itself. The drama of the balance of payments crisis was an essential part of the British identity crisis. In this case, and more generally, one must recognize that any particular point that is made about Australia is not necessarily unique to it. In the 1950s, some of the English export crisis rhetoric was exported to Australia, although for Australians the same words could have different meanings, in particular the difference between primary industries and manufactured goods. One of the regular difficulties for Australians in finding their own definition of reality comes from their existing in a wider world of rhetoric.

of cavalry charges. In the La Trobe Library in Melbourne, *Black Thursday, 1851* shows thick clouds of smoke, senseless action, emotionally exalted humans, writhing animals, an impression of a grand and tragic occasion. It was done by William Strutt, an Englishman who lived in Australia for eleven years and wanted to paint history. Lacking a battle, he chose the day in 1851 when farmers burning off around Port Phillip overdid it; the whole district burst into flames and the temperature in Melbourne rose to 117°F. The painting is stagey, overdone, melodramatic, but the fact that the victims of the occasion seem to be enjoying themselves suggests another point – the stupefied excitement with which the exploiters of Australia went about their looting was like a great, boldly-led cavalry charge: it was almost as if the ruin they caused was exactly what they had intended.

But Australians sometimes seemed to accept with melancholy satisfaction that things didn't always work out. One might compare *Black Thursday* with Piguenit's *Flood on the Darling* in the New South Wales Art Gallery: in it things are so quiet and still that the disaster, the flood itself, seems part of the natural order – as it is. This is the way things are meant to be. For a generation or two the single most popular poem about Australia was Dorothea Mackellar's *My Country,* with its boasts of Australia's brownness, droughts, floods, heat, famine, thirst.

For as quick a despoliation of a big area as can be found anywhere in history, consider what happened to the Western Division of New South Wales, an area somewhat larger than Great Britain. These western plains had very little rain, but although the existence of soil and plants was fragile, the set-up was provident: at different places saltbush, mulga, mallee or native grasses were there as ground cover to protect the springiness and sponginess of the soil, so that the small amount of rain that did fall was absorbed. Into this frugal but workable balance, busy humans, spreading along the Darling in the 1870s, introduced a river life of paddle-steamers and river ports serviced by camel trains, joined in the 1880s by railways to Bourke from Sydney and to Broken Hill from Adelaide. The future promised continuing expansion: to the myth that rain followed the flocks had been added the myth that flocks followed the flocks or, as a government commission put it in 1883, 'judicious stocking undoubtedly increases the capability of the country to carry sheep'. Firms and syndicates moved in to make money: one station was nearly a million hectares; eight were well over half a million; one had its own tramway, from woolshed to riverboat wharf. But stock were tearing away at the ground cover of grass or saltbush and axes were chopping down scrub. Natural providence was being eaten and chopped away, and when drought came in the 1890s sheep pawed the ground, ate the roots, stirred up the dust, and died. From fifteen million sheep in 1891 the numbers dropped to fewer than four million in 1903. Now when it rained the advantages of the old provident frugality had gone: with the ground cover torn out, rainwater evaporated. A new natural order developed in the west – a natural division of the soil into fine particles that blew off as dust and larger particles that piled up as dunes of sand. When all the topsoil was blown away there were left only claypans, which grew nothing. In a couple of summers in the 1940s the storms of dust from the west blew so thickly over Sydney, a thousand kilometres away, that street lights were turned on in the mid-afternoon and some of the dust finally settled as a pink smear on the snowfields of New Zealand.

The bush and its most popular individual species were praised in a thousand poems, but when it came to exploiting natural resources trees were seen as weeds. To the early settlers forests were obstacles, to be cut down or burned down: timber licences cost next to nothing. On the north coast of New South Wales, in the Richmond Valley, so richly forested that it was known as 'The Big Scrub', cedar-cutters worked their way up the river chopping down all the cedar they saw, floating the logs in rafts to Ballina and its sawpits, derricks and schooners. Then they began working up the mountains after pine, ash and cedar; they would leave the logs in the beds of creeks that flooded three or four times a year, washing the logs down the river. Steam sawmills were set up; paddle steamers went up and down river. When settlers cleared their holdings they simply cut down the trees, left them to dry for six months or so, then put a firestick to them: rosewood, tulip, sandalwood, cedar, white beech – the favourite woods of cabinet-makers – all went up in smoke that hung for days over the valleys. By the 1880s the cedar and pine had gone, and timber-cutters were working the hardwoods. At Lismore, in memory of these atrocities, they now have an old cedar log laid out in state beside the

Civic Centre. The log has its own roof. Beside it is a gas-operated barbecue donated by the Lismore Jaycees.

'Ringbarking' became part of the language, the Australian word for a way of killing trees invented by east-coast American Indians, in which a ring was cut into the trunk of the tree to cut off the sap and starve it to death, so that although the dead tree trunk would remain, more sunlight and nourishment would get to the grasses. At a time when 'clearing the land' was as much a display of practicality and virility as men having their hair cut short-back-and-sides, one of my Hunter Valley memories is of old dead trees, pale grey, sticking up out of brown stubby grass: the bleached bones of a cow or the rusted carcase of some agricultural machine might be lying nearby. The only birds in the pale blue sky were crows.

I am not simply being sentimental about trees. In fact I could feel nostalgia for those pale-grey ringbarked tree trunks, along with the pale-grey wood of the farmers' shacks and the pale-grey timber fences: now that most of the ringbarked trees have gone, the National Trust should give those that remain an 'A' classification. The point is that along with overstocking in the western plains of New South Wales, overcropping in the marginal lands of South Australia and other atrocities of optimism elsewhere, cutting down trees often destroyed the grass it was meant to improve. Material progress would have been better fostered if more trees had been left alone. When hills were cleared of trees, the soil lost the sponginess and springiness that had easily absorbed rainwater: soil particles were crammed together into a tight surface that repelled rain. Instead of nourishing the soil by spreading moisture through its sponginess, raindrops came together as streams of water that scoured hillsides and gullies, sometimes washing the soil away right down to the rock. On flatter country, stripped of natural cover, the soil also tightened, rejecting raindrops which then consolidated as sheets of water that could scour away the surface soil. With so much soil washed into them, rivers became shallower and wider and burst their banks more easily; at the same time, as less water was absorbed by the soil, after a storm the volume of water that poured into the rivers increased. Floods became more frequent and bigger.

If I were to be sentimental about trees, I would choose the trees killed by water at Lake Mulwala on the Murray. In the guide book,

Lake Mulwala is announced as 'an aquatic sportsman's paradise . . . recognised as one of Australia's leading tourist resorts . . . every modern convenience'. With a confident sense of future priorities, the Lake Mulwala yacht club was formed a year before the lake was flooded in 1939. At the Skiland Motel there is a little wooden jetty with a petrol pump: brown water beside the jetty merges into grey-blue; the bright colours of fibreglass boats bob beside the shore. Beyond them there are thousands of maimed trees, all dead. Butchered trunks stick up pale grey, out of grey-blue water, a forest of still water and lifeless wood. Several fishing boats loll in the dead forest; water skiers tease it. On the shore are the green lawns and elegant willows of the Skiland Motel, with a litter of cars and motorboat trailers. Outboard engines and women in bikinis lie here and there on the lawn. If you drive further on, and look back, the maimed and degraded trees become merely distant greyness.

Other mysteries of 'development' are seen in south-eastern South Australia. 'The South-east' can see itself as a single development unit, with its woollen mill, its pine forests, sawmills and paper mills, its vineyards and wineries, dairies and cheese factories, its processing works for vegetables and crayfish-tails, its sheep and cattle. In the dry, fragile landscapes of South Australia, the State most deficient in resources, where a government lost office because of an argument over a dam, each of these activities is valued as a development project and gets a place in the tourist brochures. It seemed part of the good sense of development, to dig channels (called 'drains'), 1,300 kilometres of them altogether, to drain swamps so that they could become farms, using some of the water for irrigation and letting the rest flow into the sea. But now there is a fear that the drains are affecting the underwater ecology of the South-east. At Mount Gambier, 'capital' of the South-east, the crater lakes are a tourist attraction, especially the Blue Lake, which turns to grey in early autumn and back to vivid blue before summer. Once, no matter how much water was pumped out of it, the Blue Lake always maintained the same level: now it doesn't. The underwater ecology faction blames the South-east Drainage Board; others blame the water demands of the decentralized industries in Mount Gambier. Across the road, in a sister crater, its slopes planted with pines and beeches so that it looks the kind of extinct crater you might find in any English gentleman's park, the

Leg of Mutton Lake ran dry a few years ago. Now, mysteriously, water has come back to part of it.

Some of the greatest mysteries of 'development' can be found in irrigation. For example a by-product of the irrigation channels that take water out of the River Murray is that they produce good food for birds that previously used to eat grasshopper eggs on the dry plains; this is one reason why there are now so many devastating grasshopper plagues. The water in the $50 million Ord River Dam encourages the growth of pests that then destroy the crops made possible by the water. Cotton crops in the Ord scheme are so troubled by pests that in 1974 cotton-growing was temporarily stopped. The water may have no final use other than that of a tourist resort. Science has produced pesticides to use against insects that proliferate from such disturbances but, according to the Queensland Government Chemical Laboratory in June 1974, one result is that the proportion of insecticides in mothers' milk runs from seven to thirty-eight times higher than the proportion recommended by the World Health Organization for the milk from cows.

Most native insects showed no interest in plants introduced by the white men. The native grasshoppers and certain caterpillars and plant bugs liked them extravagantly, but usually when the Europeans introduced a plant or an animal they also managed to introduce the insect that could infest it: introduced bugs, moths, weevils and aphids eat introduced vegetables; introduced fruit flies, codling moths, scale insects and ants attack introduced fruit trees; introduced wood wasps kill introduced pine trees; introduced grain moths, rice moths and maize moths eat introduced grain, rice and maize; introduced flies infest introduced sheep, cattle and horses. In the nineteenth century Acclimatization Societies imported starlings and blackbirds, which now attack orchard fruits, and house sparrows which attack wheat; they also brought in live garden snails for these and other introduced birds to eat, and the snails became a pest. Introduced rats and mice eat grain, introduced foxes kill farmers' stock, introduced buffalo, pigs and donkeys have run wild and become pests. Australia is infested by onion grass, cape weed, boxthorn, soursop and other plants from South Africa; burrs, lantana, water hyacinth and other plants from tropical America; clovers, blackberries, docks, thistles and other plants from Europe. Prickly pear, brought to Australia as a pot-plant, had infested four million hectares by 1900, twenty-four million hectares by 1930 when the Council for Scientific and Industrial Research had one of its best-known successes by spreading thousands of millions of eggs of the *cactoblastis* moth from Argentina and South Brazil among the prickly pear infestations, destroying them in a few months. Rabbits overran Victoria in the 1860s; by the 1890s they had reached the coast of Western Australia. Rabbit-proof fences had gone up, but all of them were built too late. Until the Commonwealth Scientific and Industrial Research Organization's introduction of myxomatosis to slaughter them, rabbits seemed as Australian as bushfires, floods and drought.

From the point of view of the Aboriginal inhabitants of Australia, the greatest of the introduced pests began to establish itself on 18 January 1788, when the first of the eleven ships of Governor Phillip's little fleet dropped their anchors in Botany Bay. Yet there is a kind of innocence in these first contacts: whites rowing around the bay, looking at everything; blacks standing around looking at whites; then a superb moment, recorded by Philip Gidley King: 'They wanted to know of what sex we were, which they explained by pointing where it was distinguished. As they took us for women, not having our beard grown, I ordered one of the people to undeceive them in this particular, when they made a great shout of admiration . . .' This was not the only time whites and blacks celebrated their first meeting by looking at each other's penises. When a young Frenchman, part of Baudin's expedition, dropped his trousers after a similar request in Van Diemen's Land, 'the savages were transported with pleasure; scarcely were they convinced that he was formed like themselves, than they set up a cry of joy and acclamation that perfectly stunned us.' When the young Frenchman had an erection, 'they seemed to be applauding this condition as if it were unusual to them. Many of them, with a sort of disdain, pointed to their own soft and flaccid organs . . .' A sketch done at Jervis Bay shows white sailors and blacks sharing a feed of fish and dancing together. Some of the earliest sketches of Aborigines (you can see them in Geoffrey Dutton's *White on Black,* which shows Aborigines through the eyes of white painters) reveal an unusual combination of a sense of difference and a sense of common humanity. With titles such as 'A view in Port Jackson:

A Woman meeting her Husband who had been out on some exploit and offering him some fish' or 'A woman of New South Wales curing the headache' or 'Native man standing in an attitude very common to them all', they show a mixture of sympathy and detachment that many painters now would be too self-conscious to repeat.

One thinks of these early encounters; of how the whites could drop their trousers to show a symbol of common humanity as well as run up flags as a symbol of mastery; of the few recorded instances of whites and blacks having a good time together; and of the other, only-to-be-guessed-at occasions when this might also have happened . . . In all those furtive shovings and pushings between black women and white men in the bush shanties of the pastoral rush, although these matings were part of deals in rum, tobacco, flour, sugar, surely there must sometimes have been some intimations of a common humanity? . . . The division falls: white, black, exploiters, robbed.

The British government had not intended the Aborigines to be degraded and slaughtered: London officials sent out directives urging respect for the humanity of the Aborigines, so that they be schooled out of blackness and become members of the British lower classes. But the demands that the country be turned over to Europeans' use made it inevitable that the blacks be pushed aside and hunted down when they objected, just as inevitably as trees were killed. Like trees, the Aborigines were in possession of land the white settlers wanted: they had no British title to their hunting grounds, so they were trespassers on their own property. Using the sensible rules of economic calculation, a geographer said in the 1850s: 'it would be a libel on Providence to suppose that it was intended that this extensive portion of the earth should be forever occupied by a handful of savages.' As nomads, they defied the civilizing mission of agriculture: to them Australia was 'a common – they bestowed no labour upon the land – their ownership, their right was nothing much more than that of the Emu or the Kangaroo.'

What C. D. Rowley calls 'the guerilla war' against the Aborigines had destroyed their society in South-east Australia by the middle of the nineteenth century. Drawings and paintings from this period in Dutton's *White on Black* show them as mad savages, or as drunken city poor. Later, as their degradation became more organized, during the settlement of northern Australia where they were exploited as cheap labour, or in the reserves where they were segregated so that they could die out peacefully, some of the paintings and drawings became melancholy; but others treated 'the blackfellows' as ignorant clowns, good for joke-lines. Perhaps the most famous drawing of an Aboriginal in my youth was the black man in the Pelaco shirt advertisement who said 'Mine tinkit they fit'.

The Aborigines were not given the same dignity as the native plants and animals of Australia: plants and animals were destroyed as part of exploiting Australia's 'natural resources', as the Aborigines were, but even while being destroyed the plants and animals were beginning to be celebrated in paintings and poems as good in themselves, or even as symbols of Australia; the Aborigines were not. There were a few exceptions: when at the beginning of the twentieth century the States and the cities began adopting coats of arms, if they wanted something native for Supporters, they chose kangaroos, emus, Tasmanian tigers or black swans, except for the City of Sydney, which chose an Aboriginal to help support its arms – but the other Supporter was an eighteenth-century British sailor, with a cutlass and a brace of pistols in his belt.

The 'development' of Australia can still be presented as an unqualified triumph for European civilization, along the lines of a letter in the *Sydney Morning Herald* on 25 November 1974:

> We, the white man, carved our way through the Blue Mountains and opened up the western plains to agriculture. We built roads, dams, permanent houses, fences, streets. We brought the benefits of electricity and gasoline, and discovered the uses of uranium and how to trade it. We made this country what it is today, both good and bad; and we did it all in 200 years. The Aborigines just sat on their anthills for two million years or so, developing nothing, organizing nothing, gaining nothing. Now, because we have taught them a little of what they could have had, they want it all in one fell swoop. I say 'no'. Give them their rights all right – but strictly at the level to which they have contributed to my Australia . . . and not a brick more!

In more moderate terms, the turning of Australia to European use can be defended as a process in which, on balance, intelligence prevailed more usually than folly, but one must also concede the many victories of folly. Australia's 'development' can be seen, on balance, despite disasters, as a human success: Australian foodstuffs, fibres and minerals have helped clothe the world and feed it, and helped give it shelter, tools and sources of energy. But this view is reasonable only if one also recognizes the greedy looting and the blunders of even reasonable men, and understands that not all the depredations associated with turning Australia into a great resources factory were necessary to this purpose. A little more scepticism might have produced fewer atrocities.

CHAPTER THREE

Money Made Us

During debates in the New South Wales Legislative Council in 1853 to determine a new constitution for the colony, those who feared the new democratic ideas expressed concern that New South Wales was becoming 'a money-loving community' in which 'many people think of the acquisition of money only – and nothing else'. The rich landowner James Macarthur quoted Polybius on Crete: there was 'the danger of a deeply rooted, sordid love of gain becoming the prevailing character of a community and obtaining undue influence in the public councils'. Citing the United States and Switzerland, he spoke of the evils of 'a democratic spirit, conjoined with a sordid love of gain' and trusted that 'debasing influences such as these will never be suffered to become paramount here'. During the same debate, W. C. Wentworth explained that when calling New South Wales 'a filthy lucre-loving country' he 'did not mean by this that the country itself was filthy, but the people were filthy and lucre-loving'.

As it became a commonplace that Australia was a sordid money-worshipping society, the ordinary Australian people were blamed: here they were with all this money and they didn't know how to spend it properly. But perhaps the reason why Australians were seen as more than usually concerned with getting money was that it was the rich, not the ordinary people, who didn't know how to spend it. The very thinness of the attempts of the élites at more specialized cultures left Australia looking rather bare. It was not that more money-grubbing went on in Australia than in Italy, or Britain, or Greece, or Hungary, but that not much else was seen to go on, or that what else did go on was distasteful to exponents of derived and provincialized specialist cultures. Or it was invisible: because it was not written about in the books they had read, they did not see it.

All the same, contemporary Australia is a money civilization as other modern nations are.* The 'radiant, mysterious, dangerous' principle of money can move Australians deeply, providing some of the most sublime values and symbols of social order and much of the meaning of individual lives, particularly in the ideas of *price* and *income*.

Income

Respectability, a true Australian virtue, as old as the reformation of so many of the convicts and their 'self-respecting, moral, law-abiding, industrious and surprisingly sober offspring', can be indicated by a person's attitude to his or her *income*. It is not the size of the income that determines virtue or vice, but the reverence or irreverence paid to it. Taking life seriously is a question of taking an income seriously. One of the significant events in Australia's history is the opening of a savings bank in 1819 in New South Wales to help mechanics, servants and labourers learn the virtues of 'economy, industry and matrimony'. Two initiation rites into being a respectable Australian, a true citizen, have been a savings bank account opened during one's school years and a small insurance policy taken out in one's name. Cheque book, department store credit card and Bankcard, along with driver's licence, mark the passage to maturity. Good citizens' names are translated into numbers, magnetized and stored in the memory units of computers but they never occur in the secret magnetic exchanges between those sections of computers' memories concerned with bad credit ratings. To be a good citizen you 'live within your income'. Life is gravely measured out in the slips of paper that record take-home pay, increments, tax deductions. Worthiness is further demonstrated by the mortgage with which a suburban home is paid off. Faith in the future of Australia and the human species is shown by taking out reserve units in a superannuation scheme.

The worthlessness of the counter-respectable, the 'larrikins', archetypal opposites of the 'suburbanites', is also revealed in

*This book is not limited to assertions of Australian 'uniqueness'. An obsession with the 'unique' can misrepresent what one is writing about. It can mean that one becomes shy in discussing fundamental matters.

attitudes to money. The 'larrikin' holds the coins and notes of the currency in guilty delight, and profanely gambles on poker machines, at T.A.B.s, at the races, at lottery offices, leaves them in spilt drinks at bars or in waitresses' trays, passes them over counters into shop assistants' hands on pay nights or gives them recklessly to friends. A larrikin 'lives above' his/her income. Larrikins see money as a measure of conviviality, companionship, affection. Money is to be shared out, spent in company, given to friends. By 'wasting money' they proclaim their humanity. The respectable and the larrikin are quite likely to exist in the one person. At night, before going to sleep, the respectable side of the person fantasizes about retirement and superannuation; the larrikin side fantasizes about a big win in the lottery.

Attitudes to incomes may determine moral worth, but the *size* of incomes can turn human beings into objects, arranging them in order of significance as if they were commodities. This is most obvious in hiring people for jobs: most Australians who sell their own labour, like workers in other industrial societies, are price-ticketed as if they were packaged goods. In lists of what people should earn (industrial awards) remote authorities put a price on types of jobs. By these remote and mechanical procedures assertions are made about what people are worth. As in other money civilizations, someone with individual bargaining power – a glamorous executive or a famous public entertainer perhaps – might be spoken of as a 'valuable commodity', as if it were a special distinction to regard a person as being valuable in the same way as a *thing* can be valuable.

Apart from these precise gradings, the importance coming from size of income can be ambiguous, even mysterious. There can be assurance in being 'well-off', 'well-to-do', 'comfortably off', and stark wonder in being 'worth a great deal', 'wealthy', 'very rich', 'rolling in money', 'a millionaire'; extra radiance can come from a sense not only of income, but of *property*, of owning land, buildings, companies; or from the more abstract idea of *investment*, of possessing magic paper, perhaps not even possessing it but leaving it to someone else to record its ownership. But while being rich gives a person social bulk, greater personal space, 'distance', other matters not connected with income or property also affect how people are regarded; and of course there are different kinds of esteem for different ways of getting an income. Social positions of Australians can be defined by income size or property ownership, but these are only two grids in the maps of their perceptions of each other: there are other overlays. However none takes away from the mathematical precision of income-grading.

The exactness of money as a means of human measurement becomes all the more strange since an income, if large, cannot even be seen. It is merely an *entry*. Of some Australian millionaires it is said 'they are so rich they don't have to carry money'. Their power comes from hidden and distant entries, part of the mysteries of *credit*, marks on paper.

Price

In the form of *price*, money is a powerful language, transforming something that can be seen and felt and touched into something that exists as a mathematical measurement. An Australian sees an outdoor barbecue set, a bunch of roses, a motor car, a pound of rump steak, a transistor, and it becomes a *price*; an object is experienced as the abstract idea of a certain number of dollars. As in other modern nations where the cult of money is dominant, money sets minds calculating and estimating so naturally that the process might almost be part of the body's autonomic nervous system. Or one might compare it with the trick used in old movies and cartoons: no sooner were objects seen than they were transformed into dollar signs on a cash register. This happens not only in daydreaming over advertisements, lottery wins, window-shopping; it also means that the question of how much things cost can be an important part, or even the main part, of conversation. The great question that matters is: *how much*? Whole evenings can be passed in talking about things not in terms of what they are but of what they cost. The price of goods and services is what some Australians naturally talk about: when they meet people they may talk about nothing else. What things cost is reality. In some places, most notably Canberra, a whole evening can be spent talking about the cost of superannuation.

Money values one object against the other. The value can be in this comparison, sorting commodities out in exact order of glamour, a process that is essential for those Australians to whom knowledge of the cost of goods and services is a fundamental part of life's meaning. It can also be necessary to pride and envy. It may not be a neighbour's new curtains or hi-fi set that a suburbanite covets; it may be the price paid for them. In the same way, in their own showing-off it may not be the design of the new patio furniture or the new portable backyard plastic gazebo that decides how much they spend, but the costliness of what they are buying. In companies making consumer goods, 'new product development' can begin with a decision about price. The product is 'positioned' in the market before it is known what it is. The design of the new product will not be considered until it has already been decided what it will cost. In many cases, cigarettes for example, the design of the pack is the important part of the 'product design'. A pack has to relate to the value put on the product by an earlier price decision.

People are not always showing off like this about money: it is a caricature to reduce the obsession with price merely to pride or envy; but the obsession nevertheless exists. For instance, if people are making a new purchase, especially if it is an unfamiliar one, say an overseas holiday on long-service leave or a new kind of domestic machine, they may decide in terms of the top amount they can afford rather than any other consideration. Tour promoters put prices prominently on each tour in their travel pamphlets not just for convenience but also for people to see which tours are near the top price they intend to pay. People are not just buying a tour; they are buying value, which they happen to be getting in the form of a tour. When an 'improvement' in some expensive line of goods occurs – quadraphonic sound, colour television, electric organs – how much can most people know about what they are buying other than the price? But the price they do know. They understand its exactness.

To pay the actual top price is not essential. It is essential for the value of a commodity that its price should exist, but it is not essential that the price should be paid. *The bargain* is an extremely important part of Australian culture. Talking about bargains is an important habit in Australian conversation. The commodity that has been valued at a certain price but sells for less is essential to the pattern of buying and selling. There are many goods of which the full price is only rarely demanded: a price is set to establish the value of the goods, then the goods are sold for less. This can be a permanent feature of the marketing policy for cheap products – their price is set, then they are sold 'reduced' – but it also applies, at least seasonally, to motor cars and domestic machines. So an important conversation for many Australians can be a discussion about prices they have paid for their machines.

And for those who don't believe that price determines value, there is satisfaction in the blasphemy of denouncing such values, a satisfaction that could not be obtained if the hierarchy of prices did not exist. For those who are not regular blasphemers but have moments of scepticism and agnosticism (at a guess, almost everyone) there is the satisfaction of occasionally denouncing a false price, as if one had caught out the god in a trick that was not worthy of him.

Inflation

In the magnetized tapes of Australian computers' memories there are equivalents of figures representing billions of dollars that do not exist except in our acquiescence: we assume that if belief in these abstractions collapses, the government could work its printing presses overtime and deliver currency for the banks to display, as if it were the Host. In the days when their Roman architecture was new, Australian banks were seen as temples of commerce; it might be more exact to see them as primitive shrines where the gods appear when they wish to manifest themselves.

The mathematical exactness of trust is an essential characteristic of a money civilization: activities thought of as 'economic' depend on accurate activity in the electronic circuits of the computers that account for all the figures at the end of each day's trading and in which new figures are created ('credit') because of the strength that comes from our faith in accuracy. The essential is that when the totals are taken out the figures should be correct. It is on the basis of this mathematical activity that we trust each other in ways that simplify the enormous financial complications of what we do. In 1974, with unusually high inflation, there began an unnerving increase in figures used to describe what we were doing. What we were doing was much the same: but the figures had become greater. Nevertheless they were still accurately added up each night. None of the people doing the adding up ran out of their offices into the street crying out, 'The figures are too great. We can't add up any more.'

For a couple of decades we had developed more and more confidence in figures describing types of human activity spoken of as 'economic'. These figures had developed a sacred character. There were devout acts of scholarship. Revered, if often mysterious, texts were produced. There was expansion of specialist studies in economics as part of the general expansion of the knowledge industries that, from the nineteenth century, have dominated universities. And the arithmetic units of the computers, so much better at sums than humans, added to the belief that progress could be measured by mathematics.

Something more was required of figures, of course, than a simple increase in totals: if all the figures went up the result was called inflation. But if, in the process of them all going up one special lot showed a superiority over another special lot, it was known as 'growth'. One possible explanation of the inflation crisis is that the emphasis on increasing the total figures got out of control. Mechanisms for pushing the figures still operated, but something had gone wrong with fine adjustments supposed to push up one lot more than another.

Even those whom inflation had left as well off as they were before, or had made better off, were suffering from culture shocks by 1974, since so much of Australians' conversations and values revolve around price and income; and money is one of their most comprehensive languages. An important part of Australian culture was being challenged: Whitlam seemed to have failed as a guardian of the figures.

Money and the dishonouring of women

In a society where money can give a sense of moral value, goods and services that don't have a price can lose honour. They are not part of 'the economy'. The most obvious example, one clearly affecting most people's lives, comes from the goods and services that Australians provide in their homes but are not described in terms of dollars and cents – housework, cookery, house maintenance, gardening, do-it-yourself house improvement, the bearing and nurturing of the children who will make up the next cohorts in what is thought of as 'the labour force', by which is meant those who are paid for providing goods and services.

In the 1974 Boyer Lectures Hugh Stretton gave a brilliant analysis of this habit of disregarding activities with no price on them, and how this habit has distorted governments' housing policies. He saw 'two economic systems. The paid commercial system produces some of the things we want; the unpaid domestic system produces others', but our present economic theories 'make the outrageous value-judgement that the work of the domestic economy is worthless'. He showed how this convention of taking seriously only those things that have a price on them leads to inhumane blunders in policy.

It can also lead to one of the great insults with which a monetized society humiliates married women. Insofar as they stay at home and remain 'housewives' they may be praised for upholding the family, the health of the nation, and so forth, but since a price is not put on what they do, a money civilization does not give them the prestige and significance conferred by contributing to economic statistics. At times when a high birthrate has been seen as what Australia needed, women's wombs have been official providers of statistics – in the early colonial days cargoes of women were shipped out, put into the first available bed and turned into breeders – but as 'housewives' they are not an important statistic, because their labour has no price put on it, nor have the goods and services they produce. They don't get into official economic figures. Their economic importance is seen as that of 'the shopper' and great, if hypocritical, honour is paid to them for this (see chapter 14); but they are not seen as producers of goods and services. As in the use of the phrase 'working wives' to describe women who go out and work for money as well as working at home, there can even be the suggestion that by staying at home they are rather a lazy lot, not really making any serious contribution to society. Yet at the same time the importance of women who are in the work force (the people who are paid for working) is often concealed. The 'work force' is spoken of as if it is almost all men, as if the economy is too serious a matter for women. Yet usually women are about a third of the total. If the contribution of married women to the work force is discussed, it is often discussed as if it were a grave social problem, deleterious to children, weakening the fabric of society. (See chapter 13.)

At periods of expansionist national dreams bureaucratic apparatuses can be set up to bring immigrants to Australia. The importance of these immigrants is usually spoken of in terms of their usefulness as part of the labour force. They are seen as units of production, necessary to the economy. Yet the greater part of the labour force has come not in migrant ships or chartered Boeing 707s but out of the wombs of Australian women. This manufacture of one of the essential factors of production is not recognized as being related to economic activity. Yet, as Beverley Kingston says in *My Wife, My Daughter and Poor Mary Ann,* this is 'one of the most significant, continuing, and important forms of production followed by women'. The economy, however, pays honour to call girls or girls in massage parlours: they are related to movements of money that can show up as economic statistics.

Except as 'consumers', married women who do not work (apart from the few with investments) are outside the economy. The economy is male-dominated anyway, both in actual control – there is a much greater proportion of men's hands on the controls than women's; and in image – even the work force is seen as more male than it is. But most married women are not dominated in the economy: they are simply not part of it. They are exiled from it. Except as shoppers, they exist outside it. The only money they get is from their husbands; whatever money they control depends simply on the kind of arrangements they can establish with their husbands. What will happen in a future with job-provision by the economy less easy than in the now departing era of affluence, and with greater acceptance of men and women sharing household tasks, with even a possibility of more men becoming 'housewives' and more women 'workers'?

Buying progress

In one of the campaigns that provided ritual legitimization of the federation of the Australian colonies, a politician said, 'we shall create a glorious nation and meat will be cheaper.' The *Bulletin* once forecast that the future Australian religion would be 'Presbyterianism tempered by the rate of exchange'. Three quarters of a century after Federation John Gorton, writing an article in the *Sydney Morning Herald* explaining the idealism of his faith in 'genuine private enterprise', said, 'The existence of more and more companies and individuals who can be taxed (within reason) and who are kept honest by the Government's guidelines, is the best way to ensure tax revenues which, though not the only part, are *the essential part* of social progress.'

And so the great ideals of social progress are translated into cash transactions. A price is put on ideals. 'Progress' is gained by 'expanding tax revenues'. With continuing increases in living standards seen as a natural right, equality, one of the main ideals of social progress in the twentieth century, tended to become a commodity that could be bought by cash transactions: not simply by skimming bits of income from those able to afford it and giving these bits (less costs of administration) to the badly off; but more ambitiously by equating equality with economic justice and so, by various financial transactions – in the 1960s increased expenditure on education was seen as the most important – producing an 'equality of opportunity' in which everyone would have equal access to what some Australians saw as the plum jobs.

I am not here criticizing this type of programme, although it wouldn't take long to suggest that narrowing aspiration down to suburban ideals about career opportunities is an assault on human potential; but even those who agreed with such a programme might not recognize that it assumed a fairly constant increase in spending (Gorton's 'expanding tax revenues') from ever-increasing economic growth and that we are now realizing that this might not go on happening.

A second point, a more general one which includes the first point, is that the financial view of progress as a simple mathematical remedy turns all policy into a spending programme. Just as the American *nouveaux riches* as described by the social critic Thorstein Veblen displayed 'conspicuous consumption', spending money to show off, so governments tended to develop principles of 'conspicuous expenditure' by which they glorified certain priorities. Budgets became dramas in which spending money showed what mattered in life. Some governments favoured 'national development' schemes, huge assertions of the final importance of superphosphate and concrete, but when governments favoured social progress they would give their policies appeal by putting up big budgets. (A lot of that, as it turned out, might also go into concrete.) When the Whitlam government made such huge increases in the money going to education, the Aborigines and the cities, it was showing where its heart was. The effects of this extra spending had not been given much consideration. The government was bestowing on education, Aborigines and the cities the honour of making them more expensive.

The view that most Australian government policy-making is economic has been a favourite of Australian political and social critics for several generations. The following example is taken from a political science text: 'Australian politics are, in the main, economic politics . . . In the twentieth century, all Australian parliaments have acknowledged that their function is primarily to allocate resources in such a way as to satisfy, as far as possible, the conflicting demands of competing sectional interests.' Note the cool rationality of the phrases, 'allocate resources', the 'demands of competing sectional interests'. It is as if a government were a machine to estimate pressures and adjust to meet them. But governments can simply be habit-ridden, only jolted into new action by sudden vote-catching ideas or vote-losing fears, obsessed by sentiments, moods and fancies; when they engage in self-interested calculation they are not necessarily reacting to 'conflicting demands' but trying to attract marginal votes (which is a different matter). It is true that they weigh up one expenditure against another – but this can be improvised in a few weeks of slapdash budgeting to which the precision of the final figures gives apparent rationality. Some of the apparently more hard-headed, 'realistic' economic policies in Australia have come from crazy notions; but since they have been expressed in terms of money they appear thoughtful and methodical. It may be true that the 'hip-pocket nerve' can produce a reflex action that can kick a government out of office at an election that coincides with an economic crisis, but this is a different question.

Profit

When I think of the worship of money I think of the great principled sacrifice made in 1972 by Frank Packer. It would be quite wrong to say that money was all that mattered to Packer, but it would be true to say money was his god. He had many other diversions but as a serious man of principle with a view of personal values and social order, he spoke gravely of money, and of the greatness of profit. His perspective had profit as the great principle holding society together: men who made profits were the nation's benefactors. The atmosphere in his surroundings was heavy with money: there was a big steel safe sticking up in the middle of his office with money in it; stacks of papers with figures on them lay in neat batches on his desk; wherever his hand fell it was likely to be on figures; men came in and out with documents about money; people would sit around his desk and speak of profit and loss; in surprise raids he would call for the expense accounts, the petty cash vouchers, the contributors' claims, and with his felt pen scrawl out items, then wait and see who complained; in a crisis, records would be spread in front of him and he would look over the lists, point to names and order sackings; or he would order others to make economies, with the threat that if they did not do so he would make them arbitrarily; when he was holding court, dry martini in hand at one o'clock, whisky in hand at six o'clock, the conversation was likely to be about the goings and comings of money. But he did have indulgences in which money was used for other purposes. The most regularly extravagant of these was the morning newspaper he owned, the *Daily Telegraph.* He loved the *Daily Telegraph.* It lost money all the time; perhaps no one apart from Packer himself and a few of his court esteemed it; many derided it; by the kindest standards it was humdrum; but Packer loved it. It seemed like *power* to him; he would think of something and the next morning there it was in the paper. It appeared to give him political influence. It gave him interesting guests to invite to dinner, esteem when he was in London and New York, his knighthood. But I think he also loved it for itself – its racing news, the printing presses in the basement, the ledgers upstairs recording its failures, the comic strips, the newsagents' accounts, the sub-editors at their semi-circular desk, the attacks on the Labor Party, the teleprinters, the scruffy typography, the stereo department, the stock exchange reports, the letters to the editor, the lift-drivers (until he sacked them). Perhaps it also held for him reminders of promise – the excitements when he took it over in 1936, the improvizations and hopes of a younger man. Those who wanted the company to make bigger profits saw the *Telegraph* as their main enemy. There would be private meetings: for a while they would talk about improving the *Telegraph's* sales; then they would stop; they knew they couldn't get their hands on it until Packer was dead. Sometimes they would dream that he might sell it. There had been offers, but nothing happened. Then in a couple of days of private excitement the *Daily Telegraph* and the *Sunday Telegraph* were sold to Rupert Murdoch, for $15 million. Packer didn't need the money; $15 million couldn't console him for the loss of the unique pleasures the *Telegraph* had given him; but he had sold it because he was a man of principle. Fifteen million dollars, even if he didn't need it, was too large to be refused by someone who saw profit as the prime mover of human affairs. He would have denied his own humanity if he had refused it. His reaction to this sacrifice was so great that people wondered if it might kill him. Several times he cried when he spoke of it; his face was pinched and his gaze distracted; he walked slowly like a wounded old man, his hand on a helpful shoulder; his words wandered; he spoke of the dead as if they were still alive and gave orders about men and machinery that it was no longer in his power to give. Those in his office who loved him spoke of the goodness of a man who could make such a sacrifice.

At times, in a country like Australia, the word 'profit' is used as if the word itself contained the key to the mysteries of society; it can be seen as the dynamic that makes everything work either well, or lamentably. At times it is even too sacred to be directly named. In a radio broadcast, for example, Menzies praised it without mention, except in the euphemism 'reward':

> If our material civilization is to produce improved and improving standards it must have a dynamic quality. It must aim constantly at progress. And there can be no progress without enterprise; the encouragement of enterprise in the most direct human fashion, that is by the prospect of reward, seems to me to be fundamental.

On the other side, the Labor Party has always believed that control of profits or even their abolition, would answer most human disappointments. It was natural that when Whitlam became Prime Minister he should want to set up a Prices Justification Tribunal to control profits and that for some Labor people the first, for some the only, remedy against inflation was to bring profits down. They brought profits down and when they found it hadn't worked, for a few of them that was the end of their policy. For their part, some of

Labor's opponents, holding to the Packer principle that the profit-makers were the benefactors of the nation, seemed to think that the spirit of profit, if liberated in pure form, would drive away inflation. These differences on 'the profit motive' can for some people present the battle between the forces of light and the forces of darkness, the Holy Spirit and the Evil Spirit, that in other civilizations is recognized more obviously as theological.

In what way profits are a decisive consideration is now harder to estimate than these opposite creeds suggest, as any reader of John Kenneth Galbraith would now know. It is not only profit that makes a money civilization; it is also income, property, price, the general emphasis on money-making as a basis of social order, the estimation of attitudes to money as measures of moral worth, the use of money as an exact language, as a confidence-creating abstraction, as a value-creator and as a grader of persons and objects.

The classic kinds of attitudes about maximizing profits might apply to small businesses, or slightly more complicated businesses where people might still think they know what they are doing, or some (not many) larger businesses, survivals such as Packer's company; although Packer's was a public company, it was made appear in myth that he was 'the proprietor', and he, like other newspaper proprietors, but to an extraordinary degree, had the knack of seeming to run the company as if it were a corner store. But the difference is easy to see in large, abstract business bureaucracies with no sense of personalized ownership. Such formations are so complicated, and the conditions in the outside world about which they must make guesses are so complex, that they have much more serious matters than maximizing profits to worry about. To stay in business, to keep their shareholders or their overseas controllers quiet, and to increase their own salaries and benefits, the persons who run them have to produce regular increases in annual earnings and they have tried to do this by getting bigger rather than by running their firms more efficiently. In this context 'profit' means making enough to stay in business and to satisfy the nominal owners (the mysterious shareholders) or the overseas controllers: what is critically important is to continue to get funds to finance continuing expansion. (This consideration is equally important in a government-controlled enterprise.) In this context 'profit', with all of its rich associations with free enterprise as the basis of social order, may be most important simply as a legitimizing idea, as a sacred word that should be present in all serious discussion, just as in other situations there is a use of words like 'democracy', or 'the people'.

A 'government-controlled' enterprise (a government-owned enterprise run by a bureaucracy but 'answerable' in unpredictable ways to some parts of the government) can sometimes get funds for expansion without showing profits. So can a foreign-controlled enterprise (an enterprise run by a bureaucracy that is a colony of a bureaucratic business-world empire in which the top of the hierarchy is located in a foreign city); if its world controllers develop a fancy for it, an Australian branch can expand although showing regular losses, usually because this is part of an operation against a world rival; from a profit viewpoint this may not make much sense but such seasons of indulgence can last for some time – at least until things get too tough back home. Funds for expansion are not so easily raised by 'shareholder-controlled' Australian enterprises (enterprises run by bureaucracies, but 'answerable', in that unless they produce a certain level of dividend the shareholders may accept another company's takeover offer). A company will get funds to expand despite losses if it is part of a larger Australian company whose controllers for some reason or other feel like expansion and have some spare money. But in the top company it is hard for them to go on raising money for expansion without overall profits or at least the promise that some time there will be profits. (Occasionally this is done by cheating.) Continuing to get extra funds is a condition of continuing to expand business. It is expansion – growth – that is the dynamic, not profit-making. Profit-making is one of the ways that make possible continuing funding of continuing expansion.

Why is there this obsession that companies should go on getting bigger? At its most elemental, company growth feeds the esteem of those who preside over it. A great explosion of importance can come with the increase in the mass of their wealth and property. Imagine the self-esteem at his commercial height of Ben Boyd, the 1840s London stockbroker turned Australian colonial speculator, one of the 'haughty, gentlemanly selfish class', 'always devising some plan of pleasure or business', controller of two townships, a bank, a whaling station, a whaling fleet, coastal steamers, wool stores and more than 2 million hectares of sheep runs before he went broke, unsuccessfully tried his luck in Californian goldfields and then disappeared on an expedition to the Solomon Islands where he was reportedly concerned with establishing a 'Papuan Republic or Confederation'; presumably he was killed, perhaps eaten. Packer, more like Ben Boyd than like a modern company executive, had a similar sense of personal expansion through activity: as his business grew, he grew. His money, and the machines, buildings, staffs, furniture, newspapers, magazines, books, television programmes about which he could make decisions, were part of his personal substance: they gave him bulk. To these he added his horse-racing, his expensive America's Cup challenges, his knighthood, his generosities, his ruggedness, by these means giving his bulk glamour.

By people looking for easy answers to the problems of human misunderstanding he was seen as desiring power over people's minds and over governments, but I don't think that from day to day this meant much to him. Others may have tried to use him for these purposes, but when he went in for them himself he wasn't much good at it. The power he wanted was the power of size and achievement. It was for the sense of infinite expansion that he bullied old machines, fought for market shares and strove for baubles and trophies. And usually, when he used his *Daily Telegraph* in the opinion business, the power of expressing his own opinions excited him more than the prospect of influencing others: just as he wanted to control big companies and win big cups, he wanted to make a big noise and say what he thought was right. To try to influence people would have been demeaning.

For Ben Boyd and Frank Packer there was a sense of personal ownership. This was partly untrue in Packer's case in that he was using shareholders' money as well as his own, and, as it turned out, altogether untrue in Boyd's case because all his enterprises simply rose on a bubble and burst: but they both saw themselves as proprietors and had their sense of importance extended by the size of what they were seen to own. Most modern executives don't own as much. Nevertheless, most modern executives can feel they are increasing their bulk and glamour by extending the number of digits magnetized in their companies' names in the memory banks of the computers.

However something more than satisfaction of size pushes

executives into a craving for eternal growth. What also pushes them is, simply, fear. In the mysterious shiftings of the 'anonymous market', who can be sure he knows the secrets of how to survive? For those who are competitive, continuing compulsive anxiety about their share of the market produces continuing novelty, new marketing plans, new production techniques, new advertising styles, new office systems, above all, new brands or continuing revisions of existing brands. If a company is not ever-active, ever-growing, there is a fear that competitors will reduce its 'market share'. Firms startle themselves by buying other firms or lurching into quite new lines of business, hoping that somehow, if they keep moving, the whole show won't collapse. Even monopolies keep moving, diversifying into new kinds of ventures, spreading out, afraid their luck won't last. For some this anxiety is also pleasurable: they are gamblers whose delight in growth is partly found in its uncertainty. Others are afraid of risk; they dread the excitement of new policy; but they can't avoid it. Others believe in prediction, research, programming; they move confidently and methodically into the unknown. But whatever their reaction they see growth as essential to survival. Packer, for whom the excitements of risk and the lust for achievement may have been even more compelling than the delights of bigness, was nevertheless also afraid. He could look at his properties and see how each could quickly die. Only ceaseless activity would save them. At other times even that belief went and he was left only with the stoicism of the gambler. I remember one Saturday night being uncharacteristically caught in a drinking session with him and some others in his boardroom; as everyone drank more we all agreed that life was a game of cards.

In the money civilization as well as the accuracy and abstractness of money, its carefulness and respectability, there are the gamblers and desperadoes – not only the larrikins, but many of the 'monied people' themselves. Respectability earned its great victories in the Australian colonies when all those wage earners invested in savings banks and building societies, 'owned their own homes', and joined friendly societies; but throughout the nineteenth century a large proportion of the rich were not respectable and prudent, but lucky gamblers: traders, squatters, gold-mine promoters, land sharks. Stock exchanges developed most vigorously out of speculation in gold shares. The 1960s and early 1970s stock exchange gambling on minerals came from a long Australian tradition of risk, greed, carelessness and crookedness.

The stock exchanges display the ambiguities of money. On one side they are temples of moral and social significance, of intelligence and efficiency: carefully articulated by electronic equipment, they can be seen as the backbone of private enterprise, itself the basis of social order. They represent growth, production, investment, expansion, progress, *capital*. The other side is pure recklessness: the yappings of voices at the time of a boom, the quick scribblings on boards, the telephone calls, the conning of trusting clients, the fiddles, the muddles. When the minerals boom collapsed and there was not much business in the brokers' offices, some of those who had done best out of the boom had to spend months finding out where everything was, clearing up the mess.

The shareholder has been seen as the archetype of capitalism. Yet one can say a great deal about Australia's buying and selling without talking about shareholders. In effect, big businesses now are bureaucracies concerned with the anonymous and mysterious idea of 'the shareholder' only as a threat in a takeover campaign. Even the few freaks – some media companies, some retail chains, a few others – that still look like old family concerns can do so only because shareholders are kept in their place. People from certain rich families remain company directors in big companies that are not foreign-owned, but this is less because they have financial control through their shareholdings than because they are part of a self-perpetuating social oligarchy of rich office-holders. The major shareholders in most companies are other companies, and much of the investment money of firms is raised not by selling shares on the stock exchange but by borrowing money. The bureaucracies interlock. One can imagine that private shareholders might altogether disappear, with institutional and/or government lending altogether taking over, and although there would be no more share certificates to put in safes or deposit in banks, no more stock exchange reports on the radio, no more finance sections in the newspapers our money civilization might remain much the same. If the very rich were taxed away some of the boards would have a different look, but otherwise the running of companies might remain much as it is.

It might not be profit or shareholding that is essential to the way things have been running in Australia, but the ability of governments to produce economic policies which are consistent with growth, or which encourage it, or offset its unsettling effects. (That I don't know which word to use – 'consistent with'? 'encourage'? 'offset'? – is an example of our present predicament.) Growth has been the dynamic, not profit, although profit may have been necessary to growth. If growth no longer works – and as a principle it has been as important to government bureaucracies as to private business, both in financial policies and in manpower (the bureaucracies themselves getting bigger) – then we are in for a new period in history.

CHAPTER FOUR

The ‘New Nationalism’ of Minerals

‘Australia has been virtually rediscovered in the past ten years . . . The new exploration of the continent – vertical instead of horizontal, geophysical rather than geographical – has uncovered vast hoards of mineral wealth, along with reservoirs of oil. It is no over-statement to say that the country that has stepped affluently into the seventies is a New Australia.’ When in 1971 Colin Simpson gave this justification for calling his latest book *The New Australia*, he was saying something that many Australians by then believed.

With the minerals rush of the 1960s the export saga swung into an episode of new confidence. In 1938 the export of iron ore had been banned – partly as a step against Japanese militarism (its effect, if any, would have been to aggravate Japanese paranoia), partly to save up apparently dwindling resources. The government’s geology adviser had said, ‘it is certain that if the known supplies of high grade ore are not conserved, Australia will in little more than a generation become an importer rather than a producer of iron ore.’ With exports banned, companies didn’t bother to look for iron ore. In December 1960, with an export crisis, the ban was lifted, in the hope of sales to Japan: it was worth bothering to look for iron ore again, and eleven months later it was announced that it had been found, in the Pilbara area of Western Australia, in deposits four or five times the size of known reserves. Two years later, one mountain, Mount Tom Price, was discovered to contain more iron ore than had been known to exist in all Australia three years before. A month after the Pilbara finds, oil was found in commercial quantities at Moonie in Queensland. Almost unnoticed, new activity had started in lead, zinc, copper and beach sands mining. Large deposits of uranium and bauxite had been discovered; in 1963 full-scale production began in the bauxite fields at Weipa in Queensland and a big refinery opened at Gladstone in 1967 to process the ore. Coal export contracts were signed with the Japanese, boosting existing fields in New South Wales and prompting development of new open cut mines in Queensland. During the 1960s coal production doubled and exports of coal went up thirteen times. Discoveries of nickel and new discoveries of iron ore were made. Oil and natural gas were found in Bass Strait.

New images of Australia were thrown up. Television documentaries showed mountains of iron ore, railways built across deserts, ports being set up in the sand dunes. Pre-packaged townships with swimming pools and mini-markets were put down on bare red earth. There were camera close-ups of oil rigs, earth scoops, drills. Freighters sailed back to Japan filled with east-coast coal. Journalists flew to oil rigs in helicopters from Melbourne. While the real developments were by big firms with real assets and real contracts, a festival of speculation in new companies allowed communal rejoicing on the stock exchanges in London and other foreign capitals, as well as Australia. Promoters with little more than leases of scrubland and good letterheads raised millions of dollars for companies not one of which, at the time of writing, has yet produced a dividend; sometimes these speculative shares opened at prices up to 1,000 per cent above issue prices. In a drama of hope and penitence, shares in Poseidon nickel jumped from a few cents to $280, then collapsed. But while, in the manner of stock exchanges, money circulated to no productive purpose in an irrelevant drama of greed and fear, out where the mining was actually happening the statistics got more impressive every year. Pre-eminent in wool, and prominent in beef and wheat, Australia now boasted of being one of the world's five main producers of bauxite, iron ore, tin, nickel, silver, lead, zinc, manganese, uranium. In 1974, at the United Nations Conference on the Law of the Sea, it laid claim to exclusive possession of raw materials on that one tenth of the world's continental shelf that surrounds Australia, a resources area roughly the size of India. There has never been such a variety of 'producers'.

In particular, a new kind of Western Australia was created. Western Australia saw itself as the centre of the 1960s mineral expansion, and changed from a kind of envy of 'the eastern states' to boasts such as, 'In fifty years, or less, Western Australia will be the most important economic unit of the Commonwealth', or even,

'Western Australia is one of the fastest growing economies in the world.' Founded in 1829, at a time when the Union Jack was being run up here and there over small settlements in remote parts of Australia, and then hauled down again when they failed, the first settlement of Western Australia did not take long to fail; but it was allowed to stay anyway. It was the last colony to have a run of luck, with an irritating fifty-five years to wait before its first gold rush, although there was the consolation that its gold-rush period coincided with the 1890s depression in the east. The long wait, its extraordinary isolation (separated from the rest of Australia by one of the larger deserts) and the absurdity of its size (two and a half million square kilometres) produced such a feeling of detachment in West Australians that the majority vote for secession from Australia during the great Depression remains one of their historic memories: when they sulked they were still likely to reach for secession. Now, with the minerals boom, they were able to knock down many of Perth's old buildings and put up new ones that made it look more like the eastern cities. It was satisfying that for a while, Charles Court, then the West Australian Minister for Industrial Development, became one type of ideal Australian statesman – a man of contracts, statistics, blueprints, projections, development plans, hard facts.

From a wider view, the minerals boom, which continued despite the stock exchange crashes of the early 1970s and the inflation panics of the mid-1970s was one of those convulsive economic dramas that changed Australians' view of themselves. In this it was the equal of other great rushes: the squatters' rush to the grasslands in the middle quarters of the nineteenth century, the 100-year rush (1860s to 1960s) to take up small farms, the great city-building booms of both nineteenth and twentieth centuries, the twentieth-century rush to build factories. It brought Australians possible new definitions of Australia and of its image in the world. They could see their country as bigger and more important and, because the frequent T.V. shots of mining equipment gave the false idea that manufacturing activity was going on, more sophisticated: in projecting export figures there were exultant forecasts of the humbling of farm products by the products of mines.

Maps had suggested an Australia whose size and small population made it weak; but statistical tables now suggested an

Australia whose mineral resources made it strong. A stock part of certain kinds of speeches and articles was to point out that Australia's G.N.P. was greater than that of all the countries of South-east Asia combined. Australian prosperity had previously been shrugged off as high per capita matter but insignificant in total, no real strength to it, but it was now discovered that *in gross terms* the G.N.P. tables rated Australia very high. John Gorton's 'new nationalism' was largely a euphoric pride in the newly-discovered deposits of minerals.

The 'new nationalism' of minerals was related to a pride in trade that was no longer simple and British, but mature and cosmopolitan. In the mid-1960s Japan replaced Britain as Australia's best customer; at the start of the 1970s the United States replaced Britain as Australia's second best customer; in the mid-1970s New Zealand replaced Britain as Australia's third best customer; there were forecasts that Britain would not hold even fourth place. Equally, Australia no longer bought as much from Britain: at the start of the 1950s nearly half Australia's imports came from the 'mother country'; by the mid-1970s imports from Britain were down to about fourteen per cent with both the United States and Japan supplying more goods to Australia than Britain did. The decision to abandon pounds, shillings and pence for dollars and cents and the decision by Harold Holt's cabinet in 1967 to keep the Australian dollar steady while Britain devalued were taken as an important assertion of Australia's independence, perhaps unparalleled in financial matters since the decision in 1910 to establish an Australian currency; but by the time the Whitlam government was making its changes to the exchange rate, it seemed normal that Australia should do what it wanted with its own currency and there wasn't much comment when Australia pulled its remaining reserves out of sterling, leaving only enough to cover its sterling trading. The main source of new capital investment was not Britain but the United States; there were excited hopes about raising investment money in Japan and in Western Europe; there was talk about playing off one against the other when expectations developed that a uranium enrichment plant would be set up, a great monument to Australian patriotism, embodiment of the dream of acquiring both higher profits and higher civilization by exporting metals processed rather than in their 'rawest state'; when the Shah of Iran visited Australia, politicians had trouble keeping their minds off his cheque book; Rex Connor, Whitlam's Minister for Minerals and Energy, began to dream of what he would do with four billion petrodollars when they were raised by a Pakistani go-between named Khemlani . . .

Although there was still some of the old financial xenophobia (for Malcolm Fraser, to borrow petrodollars was to 'put Australia into hock to the Middle East countries'), Australians, in the 'new nationalism' of changing trade patterns, could see themselves come of age; more sophisticated, in the diversity of exports and range of techniques; more cosmopolitan, with trade deals transcending political faiths and ethnic values; more independent, with a newly-defined strength in resources. In a nation with such a strongly developed cult of the export, it wasn't surprising that when exports changed, the way Australians saw themselves began to change, although the strength of old fashions was such that changes were patchy, with much opposition from those who still clung to older ways.

When Whitlam took over as Prime Minister, all this pride in minerals and maturity in trade was boosted by a twelve-month $2,000-million trade surplus that brought total foreign reserve funds up to $4,800 million. In a country so strongly self-defined as an export country, this surplus, along with the growing bounciness of the mineral years generally, helped increase even the Whitlam government's confidence. Over its whole opening period it suggested that Australia could now afford to pull faces at foreign investors and tell them it didn't want their money. The euphoria of the mineral finds had driven Gorton to some of the over-confidence that helped destroy him; the sheer abundance of money increased Whitlam's buoyancy – until he began to sink into it. Some of the extremes of his boldness – the historic 25 per cent cut in tariffs, the freeze of foreign investment, the removal of tax incentives for mining and prospecting, the end of the petroleum search subsidy, the reduction of export incentives grants, the ending of investment allowances to industry – seem hard to imagine without foreign funds of $4,800 million. It was a significant omen: world trade seemed to favour Gough Whitlam's version of John Gorton's 'new nationalism'.

There was some hatred, and fear, of foreign money; this was first given memorable expression by Country Party leader John McEwen in 1963, in a phrase that was repeated year after year until many people had forgotten that it was McEwen who had invented it. At a Country Party conference in Victoria he said,

> We in this room are mostly established farmers. If we don't earn enough annual income we live comfortably by selling a bit of the farm every year, and that is pretty much the Australian situation – we are not earning enough and we are selling a bit of our heritage every year.

As part of the cockiness of the minerals boom, Gorton played more strongly and more often on the theme that Australia didn't need foreigners investing in its 'natural resources' any more, although, like McEwen, he didn't do much about it. He produced his best-known metaphor in a speech to an Australia Club luncheon at the Dorchester Hotel in London in 1969: 'Until very recently it has seemed to me that the posture of Australia in seeking overseas capital has been the posture of a puppy lying on its back with all legs in the air and its stomach exposed saying "Please, please, please give us capital. Oh, tickle my tummy. Oh, on any conditions".' McMahon took up the theme by setting guidelines for foreign investment and Whitlam got some of his best cheers during the 1972 election when he attacked foreign ownership, now attributed in the new vogue term, to 'multinationals'. By 1975 concern with the selling off of the farm had become so associated with the Labor Party that Doug Anthony, McEwen's successor, sneered at the phrase during the debate on the Khemlani petrodollar loans, having forgotten, presumably, that it was created by his predecessor.

Confidence in minerals made possible the redefinition of attitudes contained in Whitlam's 'resources policy' speech in the House of Representatives on 24 May 1973. This gives a good example of the role played by Whitlam as a 'modernizer', although some of his government's later actions on resources policy were prime examples of its mastery of fiasco. On the one hand he was confronting attitudes of the past – in this case, a despairing love of the export, such obsession with the beauty and strength of natural resources and such fear of their faithlessness that there had been a policy of export-at-any-cost, demonstrably irrational (as most traditional policies come to be), but supported by declarations of economic self-interest. On the other hand he was aware of new perceptions. There was concern in the media and the intellectual journals about 'the resources crisis' and 'the environment crisis' caused by humans using the earth's resources so greedily and creating such filth that the only question was whether the human race would end by starvation or suffocation. Alongside these supranational questions were the local ones: the affronted national pride of the tummy-tickled puppy as it annually sold off bits of its farm; compensatory desires to feel more important in the world; love of an unspoilt countryside; complacency at having such high foreign reserves; and greed (maybe if we hung on to our resources we'd get a better price for them).

In his May 24 speech Whitlam crystallized what was already in the minds of many Australians. He underlined the familiar point of foreign control: 'Under the policies of benign neglect tolerated by our predecessors, Australia's national resources, their exploration, exploitation, processing and export fell increasingly into the hands of foreign concerns.' Australia's resources had become part of the plans of other nations: 'Because of our political and economic strength and stability, we are likely to become a significant element in the resources strategies of the importing countries.' This gave Australia a new strength: 'We are moving into a situation where our commercial and strategic importance to the Western world is giving us a growing political voice.' So Australia should have its own resources strategy: 'The stage has now been reached where Australia needs to develop policies of her own that take account of the fact that we are becoming the object of others' resource strategies . . . I consider the resource question will become a very important part of our foreign policy.'

In the debate on May 31, Opposition speakers nosed around the idea from several different approaches: sarcasm ('. . . a new trendy, high-sounding name' . . . 'public relations diplomacy'); high realism ('The deliberate use of the economic weapon in international politics can be a hazardous exercise'); me-tooism ('The previous government had taken action . . . to develop a resources diplomacy for Australia'). The Melbourne *Age*, which was inclined to favour the government, said: 'If we allow the big brothers to use Australia as a quarry we will not only suffer economically; we will downgrade our influence in the world to the status of a colonial territory.' The *Sydney Morning Herald,* which was inclined to attack the government, nevertheless saw it on this occasion as 'breaking new ground' . . . 'interesting' . . . 'very good sense'. Six days later it praised the government's successful conduct of the renegotiation of iron-ore contracts with Japan, 'the first, and a critical, test of its concept of resources diplomacy'. 'The ore producers would have settled for lower prices if left to themselves . . . It is a definite plus point for the government's resources policy.' In the 1974 election, Opposition leader Snedden promised Australians maximum control and ownership of their natural resources.

Whitlam had put a new item on the agenda. 'Resources diplomacy' wasn't an original idea: the Opposition were speaking the truth when they said they had been privately playing around with it too. But Whitlam gave the idea a weight it didn't have before: he made it real.

But he did nothing much else. The only practical implementation Whitlam announced when he gave his speech was that he would appoint a scientific adviser to the Department of Foreign Affairs. On a visit to Mexico he got muddled and excited and seemed to suggest the more extreme idea of an international cartel among the mineral exporters (twenty-four hours later he denied he meant this), but his critics were now using his earlier, more moderate ideas to attack him, thereby, in effect, defending him. It was only in October 1974, seventeen months after Whitlam's May 24 statement, when the Japanese Prime Minister was coming to Australia and it would have looked silly not to have something looking more exactly like a mineral policy, that a statement was quickly knocked together. It left many puzzles. Australia ended the year preaching interdependence among producers and consumers: it was now a moderate. By the time Whitlam was in Brussels he was talking with at least passing conviction of 'yellow cake' and 'enriched uranium' and newspapers used phrases like 'vast dollar bonanza'; but again nothing happened. The Minerals and Energy Minister negotiated prices for existing exporters which were probably better than the Liberals (who had been an easy touch for foreign companies) were likely to have won. But so far as new projects went Labor was so concerned with its own plans, wanting it all done *its* way, that again nothing happened. Nevertheless, as statesman, as politician, as clown, Whitlam had dramatized a change in attitude to exports and natural resources. If their luck continues, Australians might become more selective about who tickles their tummies.

If you stop for a while at Woods Point, a tiny settlement in Victoria's gold-bearing Gippsland mountains, you can go through what is now becoming a stock Australian experience: wondering what it was like back in the gold-rush days, the first great period of minerals euphoria. Look around: clean, cool air, the sparkling Goulburn River almost smothered in trees, steep wooded hills on all sides cramming down on little weatherboard houses clean and neat enough to be miniatures. In Geoffrey Blainey's book *The Rush That Never Ended* you can find that in the 1860s, in the days of Woods Point's brief ambition, it was a town of 4,000, with its own stock exchange and brewery. Several Woods Point storekeepers each kept several hundred pack-horses to bring provisions: along the mountains from Walhalla to Woods Point there were hundreds of independent reef proprietors, supplied by trails of fifty or more pack-horses with jingling bells on the muddy tracks, snow-covered in winter. But at Woods Point now you can hear a sound no longer heard in most of the other old gold towns: that noise in the bar, with its warm brown walls hung with stuffed trophies of stags, deer, eagles, comes not only from locals, passers-by or timber-cutters: some of it comes from living goldminers. Several miles on you hear the sound that once was a symbol of Victoria's golden prosperity: drive out of Woods Point past ferns and high, slender trees, imagine pack-horses, bullock drays, hillside camps, and then at Gaffney's Creek stop at a tattered tin shed among a straggle of houses where a sign says this is the A1 mine, started in 1862 and now 'the richest gold mine in Victoria', and listen to the sounds coming from the tin shed: they are from the crushing of quartz.

The sounds of quartz being crushed or the conversation of off-duty goldminers are now unlikely to be heard by most Victorians, but Victorians are anxious to reconstitute memories of what it was like to be, for a season, the world's most famous gold producer. The cult of Walhalla is a sad example. Walhalla was one of the mining townships thrown up as prospectors struggled along the spurs and valleys of the Gippsland mountains: it was the one that lasted, with a number of mines, including the richest in Victoria. For several generations it maintained a population of 4,000 (although, in sentiment, its cultists may now give it up to 20,000, a good round figure for a ghost town); houses clung in tiers to the steep sides of its hills; there was a banging all day of quartz crushers. But by the time the railways came (a 'puffing billy' narrow-gauge mountain railway, carrying the Premier on its inaugural trip), the mines were closing, so the railway came in handy for people who pulled down their houses to ship them to towns where there was still work. After Walhalla had been pulled down, they pulled down the railway. In its *Notes on Walhalla* the National Trust has added some amendments, one of which reads 'Page 6 – delete the second last paragraph starting "Walhalla now has only about thirty people" . . . The sawmill has disappeared, and the level of people dropped considerably.' But Melbourne people want Walhalla to be part of their past and though practically nothing is left of it they go there to try to imagine what it was like. On a holiday hundreds of cars and motor bikes litter the road alongside Stringer's Creek; car doors slam, cameras click; people walk in file along fern-lined tracks to the cemetery; they stare at the ludicrous remains of the bakehouse – a frame with a few pieces of wood hanging from it; an old brick gold-vault still sticks up, its surrounding bank gone; the rotunda from which Deakin urged federation is neatly kept, amongst the scrubby bushes; there are tours of an old boarding-house, an old cottage, a ride on a little train built by a group of Walhalla cultists. There is nothing of a gold town left to see; but the mountains are splendidly wild.

The cultists of Beechworth in the north-east have more to show for their enthusiasm. Gold was struck there in 1852, when the area was part of a sheep run; prospecting extended right along the Ovens Valley, creating the Ovens Mining District of which Beechworth was the capital. Beechworth quickly ran out of its own gold, but it did well out of running the Ovens Mining District, and public buildings went up in granite to establish its importance. When the gold ran out, these buildings, particularly the gaol and the mental hospital, continued to serve Beechworth; now they serve it by bringing tourist dollars. In the words of the National Trust's *Historic Public Buildings of Australia*: 'sunlight glances through leaves of autumn-gilded elms, dappling the honey-textured granite . . . ingots poured from the crucible of time.' The National Trust's

Notes on Beechworth suggest a tour that takes in thirty-seven buildings; one of them is Sinclair's Supermarket, built in 1968 with a 'very fine remodelled facade, constructed in 1968 in such a manner as to retain a harmonious blending with the surrounding existing buildings and thus retaining the atmosphere of the 1870s.' The Chinese burning towers at the cemetery have been restored by the Lions Club. But, except in its showing-off, it's not really a gold town. In fact, even taken simply as an old town, it tries too hard: its buildings lack the honey-colour, the unity and the rusticity of the pictures in the National Trust book; perhaps there is more left in the atmosphere of an old town in the pleasant main street of Yackandandah, a few miles away, and more reminders of gold in the wrecked riverbeds of the Myrtleford district further up the Ovens Valley where, among the dairy farms, tobacco farms and hop gardens, forty gold-dredges used to eat away at the river flats, turning them into gravel and stone.

Both the muck and the showiness of gold come out best in Ballarat and Bendigo and the towns around them. For muck, look at the swirled-up earth, abandoned shafts and mullock heaps of worked-over diggings. For showiness and gold-city grandeur, Ballarat has an Avenue of Honour twenty-two kilometres long and in the Botanic Gardens an Avenue of Prime Ministers, with a bust of each of them. At Sovereign Hill in Ballarat they also have a goldfields reconstruction. The reconstituted main street is of the present folk museum pattern, with the routine extras of souvenir horse-shoes at the blacksmith's, Wanted For Murder posters at the printer's, children's rides in the stagecoach, meals at the bakery, but the rest of it is a working museum of mine shafts and the machines that served them. Running beside the outraged shapes of these wooden engines is Red Gully Creek, in which at any one time several dozen tourists are likely to be swishing pans, or rocking large wooden cradles, peering for specks of gold in the 'wash dirt' they have bought from an attendant. Some tourists simply scoop up soil and rinse it, shaking and looking, and shaking again, with an absolute concentration that saves them from acknowledging the senselessness of what they are doing. With the strange engines in the background, it might be a Hieronymous Bosch torture scene: mad engines, demented people.

These attempts to reconstruct gold-rush life – there have also been television programmes (beginning with *Rush*) – are part of a general move to create a sense of an Australian past. But gold can seem glamorous and freakish. There was a past Australia in which the mining of more humble metals was also of paramount importance. But that has not yet come through as a strong Australian tradition. Its revival would give a sense of continuity, an 'explanation' of the present, with its emphasis on mining.

Since the 1920s, over the long decades of collapsed confidence – it had almost been forgotten that there had been such an Australia. In these decades of enervation there were nine conferences called to talk about holding a national geological survey: but nothing happened. The United States, Canada, South Africa and some of the Latin American nations were concerned with finding out what minerals they had, but the imaginations of Australian governments were repelled by such grandiloquence; they seemed to prefer land settlement schemes, setting up small farms where cheap foodstuffs could be grown for Great Britain. In 1938 David Rivett, chief executive of the Council of Scientific and Industrial Research, wrote, 'We now have the distinction of being the only Dominion in the Empire without a National Geological Survey.' When Geoffrey Blainey published his history of Australian mining, *The Rush That Never Ended*, in 1963, it seemed an odd kind of title: many people thought the rush had ended decades before. In fact new aspects of the rush were just beginning.

The emphasis on gold, which is a special case, can mar the sense of continuity. The Coal Creek Historical Park at Korumburra in Victoria is a useful exception: it has begun the reconstruction of a nineteenth-century coal town, on the site where black coal was discovered in 1872 by a passing selector: its poppet head, mullock heap, miner's cottage, section of a mine tunnel, railway track given authenticity by the Scotch thistles beside it and mine manager's cottage given authenticity by the plastic scones in its kitchen, have the makings of a reconstruction as successful as Sovereign Hill. Other folk museums could record the great nineteenth-century successes of the copper mines of South Australia, Tasmania and New South Wales, the tin fields of New South Wales and Tasmania (for the decade of the tin boom, Australia was the world's largest producer). There could also be commemorations of the innovative successes of Robert Carl Sticht, inventor of pyritic smelting,

A. D. Carmichael and Leslie Bradford, inventors of new processes for roasting lead ores, of the experimenters who worked out the flotation processes; there could be a reconstruction of an early School of Mines or commemoration of the formation of the Australian Institute of Mining Engineers.

At Broken Hill there is in fact a kind of living museum along the line of lode of its great silver-lead-zinc deposits. With its silhouette of head frames and dumps the plundered, broken-backed stretch of the Barrier Ranges from which, since the 1880s, so much wealth has come, runs straight through the town, but behind the fencing it seems unused. On a tourist minibus tour it comes back to life. Cages empty miners. Skips empty ore. Ore crushers pound. Conveyor belts roll into processing mills. Dumps of new concentrate are scooped up and trucked. The bus passes fragments of old mills, eroded foundations, bits of walls, subsided plants, rusted boilers, mounds of muck, wrecked engines, ruins of old smelters shaped like martello towers, slag dumps shining in the sun like hills of black glass. In a hollow, the gutted engine house of the abandoned Kintore Shaft, with a decorative frieze on its walls, a splendid complex of wooden beams in its roof and long, graceful windows, is like the town hall of a progressive suburb in the late-nineteenth century. An artist is sitting outside it, beside a pile of lead concentrate, sketching it. In the largest of the open cuts two of the old ladder shafts of the 1880s remain. One of the curiosities pointed out to tourists is an outcrop of ironstone, a few metres of it – almost all that is left of the original 'Broken Hill' before they dug it away. Now they are digging into the honey-coloured 'hills of residue', bulldozing into the contents of old dumps to cart them off and process them all over again to get some more of the goodness out of them. A mile away, under the Imperial Lake, a large artificial lake for sailing and canoeing, drills are bringing up new mineral finds that may keep Broken Hill going for a few more decades.

There is a difference between the truth of the statistical tables which show the recurrent (and at present growing) importance of Australia in the export of minerals, and an imaginative realization of what these tables mean. Blainey's book, the folk museums and other reconstructions can help make the statistical tables imaginatively true; they can help give meaning to the idea of an Australia in which minerals have always had economic importance.

The T.V. documentaries, the politicians' speeches, books like Colin Simpson's and other manifestations of the 'new nationalism' of minerals also begin to give meaning to the statistical tables, so that ultimately people might accept this 'new Australia'. Despite his follies, the obsessions of Rex Connor as Minerals and Energy Minister were part of this drama of a new realization of what Australia might be. Connor spoke of Australians being 'white Arabs', but he may not have fully developed the potential of this idea. Could the emphasis on Australia as a resources processor and exporter reach a stage where so much money would come in that Australians could shut down some of their more inefficient industries, import more goods from other countries, work less, enjoy their leisure more? Such a speculation would challenge the habit of seeing the export as a master that must be served, rather than as a servant.

CHAPTER FIVE

The Fall of the 'Pure Merinos'

As you drive along the Cobb Highway in the flat country of the Riverina, between Deniliquin and Hay, you find, not long after the Pretty Pine Hotel, a statue of a merino ram looking down from the left-hand side of the road. It is the merino in imperial mood – horns like warrior's helmet, rolls of wool suspended from its neck like chains of office: an ancient Assyrian conqueror. The statue is of the famous Peppin merino, bred at Wanganella last century by George Peppin and his son at Australia's most famous stud: it produced strains so successful that more than half the sheep of Australia and South Africa and many of the sheep of New Zealand and Latin America are now descended from Peppin stock.

Like an emperor, the Peppin ram had its statue, and like an emperor its face was on the coinage. Until the change to decimal currency the head of a Peppin ram was on one side of the Australian shilling, 'tails' to the head of the English monarch. The cult of the merino reached such heights between the two world wars, with Australians expected to congratulate themselves for living 'on the sheep's back' that the merino ram could seem the typical Australian. Tom Roberts's nationalist paintings 'Shearing the Rams' and 'The Golden Fleece' were hanging in major galleries; Australian history had been so written that John Macarthur's breeding of Spanish merinos early in the nineteenth century seemed the most significant event in the colony's early years; a popular movie was *The Squatter's Daughter*; national tradition was reflected in photographic studies of rams in newspapers and magazines, horns gracefully curling, silken prize ribbons garlanding their necks. No mere human could provide the reassurance that came from reports of record prices brought by prize rams after the annual sheep shows.

There was such confidence in the careful breeding that had

produced the merino that it may have had something to do with the fashion that for a while developed of squatters marrying their cousins: they wanted to improve the breed. The extension of ideas of stock-breeding to humans had other manifestations: at the first States-Commonwealth conference on Aborigines (1937) optimists suggested that the blackness of Aborigines could be 'bred out' – like black sheep. The phrase 'pure merino' had been coined in the 1820s to denote settlers without convict taint: now it had the more particular use of signifying those born into the socially elect, the pedigreed. There was even prestige to be gained from the close relation between wool and wars: prices went up not only in world wars, but during lesser episodes such as the Russo-Japanese War of 1904-5. In the Korean War wool had the greatest of all its booms. Even when wool was threatened in the 1950s by the commercial success of synthetic fibres, it was a tribute to the merino that Australia therefore seemed ruined: if wool was to go, there could be nothing else to take its place.

The only product to be personified, even if by an animal, wool was the supreme export cult. In fact its percentage of total exports was believed to be much greater than it was. It ran at somewhere around 40 per cent (up or down) for most of the century, but it was often given credit for the whole 80 per cent or so contributed to exports by all farm products (until the mineral boom brought this down to about 50 per cent). Because of efficiency in growing and handling, wool's total contribution to employment was low.

To a wool man, to make such calculations could seem insulting. His sense of importance was based not simply on wealth, but also on an identification with national prestige. I was having lunch with some of them – brokers, growers – at the time that minerals were beginning to rise in the statistical tables: for the early part of the lunch they talked about wool's survival against synthetics and they did so in the prudent, intelligent, calculating language of big men in an industry who can always look for a way out. When I said something about minerals they became irrationally angry. It wasn't their sense of profit that was disturbed, but their pride. However much wool might prosper in itself, it was insulting that it might be placed second to iron ore, even worse that it might later run third to bauxite. By 1974 a further insult was being proclaimed for wool: export of coal was about to become more important. Pride was among the promptings of those who opposed proposals in 1961 and 1966 for a floor price scheme for wool, in which the government would bid for wool at the auctions, when necessary, to keep its price up. When the Country Party, in the panic of the price crash of 1970, was at last able to set up a reserve price scheme, that seemed an end to wool's great prestige. Wool had lost its honour. By falling back on government protection it became just like other industries. And some of the rest of us, denigrated by this animal worship, were happy to see its end. Part of the 'new nationalism' of the Gorton period was delight at our final release from having to honour the sheep.

All fashions go . . . but when I was a boy it seemed unlikely that there could be such a turnaround in the world that even the immutable truth that Australia rode on the sheep's back might be challenged. Hitler might bring down the British Empire, but there would still be the merino sheep. Of course, to some the honour of the sheep still remains: along the Hume Highway, at the approaches to the township of Gunning, there is a big faded hoarding which says 'Welcome to Gunning, part of the richest wool growing area in the world'; twenty miles on, between the hoardings for hotels and service stations there is 'Yass: The fine wool hub of the world' – faded leftover banners proclaiming the excellence of an old faith.

Sixty miles on from Yass, at Gundagai, the kiosk beside the pioneer monument is bright with souvenirs, piled up its walls: bullock driver dolls, swagman dolls, Waltzing Matilda tea towels, drovers' colouring-in cards, babies' bibs decorated with cattle dogs. Outside, behind yellow rails, is the statue of a bullocky's dog sitting on a tuckerbox. A wishing well, for offerings, is in front of the shrine. In the souvenir shop they have replicas of the statue done as egg cups, teaspoons, bells, statuettes, pencil sharpeners, mugs, key rings.

The merino may finally have failed in its dominance of Australian values but it isn't an accident that the souvenir dolls at Gundagai portray the characters of the 'pastoral age'. The rush in the 1830s and 1840s to graze sheep and cattle on cheap kangaroo grass is as good an example as you can get of one of the main themes of this book, how economic changes in Australia have been associated with the creation of new social types, new customs, new fashions in the arts, new ways of looking at existence. The rush to get rich by growing wool created many of the tokens of Australianness and even though, like the boastful hoardings of Yass and Gunning, these tokens are now fading there is still the force of nostalgia in them.

The vigour of the pastoral expansion threw up a society within a society, a unique society, with its own institutions, moods and repertoire of 'types', with new visions, priorities and definitions of reality and its own forms of fancifulness, all of which achieved a kind of national glamour. It had its own rules – a cultivated crudity, an enforced openness of manner, imperatives of hospitality – and for many people its manners came to represent national characteristics. Its particular developments of the codes of 'mateship' were presented by some as a national faith; the importance of the shearers' unions in the early drama of trade union struggle seemed to give some distinctively Australian and rural concepts of brotherhood to the idea of working-class solidarity. Theories of a collectivism that developed from the pastoral frontier (ignoring the individualism of other Australian frontiers) were used by some social critics to explain a great number of Australian habits.

Pastoral-age words formed our perceptions of Australian landscapes as effectively as Arthur Streeton's paintings of rolling brown grass stretching out to blue hills under pale skies: *paddock*, *station*, *property*, *backblocks*, *the outback*, *stock route*, *skeleton flats*, *waterhole*, *homestead, woolshed*, *stockyard.* A chic revival of pastoral-age songs began in the late 1940s. (The songs themselves were being sung throughout the twentieth century, but it was in the late 1940s that they were *revived*, and sung in pubs, wine bars and coffee shops.) Now the children of people who were then students learn songs about shearing sheds, and ask their parents (who won't necessarily know the answers) the meaning of work terms like *ringer*, *boss of the board*, *snagger*, *colonial-experience man*, *tar-boy*, *barebellied yeo*. 'Waltzing Matilda' is one of the Australian songs considered seriously for a new national anthem. The Chinese played 'Click Go The Shears' when they gave Whitlam his banquet in the Great Hall of the People.

As often happens in sudden new economic thrusts, the pastoral age threw up new caricatures. These types, as part of what was to become the more general originality of life in *the bush,* were unique: *the shepherd* ('a crawler after sheep'), despised by everyone except *the hutkeeper*, whom the shepherd could in turn despise; *the stockman*,* more highly regarded than the shepherd – looking after cattle could seem more of a man's job than crawling after sheep; *the timber-splitter*; *the hurdle-maker*; *the shearer*; *the itinerant dealer*; *the shanty-keeper* (owner of a grog shop, adept in helping the station hand 'drink his cheque'); *the bullocky* (master of a dray pulled by six or more paired bullocks, the wool piled on the dray as high as a haystack); *the drover*; *the new chum*, *the old hand*. Then, later, *the manager*, *the pannikin boss*, *the rouseabout*, and that symbol of the nineteenth-century counter-culture and sad hero of 'Waltzing Matilda', *the swaggie*. Some of these types disappeared, but the shearers survived so successfully that they were chosen to ride horses at the head of the procession celebrating Federation on New Year's Day, 1901 (they were the only reminder of the bush in it); other types survived, to become dolls on the shelves of the souvenir kiosk of the pioneer monument at Gundagai.

Among them was the grandest of these types – the squatters. They have now shrunk, compared with their ambitions, into such modesty that the word itself might seemed outmoded except in the wining-and-dining vocabulary of the young executive's night out: The Squatters' Bar in a hotel-motel . . . Squatters Punch as an aperitif . . . Squatter's Mixed Grill, placed on the menu between Drover's Special and Cattleman's Steak. Nevertheless I shall use them as an example of an Australian social type whose creation is associated with particular economic circumstances. Their history is an important part of the Australian story; and even now, there is still some force left in the idea of the squatter.

Thrown by economic circumstances into the aristocratic situation of being masters of great stretches of land, squatters made the only real attempt in Australia to form an indigenous upper class of the traditional kind (a rich, hereditary landed interest, with wealth, power and honour). For a while they seemed the only 'pure

*It should be remembered that there were cattlemen as well as sheepmen in the pastoral age. In some areas there were more cattle than sheep. One of the effects of the merino cult on school history writing is that it represents the squatters' expansion as a phenomenon affecting only sheep.

merinos'. When people speak of the lack of an upper class in Australia they speak of the squatters' failure. Even when people speak as if there were an upper class in Australia, by describing its characteristics they may still speak of the squatters' failures: the crass inability to clothe self-interest in public concern, the derivativeness, the inability (apart from such fruits of the squatters' autumn as Patrick White, Russell Drysdale and a few others) to throw up men of original culture.

One way of watching the squatters come and go is to take an overview of Victoria, which was created because white people seized hunting lands from brown people to graze sheep and cattle on them. Some of the land-seizers sailed from Tasmania in the mid-1830s and set up little ports where Portland, Geelong and Melbourne now are. Their ships carried what they needed: food supplies and tools, sheep and cattle, bullock drays and bullocks, stock feed, building materials, pigs, poultry. Take Geelong: in 1836 the squatters start arriving, landing their stores and their sheep in 'the noble harbour' of Corio Bay and taking over Aborigines' land for grazing. In 1838 some of the first squatters move inland, concerned that the government might sell off the coastal land: some tents are set up on the beach, to act as a store, then a wooden building . . . a town is laid out, land sold; small suburbs develop; by 1848 Geelong outstrips Melbourne in the value of the wool it exports from its pastoral hinterland.

About the same time as the landings at Geelong, Surveyor-General Mitchell from Sydney crossed the Murray River on a showy exploring expedition, in which his marching column included herds of sheep and cattle, carts and boats on wheels, as well as convicts and soldiers. Two men marched with barometers, bearing them as Roman legionaries carried their *fasces*. Mitchell proceeded with the military precision of an invasion into what he named with typical gush 'Australia Felix'. As he stood, 'the first European intruder on the sublime solitude of these verdant plains', he 'felt conscious of being the harbinger of mighty changes', contemplating 'a country ready for the immediate reception of civilized man', 'destined perhaps to become eventually a portion of a great empire'. Overlanders from New South Wales burst into it almost as soon as he got back to Sydney, following the wheel-tracks of his expedition until they found unoccupied grass.

Less than twenty years later, in the 1853 debate on a new colonial constitution, the squatter created by these wool rushes was seen as the prototype aristocrat:

Of all the dependencies of the British Crown, there is none, and never will be any, where such large fortunes in land exist . . . we have among us, and we shall have among us to the latest generation, our Shepherd Kings . . . men of this class, in ages long gone by, were . . . founders of the greatest and most celebrated cities and nations of antiquity. Who but this race founded Ninevah and Babylon, and subjugated surrounding nations?

In Argentina, when new wealth came to a landholder from the combination of export demand and British-financed railways, he was likely to build a French château or an Italian villa on his *estancia* and set up a nobleman's park. In Victoria, while many squatters were satisfied with a large, expensive homestead with wide verandahs and enough rose gardens and exotic trees to cut it off from the rest of Australia, the more fanciful put up large nineteenth-century English gentlemen's mansions of up to forty rooms. Towered, turreted and arcaded in the Italianate style, built in basalt, with a village of stables and outbuildings behind them, these mansions were surrounded by large gentlemen's parks of ten or even twenty acres with flower gardens, vegetable gardens, orchards, glass-houses, and imported oaks, elms, cypresses, pines, willows, peacocks and pheasants, beyond which grazed the flocks of merinos. One property had its own railway station. As their influence at last began to weaken, the squatters seemed even more extravagant in their living: it was the beginning of their autumn and they showered gold. They were a mysterious presence hidden by their vast paddocks from the eyes of other people; they had become even more magical because they were under the spell of a distance that divided them from all others.

In Buenos Aires the *estancieros* became patrons of horse racing and in Melbourne the squatters were likely to spend small fortunes on maintaining racing stables, so that in the style of the rich of ancient Rome both *estancieros* and squatters displayed civic virtue by subsidizing public games. In Buenos Aires *estancieros* demonstrated their exclusiveness by membership of three clubs; in Melbourne the most honoured squatters dominated the Melbourne Club, whose bland facade 'would not at all disgrace St. James's

Street'. The richest or showiest maintained town mansions, and held weekly balls during the long 'season' they spent in Melbourne.

Many of the Argentine *estancieros* were Anglophiles. The Victorian squatters saw themselves not as Anglophiles, but as the real thing: *gentlemen*. They were *British*. Although as uniquely Australian in economic circumstance as bullockies, shearers or swaggies and, if international comparisons were to be made, more like Argentinians than like the British, they saw themselves as honoured standard-bearers in Australia for British civilization. ('Honoured' here is not the same as 'liked'.) For this reason they became important in defining what Australians understood British civilization to entail. Some families were automatically members of the Government House set, no matter who the Governor was. They coveted British knighthoods and awards, although they rarely engaged in sufficient public service to justify getting them. They sent their sons to Geelong Grammar, which was as English a 'public school' as could be set up in Victoria, and if they could afford it they would then send them on to Oxford or Cambridge while, in the English manner, they might send their daughters to finishing schools in Switzerland. The men wore English suiting; in the London manner, their wives wore French dresses. They spoke of 'the old country' and 'a trip home'. But the Britishness of the squatters was of an attenuated type: it was the Britishness of Edward VII – flashy, plutocratic, horse-loving (although not as tolerant of Jews).

They lost overt political power before the *estancieros*: the new fashions of democracy frustrated their hopes in the early 1850s. But for as long as they could get away with it, squatters in Victoria, as in the other colonies, tried to dominate political representation and the administration of justice. The strength of the pastoralists at the time the colonies established their new constitutions in the 1850s helped set two important precedents in Australian politics: powerful upper houses chosen on unrepresentative principles, and a general bias in electoral distribution in favour of rural areas. Even though their influence weakened, some squatters were members of the Legislative Council, the undemocratically chosen upper house of the Victorian Parliament, and by their influence over Melbourne's 'society' (the clubs, the racing set) and the commercial and financial groups, they could influence other Council members, by these means consistently trying to stem the flow of democracy in Victoria.

Then came the decline. Drought broke some of them, or rabbits infested their pastures. When land reform came, stations were subdivided. Some of the smaller farms that were cut out of the old stations still produce wool and fat lambs now, but others were turned over to dairying, even vegetable-growing (potato fields where the merinos once grazed). Finally, with the floor price scheme for wool, the words 'squatter', 'pastoralist' and 'grazier' began to be replaced by the more efficient-sounding 'wool-grower'. The 'Shepherd Kings' had become 'wool-growers'. Some of the mansions, built out of old volcano lava to last forever, fell into disrepair and were pulled down. Of those that stay up, some look dowdily over-dressed among the busy, prosperous farms whose successful owners read the Hamilton *Spectator* advertisements for swimming pools, take-away Continental food, fibreglass boats. One farmer built his cottage in the garden of one of these old mansions and turned the mansion itself into a storage shed. Those houses that are still maintained, sometimes by city money, or by companies, are likely to be photographed and classified by the National Trust, even used as film sets. A few monuments to the squatters' honour remain in Melbourne: a mansion or two in a suburb here and there. The old offices and warehouse of a pastoral firm, a strong, dark, dignified basalt building which has the calm solidity of the Riccardi Palace in Florence, is given a 'B' by the National Trust. The Melbourne Club (classified 'A') is still there, its assured facade confronted on the other side of Collins Street by a building 'development', product of a construction rush reminiscent, in its gambler's hopes, of the squatters' rushes of the 1830s, the success of which produced the Melbourne Club. In the post-Menzies era, during one of the Liberal Party succession disputes, television and newspaper pictures were taken of the carved doors of the club, set between two carriage lamps, as reminder of its continued power.

Of course all of this is over-generalized. It is most true of the Western District of Victoria and, to a lesser extent, of the Riverina in New South Wales whose pastoralists have usually seen themselves as really belonging to Victoria. Large pastoral buildings still survive, especially in the north of Australia, and many pastoralists lived less ostentatiously than the Western District and Riverina squatters. But the character of the squatter as presented here is an important type in the national repertoire, as villain or hero. The idea of the squatter can still be used as a conceptual tool.

As a national villain, the squatter mounted on his thoroughbred was comforting to several generations: hatred of the greedy, snobbish land monopolist successfully sustained hopes that an easy answer to life's inadequacies would be found in 'unlocking the land', 'bursting up the big estates'. And the political habit of having powerful upper houses chosen on unrepresentative principles is still one of the peculiarities of Australian politics, even if the squatters are no longer of particular importance to them. But as an admirable type, the ideal of a squatter, sympathetically simplified, could also affect the conduct of many other country people – and not only country people. In their high summer and golden autumn the squatters, monopolizing honour as they monopolized land (an honour that could be hated as well as loved) were critically important as an example of how you behaved if you got to the top. Earlier there had been the English gentlemen who were sent out as officials, and even after self-government there were still English bishops, generals, governors, admirals, headmasters, professors to show Australians how to behave, but squatters were masters of three different kinds of native magic – the magic of possession, of aloofness and of national significance. They were not only rich, but honorifically so, owners of bales of wool as well as overdrafts and letters of credit: to the glow of money they added the radiance of land. At the same time they put an unmatched distance between themselves and others: they were unobserved on their estates; even their annual public local ritual, the picnic races, was conducted so exclusively that it was one of the proudest affirmations of their aloofness. And in two national matters of overriding gravity, sport and the balance of payments, they were essential: they were masters of the secrets of those two prestigious phrases, 'the races' and 'the wool clip'.

For those who imitated them, what was there to imitate? Mainly the mysteries of being a gentleman. They were not in the ordinary sense a culture-bearing elite – the refinements of Western civilization were beyond them; they were bearers of forms of British snobbery simplified for the Imperial export market. These included scorn for education, except as an expensive caste mark, a way of developing 'character' and training the voice of command: the Australian private school education, it was said in 1910,

> breeds a . . . man who can rise to the top, who can face difficulties, who can lead others, who can manage affairs successfully; a man who may be neither smart nor doctrinaire not scientific nor original, but in whose hands any piece of business is safe which entails the management of men.

The pride of possession was also important, the aristocratic virtue of *being there first*, of scaling honour chronologically so that whoever first got land was best, with the accompanying exclusion of also-rans: the motto of the Melbourne Club was *rara avis*. Loyalty to the Crown and to the Old Country were essential, and except for a few odds and ends, so was suspicion of most things that were Australian.

It might seem eccentric to have spent these paragraphs on such an exploded force as the squatters, when I could have been writing about managing directors or the heads of government departments. But I wanted to make it clear that to say that Australia has no generally recognized upper class is not the same as saying that Australians are all egalitarian. And the squatters set (or strengthened) certain prevailing styles and tones. Managing directors now belong to the Melbourne Club; the heads of Commonwealth departments, the Menzies knights, used the Commonwealth Club in Canberra in exactly the way the squatters knew a club should be used. Even more to the point: Malcolm Fraser is a rich pastoralist from the Western District of Victoria. It was not until 1975 that a squatter became Prime Minister of Australia. It was significant that he got there after the intervention of Government House.

CHAPTER SIX

Standards of Civilized Excellence

When the Romans found they were suffering an economic slump at the beginning of the fifth century B.C., they took realistic action: farmers had always sacrificed to Ceres, the goddess of growth, but to put relations on a stronger basis the cult to her was made official, with special rituals, sacrifices and festivals. As a personified 'Agriculture', Ceres is still given esteem in Australia: she may appear as one of the four figures in a fountain paying baroque honour to Governor Phillip in Sydney's Botanic Gardens; or as the carving of a naked woman in that holy place, the Shrine of Remembrance in Melbourne; or as a live girl, dressed in a bikini, sitting on a papier mâché cornucopia in the procession opening a festival in a country town. Agriculture, totemized as a wheat-symbol, has been celebrated on objects varying from triumphal arches to the present two-dollar note; as a cult it is maintained by the six State Royal Agricultural Societies, and the nearly 600 lesser agricultural societies which organize the annual 'agricultural shows' that have given every town of any size its 'showground' and provide Australians with one of their important festivals.

Agriculture was one of those abstract nouns used by Michael Massey Robinson, poet and convicted forger, in the odes he wrote each year in Governor Macquarie's time and read at Government House levees celebrating the King's and the Queen's birthdays. Agriculture, Arts, Commerce, Industry, Reason, Learning, Labour, Freedom and Justice would all flourish now that 'Britannia's sons had come forth, to brave the dreary perils of the lengthening wave'. With experiment, care and thought, agriculture, one of the necessary arts of civilization, would be part of that improvement which had become fashionable in Britain amongst great landowners, including King George III himself. A special school of painting developed, the 'agricultural school', to portray noblemen in front of their barnyards. It was this sense of aiding civilization by thoughtful improvement that was so affronted by the gamblers' untidiness of the squatters' rush.

The squatters seemed nomads defying one of the necessary conditions of civilization. Australia could not be civilized if it was to be one great sheepwalk. To emerge from barbarism, it would have to grow crops for a living. Even when they settled, the squatters were seen as plunderers of 'the natural pasture, the abiding source of wealth': they were a defiance of reason. When they spoke in their own defence they seemed to confirm their guilt, with a view of Australia as 'illimitable waste' with no other value than as a place for stock to nibble the grass.

Such ideas were first challenged by the colony of South Australia. It opposed the pastoralists' gambling with such confidence that it still sometimes sees itself as the most civilized and thoughtful part of Australia. South Australians with this kind of memory weren't surprised when, for a while in the late 1960s, with Don Dunstan and Steele Hall, they seemed to have the only modern political leaders in Australia; or when, despite Federal Labor's debacles in 1975, in a State election they held firm to a political centre of reason and moderation by returning Don Dunstan. Colonial South Australia had to suffer the barbarism of sheepwalks on the fringes of its settlement, but it was as determined for the civilized order of wheat-growing to be the prime reason for its existence as it was determined to be a society not of convicts but of free men. At the start it was the only colony in which ideas such as thrift and hard work could credibly seem more valuable than the idea of luck. But the luck was there: the only reason it was the first colony to have general success with family-sized wheat farms grouped in orderly settlements was that land suitable for wheat was near its coast; suitable wheat land in the other colonies was in the interior, useless until the railways came.

Nevertheless there was a comfortable sense of order, rare in early Australian colonization, in the confidence with which South Australia was 'determined to become one of the first agricultural colonies in the world'. Consider the signs of progress: the criss-crossing of surveyors' markings on maps; towns, each modelled rigidly on Adelaide (unlike those of the eastern colonies that were modelled on the grid-like town-planning principles of imperial

Rome); stone farmhouses; fences of iron wire pulled tightly through wooden posts; flour mills; the twenty-eight little wheat ports, five with their own short railway lines, that were established around the two gulfs; the ketches, brigantines and barques loading the wheat as part of a process leading to export to the East, southern Africa and Mauritius . . . But stop there. The Australian sense of the absurd has its victory. Settlement became too confident. It spread too far. With unexpected dry weather in the 1880s, marginal settlement collapsed. Hundreds of thousands of acres were abandoned. Empty farmhouses crumbled back to lumps of stone.

However it wasn't such a fiasco as the farm failures of the other colonies. The belief in agricultural improvement, in the benefits of experiment and care and thought, had its first success in South Australia at a time when, generally, Australian farming practices were a generation or two behind Britain. Australia's first contribution to the industrial revolution was probably the invention in the 1840s of a stripper-harvester by John Ridley, South Australia's first miller; trials of combine harvesters in the 1870s began a process of improvements; special tools and techniques were developed to lessen the despairs of breaking in the tough mallee country; by the 1880s, at the South Australian Agricultural College, phosphate deficiencies had been identified as the main cause of declines in harvests. The South Australian Agricultural College was the first in Australia, but the improving approach was spreading to other colonies. Departments of Agriculture and agricultural colleges were set up and the universities trained graduates to staff them and to conduct researches of their own. It was slow work, done on skimpy budgets by dedicated men. William Farrar, breeder of the drought-resistant 'Federation' wheat which became the most popular wheat in Australia and is now commemorated on the two-dollar note, made combinations of wheats, 200 to 400 cross-breedings annually, trying to produce strains that would best suit Australia's soils, climates and diseases, and for half that time he had to rely on his own resources; even when the government made him official 'wheat experimentalist' he didn't get much money.

It was only after the Council for Scientific and Industrial Research was established by Bruce in 1926 that Australia really became a country that would have pleased King George III in his role of enlightened farmer-improver. A famous photograph of Bruce, taken in 1923, shows finely-chiselled features, plus-fours, long cigarette holder, one foot on the running board of his Rolls Royce. But if the eighteenth-century 'agricultural school' of painting had survived into the 1920s (there were so many other unlikely survivals that the idea is not altogether absurd), Bruce, through his creation of the C.S.I.R., could have been painted as a Great Improver, posed in front of a meat-freezing plant or a fruit cannery.

The C.S.I.R. had been ten years coming. In January 1916 Billy Hughes opened a conference called to consider setting up a Commonwealth research organization, with a gush of aspiration:

> Science can make rural industries commercially profitable, making the desert bloom like the rose . . . Science can develop great mineral wealth . . . It can with its magic wand turn heaps of what is termed refuse into shining gold . . . Science will lead the manufacturer into green pastures by solving for him problems that seemed to him insoluble. It will open up a thousand new avenues for capital and labour and . . . will help [the people] to clear thinking; to the rejection of shams; to healthier and better lives; to a saner and wider outlook on life.

All that followed was an Advisory Council. Two years later a bill was drafted to set up a Commonwealth Institute of Science and Industry but another two years elapsed before anything happened. Politicians turned the proposal into controversy: the Institute would involve 'huge expenditure'; it was a threat to the States; it would be cheaper and better for Australia to depend on overseas research; scientists were impractical men anyway, 'not caring to do productive work', simply out to get 'soft jobs in magnificent suites of rooms in Melbourne'. The Institute was, said the *Age*, a 'mad scheme'. When it was set up in 1921, it was short of money, research facilities and scientific staff; it was mainly a co-ordinator of other people's research (which included investigation into the tanning properties of Queensland mangroves, the use of mechanical cotton pickers, possible commercial uses of seaweed, the cultivation of flax, the import of carrion birds to combat the blowfly pest, defects in Australian leather, ways of combating infestations of cattle ticks, prickly pear, St John's Wort, the buffalo fly, white ants, the Squirler disease in bananas).

When Bruce decided to set up the C.S.I.R. to replace the Institute most of the decisions were made in three weeks, despite resistance from universities and 'pure' scientists. The founding bill got through parliament in a month. Like Hughes, Bruce addressed a conference of scientists, but fashions in rhetoric had changed. There was a brisk emphasis on practicality and modernity. To 'progress with the times' Australia needed 'the most modern and efficient . . . scientific methods'.

The C.S.I.R. rented some rooms in Melbourne and set to work with soil surveys; with investigations into the use of native timbers, nutritional factors in the sheep industry, ways of preserving fence posts and railway sleepers, of preserving beef, of transporting citrus fruit; it looked for methods to combat wheat rot, tomato wilt, and blue mould in tobacco, scourges in pineapples, bananas, apples, as well as buffalo fly, white ants, blowflies, black disease in sheep, pulpy kidney, the Kimberley Horse Disease. With the assuredness of the eighteenth-century English noblemen contemplating the new possibilities of clover and turnips, scientists in the C.S.I.R. applied methods of Improvement to Australian agriculture.

The Commonwealth Scientific and Industrial Research Organization, as Bruce's C.S.I.R. was renamed in 1949, now has a staff of six and a half thousand people. It still pays tribute to eighteenth-century standards of civilized excellence. By rational calculation and intelligence it has won great victories in research on soils, plants and animals; and it has brought to Australia more than 35,000 plant species to experiment with for pastures, forage or crops and made remarkable world contributions in the biological control of pests, in combating plant and animal diseases, in the control of water evaporation, in wheat and sheep breeding, animal nutrition and fertility. It has been a pioneer in making woollen textiles mothproof and waterproof and in the use of minerals to offset deficiencies in soils.

An improving aristocratic landholder would have appreciated the economy of style in the C.S.I.R.O.'s 'cobalt bullet', a pellet of cobalt injected into animals, which throughout their lives liberates cobalt to make up for trace-element deficiencies in soils. Or in its feed supplement which produces beef and butter with a higher-than-usual proportion of polyunsaturated fats. An aristocrat's desire to preserve his opulence would have approved the

C.S.I.R.O.'s present research on ways of inducing the woollen fleece to fall off a sheep so that no shearers need be employed to cut if off. He would have admired the good husbandry in the idea of importing dung-beetles to dispose of the cowpats that despoil pastures, while the mites that live on the beetles attack the maggots that grow into flies.

In its annual report the C.S.I.R.O. displays its achievements with aristocratic laconicism (laconic, because it merely gives examples, without being comprehensive; aristocratic, because it is nevertheless showing off, with a studied negligence). Among other things, the 1973-4 report happens to mention use of soil surveys in urban planning methods for revegetating mine dumps, study of the ecology of rain forests and the biology of the bandicoot, methods for speeding the weight increase of lambs by artificially induced sterility, study of the galah, methods of predicting the passage of schools of jack mackerel from aerial surveys, development of new yarns for fine-gauge knitting wools, control of insects in grain silos by aerating them with cold air.

'Few countries, if any, have given agricultural research the degree of priority that has been accorded to it in Australia,' says D. E. Tribe in the magazine *Search.* The C.S.I.R.O. spends more than half its budget on agricultural research; the State governments somewhat more than the C.S.I.R.O.; the universities also have research programmes. But nobody outside cares much about all this. There is a strange division between the honour given to the mythologized rugged virtues of the farmer and the widespread public ignorance of the laboratories and experimental stations of one of the most research-intensive industries in the world. When they speak of their successes Australian farmers are likely to speak of rural virtue in terms that could have been used by a Roman orator; they are not usually likely to boast that Australian farming is 'research-based'.

Yet there is worthiness in it for them too. The farmers make the research work. They are used to the idea of industry research funds and levies and they can absorb the suggestions of research more quickly and usefully than almost any other farmers on earth. Research findings are rapidly transformed into techniques on thousands of farms that produce statistics of almost unparalleled productivity. Bruce's briskly expressed hopes have come true.

Using 'the most modern and scientific methods' Australia has 'progressed with the times'.

The 1973-4 report of the C.S.I.R.O. was concerned not only with agricultural research. With its studied negligence it also happened to mention research in a remarkable range of fields including possible changes in the world climate, the probable impact of a Melbourne power station on local fog, D.N.A. repair in bacterial cells, the leakage of energy from microwave ovens, new treatments for copper ores to eliminate sulphur dioxide pollution, methods for de-watering industrial waste, a new microwave approach and landing guidance system for aircraft, invention of a light-scatter detector to improve fire alarms, improvements in office acoustics, production of a prefabricated panel to reduce the time spent in house construction, improvements in the atomic absorption spectrophotometer, discovery of organic molecules in Sagittarius B2, a dense cloud of gas in the Milky Way, and of a high concentration of molecules in the nuclei of galaxies NGC 253 and NGC 4945.

The C.S.I.R.O. runs one of the world's most important radio-astronomy programmes, aristocratic and expensive. Throughout Australia there are other scientific research programmes: in medical institutes, for example. According to Dr Derek J. de Solla Price, who worked out a way of measuring these things, something like one in sixty scientific breakthroughs takes place in Australia. The mathematical exactness is purely metaphorical, but if you follow it, this would place Australia as the tenth-ranking science nation, after the United States, Russia, Britain, Germany, France, Japan, Canada, Czechoslovakia and Hungary, just before Switzerland.

But according to the first Australian Minister for Science 'there are absolutely no votes in science in this country'. It is one of the paradoxes of Australia that a nation wanting so much to 'come of age' by testing itself successfully against other nations has taken so little pride in one of the fields where it passes the test. Not only are there no votes in science, there is very little honour in it. This doesn't mean that scientists don't have personal prestige: the surveys suggest they do. But science as an idea is not given the public honour that its success might suggest it has earned. When agriculture, once seen as the civilizer of Australia, is praised, it is praised in terms of hard work and individual effort, although these have nothing to do with its unique success. (Farmers can work hard in poor countries, but it doesn't do them any good.) There is no reference in praise to those eighteenth-century terms of civilized excellence that led Michael Massey Robinson to exalt 'Reason' and 'Learning' as well as 'Agriculture'. Yet these aristocratic ideals have been met in the twentieth century.

The agents of this view of civilization are now the Ph.D.s, the 'researchers', the 'experts'. Some of them began to define themselves at school as 'scientists', different from the others. At university they could begin to see themselves as joining a select world group of investigators who speak with a precision unknown to other humans, in a cosmopolitan language passing over national barriers, and who have standards of excellence that are not subjective but measurable. After taking an undergraduate degree, they gained post-graduate scholarships from the government and worked in a university laboratory for three years or more, with a supervisor, and at the end of it produced a Ph.D. thesis which was then meticulously assessed. Some then lined up for scholarships to do post-doctorate research at a foreign university.

According to those who are in the game, in the world of the Ph.D.s there is more status in 'pure' than in 'applied' research and more in university jobs than jobs in colleges of advanced education or government research agencies such as the C.S.I.R.O., although these carry more prestige than jobs in private industry. In these distinctions Ph.D.s do not display the sense of usefulness that marked eighteenth-century aristocrats, although the idea that ultimately discoveries in pure science are likely to be most useful is now received wisdom, but they experiment and take thought about what they are doing with an efficiency merely dreamed of in the eighteenth century, although they can also display a narrowness in learning and in general intellectual cultivation that in the eighteenth century would have seemed barbarous.

The supreme artefact in the world of the Ph.D. and of 'the researchers' in general is *the paper,* an expression going back to the beginning of modern science in the seventeenth century, and now meaning a report on research findings published in a scientific journal. A Ph.D. thesis is often assessed in terms of how many papers it will make: it might make two papers, or two and a half papers; or it might be criticized as not being worth more than one paper. In this sense, as Donald G. Macrae pointed out in his book on Max Weber, the Ph.D. thesis is similar to the token of craftsmanship that used to be produced by the apprentice when he had finished serving his time. A Ph.D. thesis shows that the candidate is a craftsman in the production of papers, which is the prime business of the learning industry.

The paper is a deposit on a growing mountain of learning. Knowledge can be seen as accretive, piling up, progressive, until some original-minded person produces a paper that makes nonsense of a whole mountain, whereupon another mountain begins to form. In this way a paper can be assessed by the extent to which it contributes to knowledge in one of the particular learning industries. The importance of a paper is often rated by how hard it is to get into the journal in which the paper is published: the more papers a journal knocks back, the greater value there is in being published in it. Later assessment of the importance of a paper can come from the number of references it gets in other papers in learned journals: sometimes the number of footnote references to it is counted as a measure of a paper's excellence.

There was a time when, if some colonial gentleman 'gave a paper' to the Sydney School of Arts, it meant a learned amateur's disquisition on some matter of literature or science. Now, when a committee at a university or a college of advanced education sits to decide on the appointment or promotion of a scientist or technologist they count the papers he has produced. The value of papers to careers can determine what research is done: according to a report of the A.N.Z.A.A.S. Science Policy Commission the most rapid promotion in the C.S.I.R.O. goes to those with frequent publication of papers reporting basic or 'pure' research; papers on 'applied' research are sometimes considered of lesser status, so in spite of their use to industry they may not count so much towards promotion; the report also points out that some fields favour production of papers more easily than others and that this might help determine the research fields of people who want promotion.

Research-based doctorate education has transformed Australian universities since the Second World War. Statistics were once quoted to suggest that Australia was the least educated of the prosperous countries; now it ranks sixth among O.E.C.D. nations in the number of students aged 20-24 enrolled in higher education.

However there are still feelings of inadequacy when people look at the statistics on money spent on research, even though it has for some time been shown that there is no necessary relationship between the money a country spends on research and its prosperity: it depends on the research, what happens to it, and to what extent a country can live more cheaply on other countries' research. There can be shame and derision when the figures for Australia's G.E.R.D. – gross expenditure on research and developments – are added up and Australia is found not to have as big a proportion of G.E.R.D. to G.N.P. as some other prosperous industrialized nations. Manufacturing industry in particular can seem rather stupid because of its low contribution to G.E.R.D. statistics. When the Holt government introduced R. & D. grants, expenditure on R. & D. went up, but what this has meant, apart from creating more jobs for researchers, is still hard to know.

At times the great successes of Australian research, especially in the farming industries, have been ignored, perhaps because the research is so much better than almost all other countries. Instead there is an incantation of statistics, on G.E.R.D., G.N.P. and so forth, as if the numbers had magic properties and would do the trick by themselves.

CHAPTER SEVEN

The Disputed Honour of the Farmer

The mallee tree, a eucalypt with no single trunk but with a cluster of slender branches rising directly from the ground, gives its name to 'the mallee country' of South Australia and north-west Victoria, which was described in 1836 as 'one of the most barren regions of the world'. In parts of the mallee country, skinny tree-sticks cram together over the red bare earth. In other parts, the mallee gums seem more relaxed; delicate branches wave over large, fleshy-leaved saltbush shrubs. Sometimes there is the simplicity of bare sand, or of limestone outcrops and stones. If you look at the mallee gum closely there can seem a graceful freedom in its light, slender branches. Sunlight filters amber and gold over quiet grey-green.

Like the brigalow tree, which dominates 'the brigalow country' of Queensland and northern New South Wales, covering the soil like a bluish-grey mist, the mallee gum clings resiliently to life: chop it down and it sends up suckers; chop the suckers and they send up suckers. To defeat this resilience, in the strange improvised techniques of early mallee farming in South Australia a heavy wooden roller was invented: pulled by horses, it would knock down the skinny branches and when they were dry they were burned off; at sowing time a spiked log roller, pulled by horses, broke up the ground enough to let in seeds and the crop grew amongst green mallee sucklings; after harvest the sucklings were burned off along with the straw. All this went on year after year, until finally the stubborn mallee stumps died. Prizes were offered by the government for new machines: a stump-jump plough was invented, with independent ploughshares, each of which could rise separately if it struck a root. These funny old machines are preserved in the Pioneer Settlement at Swan Hill, where you can sit on a hessian chair at a rough table in the reconstructed hut of a mallee settler or, outside, pat a horse in a stable with a thatched roof and walls of mud and mallee stumps. For dinner later in the Riverboat Steamer, along with Witchetty Grub Soup, Kangaroo Tail Soup, Grilled Yabby Tails, Wakool River Frogs' Legs, the menu offers Mallee Hen Soup and Wild Mallee Pig with Chutney Sauce.

The pioneering of the Mallee, and the way its memory is now celebrated is evidence that Australia's rural virtues have included hard work and ingenuity. They have also included a thoroughly stoic acceptance of disaster. In many areas it was more usual than not for a settler to fail. There were fewer than one in eight of the 190,000 selectors still on the land after the first twenty years of land selection for small farmers in New South Wales (from the 1860s to the 1880s). In the group settlement schemes in Western Australia in the 1920s, 30 per cent of the immigrant 'groupies' and 42 per cent of the native-born groupies left their holdings. Of all the ex-soldiers settled on farms between the two world wars, half failed.

These disasters came because of another strand among Australians' dreams: although the belief in agriculture's civilizing functions concerned aristocrats like eighteenth-century noblemen or the chiefs of C.S.I.R.O. divisions, there was a more general obsession that has only now died – the fixed belief that for its purity as a nation Australia needed a numerous and prosperous yeomanry, an obsession with the merits of 'the small farmer' 'the little man', supported by the craving among many Australians to own 'their own bit of land'. There was a policy of smallness for its own sake, pursued at enormous cost in tax-payers' money and disasters for settlers, their wives and children, but also achieving many successes, incuding the disruption of the squatters' dominance. The policy of 'smash the crook and speed the plough', as the *Wagga Wagga Advertiser* put it during the nineteenth-century rush for small farms, can be presented as one of the most successful land reform policies ever carried out, although because there were many blunders it is now unfashionable to do so. It ended only a few years ago when the last of the closer settlement schemes closed down (see below). By this time a new slogan had arrived, 'get big or get out' – and there were plans to reassemble some of the big estates that had been cut up. The idea of getting people into the country now took the form of 'decentralization' – city people were no longer required to become farmers, but to migrate to country 'growth centres'.

In the new industrial cities of Britain in the nineteenth century a myth grew among the poor that a rural arcady had existed before the dark satanic mills went up, a green and pleasant dream-time in which it had been a Briton's birthright to have his own fields to till. Immigrants brought this myth to Australia and demand for a bit of land became a driving political impulse. (For men anyway; women seem to have been merely part of the equipment.) It was backed by notions of what nations needed to survive: 'what we want to make a great, powerful and happy people is not a race of aristocrats . . . but a race of hard, shrewd, intelligent and industrious men, whose object will be to develop the resources of this country.' 'There is nothing more noble on earth than agriculture . . . Small farmers are the very backbone of the community.' Australia must achieve 'a territorial democracy' in which every man might sit under his fig tree while the vine brought forth her fruit and the wilderness blossomed as a rose. 'If we . . . boldly throw open our lands to the occupation of the energetic, willing and intelligent minds now flocking in upon us, we may . . . create a little England in Australia which shall set an example to the world.' In this little England, once the monopoly of the squatting lords with their serfs was overthrown, the deserted interior would present a beautiful scene, a thousand farmhouses with flourishing English gardens along each creek.

This was the rhetoric of the first war against the squatters. The 'monster monopolists, comparable only to the Persian satraps of yore' were attacked from the 1860s onwards by a series of Land Acts which enabled 'selectors' to obtain small holdings (up to several hundred acres) on the squatters' leasehold runs, with a deposit and easy terms. In Argentina the great landholders remained: the *gaucho*, a stockman almost as wild as the stock he rode down, was tamed into a cowhand, and the typical worker on the pampas became the *peon*, the exploited day labourer. In Australia the great landholders were forced to allow the growth of small independent land-owning farmers. The new economic class created was not the labouring *peon*, but the *cocky* ('cow cocky', 'wheat cocky', 'cherry cocky', 'cane cocky', etc.), the small independent farmer. For many, the first test of democracy and of all political principle was land reform, and the destruction of the land monopoly. Joseph Furphy makes fun of this in *Rigby's Romance*.

Tom Collins, yarning away on the bank of the river, finds it enough to say of someone, 'I tell you he's an advanced Liberal, and firm in the faith. He approved of the Land Act of '65 and the amending Land Act of '68.'

An insouciance which believed that 'anyone can be a farmer', meant there was no training of selectors, most of whom knew nothing about farming; usually they didn't have enough cash to see them through, and the size of the holdings was often too small for Australia's climate and soil. It was a rush, like the preceding pastoral rush and the gold rush: taking a selection was a gamble, you tried your luck and gave it a go. But it was commemorated (sometimes exaggeratedly so) as a drama of failure, whereas the other two rushes, on the whole, and sometimes exaggeratedly, were commemorated as dramas of success.

In the 1880s the radical idea of a land tax 'to burst up the big estates' was instituted in South Australia, from where it spread, to be finally taken up by the Federal government, after the Labor Party declared it the main issue of the 1910 election, which it won. In the 1890s the even more radical idea of farmers' communes had been tried, and failed. Another radical idea, later known as 'closer settlement', succeeded. It began in 1890 in South Australia: governments gave themselves power to take land from the big landholders arbitrarily, on the government's purchase conditions, subdivide it, and sell it on easy terms to settlers. This time there was more ancillary backing. In closer settlement, the rate of failure was less than in free selection.

New rhetoric developed. 'Almost all the evils Australia is suffering from are traceable to land monopoly.' 'Our cities are congested because of this monopoly. It is largely responsible for our unemployed. It has driven thousands out of the Commonwealth during the past few years and it impedes us in obtaining any substantial increase of population from abroad.' Magic figures were sought: the population could rise from five million to – fifty million? a hundred million? Talk of an 'eightfold increase' had a season. Part of the magic of figures was to dispel fear: 'A mere handful of people occupy the continent . . . unless we are able to show that we are able to hold it against all-comers . . . we will not be allowed to hold it for long. We must, therefore, fill up the blank spaces.' There was also a feeling that prosperity would rise directly with numbers and the only way to attract people was by offering them land to farm: 'Unlock the lands and there would be something to entice the people to Australia.' 'Prosperity would attend every branch of life and every class of industry.'

The town of Barmera in South Australia is a monument to this kind of rhetoric. Once there was only Lake Bonney, one of the two largest lakes in the Murray, amidst the desolation of the mallee. Now the approach to the blue lake is over smooth gravel roads past a long sweep of green lawns, tree-shaded; pleasure boats are moored beside a sloping beach; people swim, sunbake, sail, lie on the green grass and drink iced drinks. There is a monument that announces that Sir Donald Campbell used Lake Bonney in an attempt to break one of his own water speed records. The guide book says Lake Bonney is 'South Australia's aquatic playground'; Lake Bonney reached this eminence because, after the First World War, irrigation water combined with the red dust beside the lake to allow vineyards, orange groves, apple and pear orchards to flourish, and the town of Barmera was created. Barmera was a 'soldier settlement' town, one of those places doubly holy because of the combination of small farms and warriors; as in the Roman Empire, old soldiers were given their acres, sometimes creating whole new towns and districts. The last of them established in Victoria is Robinvale, in a horseshoe bend of the Murray River, developed in the late 1940s to farm citrus fruits, grapes and olives. Robinvale's small shopping centre, set at right angles to the highway, looks like a less ambitious new suburb in Melbourne. Two arcades are planned, to bring it into fashion. Beside the air-conditioned pharmacy, a vacant building site shows red mallee earth.

Towns like these have been created by design, unlike most older towns which grew by accident around barracks, convict stockades, fords, punts, goldfields, court houses, railheads, inns, river ports, seaports. These new towns grew because of the European utopian tradition of the virtue of yeoman smallholders, and many older towns were reinvigorated to serve the same purpose. However, all the subdivisions, bounties, rural credit schemes and other reform devices that went into their creation failed to produce a sturdy independent yeomanry. There was to be no class of Australians with a deep love of the land, happy with only a modest surplus from a variety of crops: instead there are men who imagine that a successful life depends on world commodity prices; they make money or lose it by selling highly specialized products in a completely monetized market.

The greatest monuments of the Australian countryside, helping to give life meaning, are the places where the farmers' commodities are stored, or processed. At Rutherglen, in northern Victoria, it is the large dazzling grey metal storage tanks of the winery; at Rankin's Springs, in the Riverina, it is the wheat silos, one towering over the town like a castle, others like fortified towers along the road. In the South Australian irrigation town of Berri, among the low, pale buildings meaning is found in the fruit packing sheds. At Beachport in South Australia, beside Rivoli Bay, named by the French navigator Nicolas Baudin after a French duke, the Fisherman's Co-operative Canning Factory, set up to turn South Australian crayfish into 'Beachport Lobster Tails' for sale in the United States is by far the largest building in town. Paper mills and packing sheds brood over Tasmania. In Queensland ports the tourists' tour of the town always includes as a highlight a visit to the local sugar mill; inland, it might include peanut depots or bulk tobacco sheds. On the north coast of New South Wales among the butter factories, cheese factories and fruit packing sheds symbolism becomes explicit: at the banana town of Coff's Harbour there sticks up, as big as a railway carriage, the world's largest artificial banana. Near Nambour in Queensland, in the pineapple country, there is a building fifty feet high disguised as a pineapple, which has an observation deck and a Polynesian Room with a tropical restaurant and gift shop.

It is more than a hundred years since the new economic class of 'free selectors' began to acquire real consciousness of itself as a defined type threatened by other classes, and almost a hundred years since it established organizations to protect its economic interests. At first wheat farmers were the most active in forming pressure organizations to support this newly-defined sectional interest – at much the same time as wheat farmers began to feel their strength in Canada and the United States, and for much the same reason, the new market opportunities brought by the railways. With an enthusiasm that made the blood stir, using words as emotive as *rail freight*, *bounty*, *fertilizer* or *bulk handling*, the small farmers came together in political action. In the United States and Canada, the new farmers' parties later merged into the older parties but in Australia the farmers' political parties produced a new creation in the Country Party, the most narrowly-based and now usually the most conservative force in Australian politics. Although the small farmers began as radicals, once they got what they wanted, they wanted to hang on to it. They have been helped in that by the unfair weighting the Australian electoral systems give to country voters, with up to a two-to-one bias. This is the most obvious widespread corruption in Australian politics. Through its unfairness it represents one of the greatest single threats to the legitimacy of institutions of representative government in Australia.

The Country Party has been one of the peculiarities of Australian politics. It helped establish the split between the cities and the country as natural to politics and life generally, appealing strongly not only to farming people (less than eight per cent of the labour force), but also to many people in country towns. The Country Party was able to present itself to country people as protector of their special interests more bluntly than the other two main political parties could normally risk when trying to appeal to special interests. The Country Party could afford to look like a mere pressure group. This didn't endanger its legitimacy, because to many country people that was how an Australian government should look. They saw the rural interest as the only legitimate Australian interest; the Country Party seemed the party of Australia's true economic interest because it represented 'the primary producers', and the uniquely patriotic party because country people were superior to city people. Bribes in the form of special government assistance to country areas – the most usual bribe in Australian politics – could seem policies of national interest. Since becoming the National Country Party, in some states simply the National Party, in order to widen its appeal, the party can no longer appeal to the country interest so nakedly, but by using emotive phrases that please city conservatives it may still be able to signal that it knows country people are best.

Country people were the first to try and draw blood from the Whitlam government. They began attacking Whitlam almost as quickly as he began attacking them, when, with his early devotion to the ideals of economic rationality, he insulted the ideals of a nationally pre-eminent rural interest by removing the superphosphate and petrol subsidies, phasing out the dairying subsidy and dropping the exemption from sales tax of fizzy drinks containing more than five per cent of Australian fruit juice, a bribe of $4 million that had mainly benefited Tasmanian apple-growers. At meetings in country towns in 1973, conservatives used the language of revolution. In Canberra, farmers on horses rode in a protest meeting – between Parliament House and the lawns in front, on which the Aborigines had already put up their protest 'embassy' tent. In the cedar-panelled Legislative Council in Hobart, where a copy of Winterhalter's portrait of Queen Victoria still dominates the members sitting on red plush sofas, speakers from both sides of the House courteously agreed on the basic right of the apple-growers of Tasmania to a share of the tax-payers' money.

In its earlier years Labor had presented itself as a party of the country as well as of the cities: closer settlement was one of Labor's main programme points when it won its first election in 1910, and it won a majority of country seats. In the 1943 election the Curtin government won two thirds of the country seats. It was one of Whitlam's theatrical achievements that in the 1972 election he put the issue of 'the cities' on the political agenda and in the 1974 budget he supported this in the theatre of figures: in one of those acts of attempted 'irreversibility', of changing policy so boldly that the other lot couldn't undo it, he backed up the talk with big budget expenditure. He held two thirds of the city seats, but less than a quarter of the country seats. In the 1975 election he lost most of the country seats left.

There had never previously been elections in which 'the cities' were put up as an issue. It has been an important crisis of identity for Australians that they have found it so hard to accept themselves as the most urban people in the world and also, because of the concentration on the State capitals, the most metropolitan and also, because their gardens spread out so much, the most suburban. Neither of the two city folk types created earlier – the 'larrikin', the 1870s city tough, and the 'suburbanite', the mild, meek conformist – have answered the need for an image, although Barry Humphries' great comic characters, more subtle and ambiguous creations than the larrikin and the suburbanite, if related to them, were closer to demographic reality in the 1970s. To make the point more general: in an export-worshipping nation where 'natural resources' carry honour, the cities didn't make counter-claims of dignity. There could be a Country Party: who could imagine a City Party?

As strong as the belief in the virtues of a numerous and prosperous yeomanry was the belief that there was something inherently evil in living in a city. This was important to the development of the collective identity of the farmers and the country townspeople: in their shared vision of the enemy they were able to define themselves by distrusting the cities. Right from the start an important part of the purifying influence of agriculture lay in its revulsion from the filth and evil of the cities and their 'idle and impoverished population'. Hysteria became even greater when it was realized, towards the beginning of the twentieth century, that one of Australia's demonstrably unique features was that of being the world's most town-dwelling society. Cities had become 'huge cancers whose ramification of disease spread far into national life' while 'the prosperity of all classes, and that of the city first of all depends on the success of the man on the land.' 'The farmer is the root of the tree. If the roots are not sound the leaves will wither.' The farmer 'gives his girls and boys to the big cities to infuse . . . red blood into a society that is constantly decadent, and whose only salvation is the virility it draws from the rural section.' 'The steady country influence' must fear the power of 'the great city-controlled parties who, like the Roman consuls of old, have to placate an over-hungry mob of city voters, howling for the expenditure of loan money.' In its manifesto at the 1910 election the Labor Party said:

> The foundation of all national greatness and prosperity must rest upon some form of agriculture or pastoral pursuits. In the Commonwealth nearly 80 per cent of the people live in towns; over 50 per cent are crowded in the six capital cities of the several States. Such conditions are unnatural; they make for degeneration, they invite disaster, they make healthy progress impossible. We must get the bulk of the people on the land.

In the repertoire of national types, the characters previously known as 'free selectors', 'cockies', 'settlers', 'soldier settlers' came together with the pastoralists to form the character of 'the man on the land'. The phrase exemplifies how in this area the emphasis on the male has been made more manifest, and is less accurate than probably in any other part of economic life in Australia. No one spoke of 'the woman on the land'. The longing for land was seen entirely as male. To be a farmer was the ancient Anglo-Saxon birthright of a man, not a woman, yet running a farm could be a family enterprise with wives and daughters as significant as husbands and sons. The closest parallel would be the family shop, but here the role of women was acknowledged: the phrase 'small shopkeeper' had no gender. The point is that farming, unlike housework, which, because no price is put on it, lies outside the definition of what is economic, is an activity that does belong to the economy. Women helped run farms, but were not seen as part of the economy.They were labourers in an economic activity on which there was a price, but they were not paid; they usually had no stake in the farms they worked for; they didn't show up in the statistics. For one view of what this might mean, as A. A. Phillips suggests in *The Australian Tradition*, Barbara Baynton's short stories about farm life show a world with a 'bitter insistence on man's brutality to women' and 'men's lusts for women and money'. The recurrent image of farm life in her stories is of the innocent woman alone in the shack: a threatening man is outside. There are other quite different views of which the opposite to Barbara Baynton's is of the farm wife as the prototype of the Australian 'Mum'. In all these versions, the farm wife, unlike her husband, is not honoured as an essential and dignified part of the Australian economy.*

In his own estimate the man on the land was an individualist, unlike the parasites in trade unions and cities; he was devoted to hard work and self-reliance; his was the purest vocation and the most natural life; at times he might have been a little slow-thinking, but his steadfastness provided the nation's stability as well as its prosperity. In his T.V. commercial for the 1972 election, Doug Anthony, the Country Party leader, walked slowly among stalwart trees and philosophized on virtue. (The trees were part of a Melbourne park.) But although city people did not honour

*Since pastoralists have become 'woolgrowers' the man on the land is now at last likely to be simplified as 'the farmer'. It illustrates one oddity in Australian social life that although George III, the colony's founding monarch, was proud to see himself as the farmer-king, the word 'farmer' is only now beginning to become acceptable enough to include woolgrowers.

themselves, and although honour was given to the country in a general kind of way, city people (that is, most Australians) have not normally granted to the man on the land the admirable qualities he has proclaimed for himself. Scholars with their eyes on the pastoral frontiers maintained that Australia was a collectivist country with little of the Americans' individualism.

There has been a recent exception, from the tourist industry, where there is a wide usage of the word 'pioneer' to describe the early farmers. Before this there was no pioneer cult in Australia similar to that of the United States. There are no Australian phrases rich in the same kind of associations as 'taming the wilderness', 'blazing the trail', 'log cabin' or 'wagon train'. The word 'pioneer' had been around (it was an early euphemism for 'convict') and one of the 1890s most famous nationalist paintings was Frederick McCubbin's triptych, 'The Pioneer'. But McCubbin's concern with pioneers seems more to understand them as fellow-creatures than to exalt their achievement. One can still feel for the young woman in his famous 'On the Wallaby Track' – imagining the young, exhausted flesh sweating into hot clothes – but she hasn't blazed a trail: she is simply following a track. The word 'pioneer' is not in the index of Ernest Scott's *A Short History of Australia*, which contained all that most of the present generation of middle-aged Australians was likely to learn at school about their country. The Australian idea of the honoured predecessor was not the pioneer but the explorer, a gallant man of failure who discovered deserts, in which he frequently died. But now a special issue of stamps has honoured pioneer life (if somewhat in the manner of the old *Saturday Evening Post* covers); a big cross-country bus service is called Pioneer Buses: there are Pioneer Tours, Pioneer Museums, Pioneer Settlements. Some anti-American crank might write a letter to the papers saying that the spreading use of the word 'pioneer' is an example of the Americanization of Australia.

While the smaller farmers began to see themselves as the backbone of the nation,* to the rest of Australia they were more likely to be either figures of fun ('cockies') or tragic failures who ended as 'battlers'. One of the two best-known celebrants of the

*This claim is usually made exclusively for farmers; while by the export test, forestry workers (through savings in imports) and fishermen are demonstrably significant.

selectors, Steele Rudd, in *On Our Selection* and some of his twenty-four other books, made the selectors funny people who faced their hardships with frontline wit; he did this with such commercial success that his comic creations also carried into seven plays, seven movies and a long-running radio serial, *Dad and Dave*, which was revived as a curiosity in 1975. The idea of small farmers and their families as funny people was carried on by other writers, and in other movies. Dad and Dave, and their womenfolk Mabel and Mum, became famous national types, even characters in dirty jokes. The contemporary good taste with which Doug Anthony philosophized among the trees in his T.V. commercials, showing concern for the environment, could have been partly intended to offset the Dad and Dave image. The other most famous celebrant of the selectors, Henry Lawson, turned them to his sometimes sad and stoic, sometimes maudlin, view of existence: the life of the selectors was lonely, dangerous, drab, harsh, meagre.

I suppose it would be mainly in children's books, that one would find accounts of the lives of farm families in Australia that allowed for the possibility of occasional human happiness, or at least showed an absence of freakishness, whether of failure or of farce. Among the great nationalist paintings there is no painting idealizing the life of the selectors as Tom Roberts' 'Shearing of the Rams' idealizes shearers: in Arthur Streeton's 'The Selector's Hut' the emphasis is more on the timber – the log, the tree, the walls of the hut – than on the selector. One does not, as in U.S. myth-making, get an impression of the moral superiority of farm life or of the wilderness being thoroughly civilized. Sometimes, as with George Lambert's 'Across the Blacksoil Plains', the wilderness is temporarily *mastered*, but it is not tamed. The mastery is as crude as the wilderness itself, and perhaps only transient. The closest one gets to the idea of farm civilization is in sentimental studies of little girls feeding calves or holding buckets of milk. Relatively 'straight' observation of work situations, or any other aspect of life on small farms, is almost non-existent. In the United States painters like William Sidney Mount could show farm people going about their jobs in a man-controlled landscape, but although this was done with the pastoral industries, it seemed impossible for anyone to paint ordinary farmers in Australia as directly as that. E. Phillips Fox did a work-picture, 'The Milking Shed', but the woman has her back turned. It was through their treatment of landscapes, rather than of the people somewhere outside the painting's frames who were running farms, that Australian painters hinted that on farms perhaps not everything was farce and failure: in the new feeling of what the art critic Daniel Thomas has called 'intimacy', trees, twigs, fences, leaves or grass, bushes, stones could seem as if humans had seen and rather liked them. By the way they painted twigs and leaves or grass, painters had begun to suggest that life might be good on a farm.

The Australian inability to find general forms of honour for farmers had something to do with shifts in the idea of honour itself. The colonies were begun in the eighteenth century and the kind of honour the squatters sought and for a while gained (even when they were hated) was an eighteenth-century pride of place, with no humbug of morality about it; but the honour the small farmers sought was the domesticated bourgeois honour of *worthiness*: they wanted to be seen as paragons of virtue whose decency and industry had earned them praise, and a certain amount of cash recognition. But the writers and artists who bestowed honour didn't use this language: those of them who admired the settlers used the language of the heroic. In Hyde Park in Sydney, inconspicuously placed, is a monument to pioneer farmers: it looks like the crude cult statue of a religion of blood sacrifice; to stress how elemental it is, the key words of its inscription are 'earth', 'fire' and 'water'. Those whom it honours prefer kind words in newspaper editorials and subsidies on superphosphate.

Something of the mixture of the banal, the heroic and the venal that can mark country life is found in the monument in the New South Wales town of Wentworth set up after the 1956 floods; a flood from the Darling met a flood from the Murray and it looked as if Wentworth, at the junction of Australia's two greatest rivers, would be destroyed. On yellow stone a metal plaque says:

This cairn was unveiled on April 20, 1959 by L. T. Ritchie, Managing Director of Massey-Ferguson (Australia) Limited, to commemorate the epic fight by the people of Wentworth and district against the record flood of 1956 and the major part played by Ferguson tractors and implements in saving the town from complete inundation.

On top of the yellow stone is a model of a Ferguson tractor.

CHAPTER EIGHT

Country Towns: Making It Last

The court house at Bathurst is one of the most successful expressions of late colonial self-confidence ever produced. Large and, with forecourt, wasteful enough to belong to the governor of a prosperous province, it has achieved bland certainty by overcoming its own complexities – which include a Doric portico with pediment, an octagonal tower with turret, stone facings and brick pilasters, a colonnade of Doric pillars, a sage-green roof, red bricks, yellow bricks and long lines of sash windows. It has brought these elements together with such sure sense of space and balance that it needs military guards, sentries and high personages to set it off. Behind the court house the Edwardian-style Macchattie Gardens would provide a place for these personages, if they existed, to stroll among lavish banks of trees, past a fernery with marble statues of almost naked women, a rotunda bandstand, a lake with swans and a fountain as contrived and billowing as an Edwardian mistress.

Beside the court house is a 'contemporary' building, the Civic (and Cultural) Centre, so absurdly out of style that one looks for some intention in it. Opposite is a large grass square lavish enough in plan to match the court house. Its trees and cannas provide an appropriate stiffness and there is a statue at each end. At one end a volunteer for the Boer War, his rifle at the ready, shelters under a stone canopy; at the other end Evans, the British 'discoverer' of the district, with his faithful native tracker at his feet, peers over the cannas. In the centre, aggressively out of style, is a red brick War Memorial Carillon, with the eternal flame at its heart framed by red plush curtains and protected by glass windows; matching it on the other side of this square is the brick-built Anglican Cathedral, a glum warehouse of God.

Australian country towns don't usually run to such formal town squares. Bathurst managed it only because the space for the square was already there before the buildings started – it was 'a desolate and sandy waste' in front of the watch house and gaol, where public hangings took place; then it was covered with some improvised market buildings; then it was turned into a blue-metal dump. It wasn't until the unveiling of the Boer War statue by Lord Kitchener when he was in Australia in 1910 that plans for a formal garden were produced. However the buildings grouped around Bathurst's unusual square are usual enough. They are typical monuments to the dignity of an Australian country town: a court house, a civic centre, a war memorial, a church. What is remarkable is that the court house isn't classical and the cathedral isn't Gothic. For a period in this part of New South Wales European civilization looked over the cleared bush with two official faces: medieval for God, classical for government, finding complexity in churches, simplicity in court houses.

The economic circumstances that threw up individual Australian country towns as way-stations in the progress of Australia as an industrialized export country were different, but in any town of any size ('size' can begin with a couple of thousand people or less) there are much the same principal buildings. For communications, there are the railway stations and the post office, and in some towns, the airport shed. The power of the capital city is represented by the police station and perhaps by a court house: in some towns the remaining government offices are housed more modestly, in others, office-palaces show off new forms of architecture and the love of governments for country towns. Faith is enshrined in the War Memorial, the Anglican church, the Catholic church, the Presbyterian church, the Methodist church, the Masonic Temple, perhaps a local monument to an explorer or the victims of a calamity, sometimes another church or two. In Woolgoolga on the north coast of New South Wales, the other church is a Sikh temple. Humanist faith in improvement used to be shown in a School of Arts or a Mechanics Institute; now there is often a new Civic Centre with a library or a Cultural Centre or at the very least a Craft Centre. Community groups may have their halls: the Returned Soldiers' Hall, the Scouts' Hall, the Country Women's Association Hall, the Band Hall. There are at least two schools – a State school, a Catholic school. Belief in both nature and nineteenth-century good form are shown in a park, and belief in agriculture in the showground (as well as the silo, packing shed, butter factory, stockyards or whatever it is that denotes economic importance in the district). In some towns a belief in manufacturing and decentralization may be shown in a small factory or two, perhaps set out in a section designated 'industrial area', at the side of empty, weedy paddocks. A belief in sport is shown in the oval, the golf course, the tennis courts, the bowling green, the olympic swimming pool. The hospital and the cemetery are likely to stand on the outskirts of town; at its centre, substance is most likely to be suggested by the bank buildings (the old ones are likely to have classical or Renaissance facades, the new ones espresso-contemporary), the hotels and, if the main street is also a highway, the motels. On the road the first one sees of some country towns is the screen of the drive-in cinema.

In New South Wales, since poker machines became legal, the buildings with some of the richest associations are the clubs that house the poker machines – the Soldiers' Club, the Workers' Club. But no single public building is likely to be regarded by a majority of the townspeople as of predominant importance in the community. Sometimes a number of public buildings may be grouped. Often they are not. Grafton in New South Wales is a curiosity: for the length of two quiet tree-lined streets, all the public buildings are together. Around the corner, at right angles, is the broad commercial street. Normally in Australia, as in most towns in the United States, the 'centre' of town is a line – the main street. It is not usually public buildings that matter most in the main street, or that determine its most significant section; this is usually decided by the position of the biggest and most popular stores. One of the most meaningful signs of progress in a town is its adoption of the latest fashion in shop construction: for the moment it is the arcade. Business men in a country town can feel more up-to-date when they have an arcade.

Assessments of the prestige of the residents are less likely to be pluralist than feelings about the significance of buildings. In Sydney, and probably in the other big cities, there is no longer any established and generally acknowledged hierarchy of prestige. Individuals may lay claim to honour; there are many snobberies, even imprints of hierarchic patterns. But the patterns are in conflict. There is not one hierarchic pattern that lies so oppressively on the city that even rejection pays it honour. In a loose sense, snobberies in Sydney are a matter of choice; you choose which sets of snobberies you belong to. In country towns (because they are smaller) it is not so easy to escape a sense that one hierarchy is so strong that even rejection of it is a kind of recognition.

I shall repeat the hierarchic pattern of prestige of my own country town when I was a boy: The 'old families' – the rich landed gentry whose stations surrounded the town – were accorded general honour (by some, the honour of respect; by others, the honour of hatred); they controlled invitations to the Picnic Races Ball and from the town they invited only members of a rich merchant family (a connection by marriage), doctors and lawyers, the stock and station agents, bank managers and chemists (but not dentists). The shire clerk went, but not the town clerk. The mayor wasn't invited: he was a blacksmith. The attendance at the Golf Club Ball was less restricted, taking in school-teachers, bank clerks, well-to-do townspeople, including shopkeepers and hotel owners, and representatives of the oil companies. The company at the Anglican Ball and the Masonic Ball was more mixed still, adding salaried railway officers, other salaried government officials, small shopkeepers, clerks and any manual workers (usually skilled) defining themselves as people who went to the Masonic Ball or the Anglican Ball. In our family we didn't know who went to the Catholic Ball. A majority of manual workers – mostly miners or railway men – did not go to balls: they could go instead to the weekly dance ('the Friday night hop'). Farmers who were thought of as 'smaller property holders' (something less than 'old family' but more than cockies) might go to the other balls, but they would not be invited to the Picnic Races Ball. Cockies were regarded as without prestige by almost everyone in town: they were mugs who worked too hard; or they were lazy buggers who didn't know any better. At the bottom, the shanty-dwellers, thought of as chook thieves, and the tramps were probably most successful in establishing their own counter-system of prestige, themselves on top.

Other towns had other patterns. Now things change – in my own town the estates of the old families have been subdivided, the population has gone up, diversity of jobs has increased, there are more managers and professional people, the manual workers are better off (when I was a boy one in ten were on the dole) but when I go back I am told there is still a more generally agreed scale of prestige than in the cities.

The country towns I am thinking of are those that see themselves as significant centres of farming, fishing or timber districts; others are simply, or mainly, mining towns or industrial towns; others, although in farming districts, may be too small for a full range of snobberies, yet it is doubtful if any is so small that it does not see itself as the significant centre of something, as is easily seen by flipping through the pages of their local newspapers. Here is a selection from summer holiday seasons.

Inspection of the classified ads in the *Riverine Herald,* from the Murray River town of Echuca in Victoria, shows that two dogs have been impounded under the Dog Act; if they are not claimed and fees and expenses paid, they will be sold or destroyed. The 'Mixtures', a group fresh from Las Vegas, will perform at Variety Night in the Working Men's Club. Kitchen teas will be held for Miss Cheryl Watson at the fortnightly dance at Bamawn Extension and for Miss Tina Constantino at the home of Mrs M. Kelly. The Echuca Ethiopian Famine Fund has raised $23.50.

In the Victorian coastal town of Portland the *Observer* expresses Portland's fears: because wharf labourers are no longer subsidized by the government, some of them are leaving the district and the port is again in jeopardy. It is said of the Minister for Decentralization: 'The only growth centre he has successfully expanded has been his ever-growing tongue.' A news report says Portland's motels, hotels and camping grounds have taken capacity bookings this capacity season, but a reader's letter questions whether tourism really benefits Portland; he suggests the civic authorities return to fundamentals like restoring the footpath in Percy Street north of Otway Street.

In the *West Wyalong Advocate* in New South Wales there is an advertisement for air-conditioning for a tractor-cabin: 'Farmers! You spend a third of your life on your tractor. Why not spend the time in comfort?' An electric organ is advertised in the classified ads. An announcement in the *Grenfell Record* says: 'You are improving the prosperity of your community when you buy from local stores . . . wherever possible buy country-made goods! Keep money circulating in your own area. This will benefit your community. Provide jobs for young people.' The Grenfell Bowling

Club is having a Prawn and Chicken Night. The *Cowra Chronicle* announces that Mr Ab Oliver was given a civic reception in recognition of the M.B.E. given to him in the New Year honours. *Love and Pain and the Whole Damn Thing,* now at the local cinema, will be replaced on Thursday by *Bedroom Mazurka.* The Cowra Pizzeria announces its telephone take-away service. The *Benalla Ensign,* in reporting the opening of a new restaurant, The Loaded Dog, points out that the 'unique features of the fine old brick building have been retained.'

The *Murray Pioneer* in the South Australian irrigation town of Renmark reports a record flow of visitors to Riverland for the holidays; about 900 people attended the open-air Snap Crackle Rock pop festival at Berri; the national gliding championships have begun at Waikerie; Sunraysia defeated Riverland at cricket in Mildura; at the Barmera trots there was the best crowd since Easter. The principal of the Waikerie High School says a new-style council with teacher and student members has been a 'successful innovation'; the 'youth and vigor' of the students is 'refreshing'. There are advertisements for the sale of vineyards and apricot orchards and reports on dried fruit stocks in Greece, Iran and Turkey. Classified ads in the *Hopetoun Courier* in the Victorian mallee country announce a Beef and Burgundy function in St Luke's spacious gardens, the availability of a good, quiet, willing cow and some point-of-lay pullets, the annual meetings of the Golf Club and the Fire Brigade Ladies, and the expected arrivals of a travelling optometrist and a travelling chiropodist.

The *Western Times* in the Queensland town of Charleville reports that in the magistrate's court at Charleville two 18-year-olds were found guilty of killing an animal with intent to steal portion of the skin and carcase; they were committed for sentence at the criminal sittings of the District Court. Sheepmen are warned to expect blowfly attacks following recent rain and are recommended to engage in mulesing, and then to take their choice from crutching or jetting. A local pharmacist advertises that his health bar sells Muesli breakfast cereals, Vegisalt and natural sea salt, goat's milk and stone-ground gluten-free cereals. A cooking column gives recipes for zucchini *ripieni* and Chinese stuffed cabbage rolls in tomato sauce. The *Central Queensland News* says the recent bushfires burned out 30,000 acres of valuable grassland. One advertisement offers to buy sunflower crops, another safflower crops, another sapphires. A 22-year-old Aboriginal woman, charged as a vagrant with insufficient means of support, pleaded guilty and was sentenced to six weeks imprisonment. At the golf club last weekend the competition was to play the course backwards; next weekend there will be a choose-your-partners competition.

In the far west of New South Wales, at Bourke, the *Western Herald* gives most of its front page to the golden wedding anniversary of two of Bourke's favourite citizens, held on New Year's Eve. Supper was 'sumptuous', glasses were kept 'full to the brim all night' and the town band played. The Regional Controller, Upper Darling Civil Defence, announces the flood position in some of the rivers that feed the Darling. A university agricultural economist has written a letter to the Bourke Chamber of Commerce saying that he wants to 'quantify the flow-on effects' of the rural crisis on a number of country towns: he wants Bourke to be one of them. In Queensland the *Central Telegraph* in Biloela ('The ONLY Newspaper Printed in the Banana Shire') reports attempts to check depredations on cotton of the weed *sesbania,* also known as supplejack or horse bean, and announces a showing of paintings by Mrs Lal Lenyon who 'is mainly concerned with the unity of the human being with the elements and the environment in which he lives'. In the *Coonabarabran Times* the high school principal says that if Australia is to become a strong nation with a sense of national destiny then its educational aims must be brought into national focus and clearly enunciated. Moree is declared one of the ten major beef cattle districts in New South Wales. The Coonabarabran Mini Land Complex, a tourist attraction, is described: its service station is made of fibreglass to look like a cave in the Flintstone television series and the seventeen foot model of a prehistoric animal guarding the garage will groan if a coin is inserted; there are novelties along the walks to the barbecue area – a giant imitation spider and its web, a quaint white bridge, a fountain made from pink fibreglass – and a miniature medieval castle with a Spanish galleon moored in the moat.

The country newspapers I have quoted from present the perplexity of what it means to be a country town in the 1970s. But my selection of items doesn't bring out the main obsession of these newspapers. This is a deeper anxiety: *how can we make it last?* There are people in country towns who don't want the population to grow any more or could even be content with a decline – they would agree with the man who wrote the letter to the Portland *Observer* saying he would sooner have better footpaths than new tourist promotions – but the dominant ideologists of country towns tend to be the boosters, and whether they like it or not the country newspaper editors usually have to be boosters too. When these towns first began to grow out of scattered settlements, 'getting bigger' was the main answer to anyone who sought some purpose in them: this desire to get bigger usually remains the first cause of those who make themselves spokesmen for the country towns. They can't think of anything else. The present fury of these spokesmen is part of the literature of male impotence, with which it shares not only the common concern with growth, but the practice of blaming others if there is a failure to grow. The craving for growth in the country towns is one of the important economic determinants in Australia and (especially because the unfair weighting given to votes in country districts amplifies their importance) the country towns are important garrisons of political fundamentalism.

Driving into Portland from the east, on a misty day the main harbour is a study in rectangles and arcs; closer, these geometrical shapes become a breakwater and wharf, a silo and storage shed waiting to be stuffed with oats, wheat, frozen meat, wool and hides. On the other side of town, at the level crossing, there are large wool stores on either side of the road, with stacks of greasy wool and long rows of stinking hides; nearby are a slaughterhouse and a freezing plant. These important buildings stand in Portland like hungry children – if Portland doesn't *grow* (this means if it is not government-subsidized), these storage spaces will be empty. At Hay in New South Wales, the travel handout *Welcome to Hay* describes the town as the 'Home of the Cobb & Co. Coach', perhaps the weakest tourist claim in the southern hemisphere, since all it means is that an old coach is on display at the back of a service station and is brought out once a week for children's rides; but after this weak opening, the producers of the pamphlet get down to the serious matters of describing what Hay does for a living and how it is going, *Wool and merino studs* – excellent ('stud merino flocks still win the highest honours at leading shows'). *Fat lambs* – show promise, *Wheat* – should try harder. *Oats, barley, rye, sunflowers, rape seed, soybeans* – very fair. *Sorghum* – unsatisfactory. *Maize* – very successful. *Melons, lettuce, tomatoes, onions, garlic* – progress is being shown. *Grapes* – steady improvement. *Pasture crops* – satisfactory. *Manufacturing* – 'the industrial area is not yet subject to a great amount of development but was set apart by the Lands Department to satisfy an existing need of one enquirer.' This is in the style of a school report because the assumption of country town growth-boosters is that the towns they profess to serve are permanently and necessarily immature: if the whole aim of these towns is to grow, they can never be thought of as grown-up. People who drive through the Hunter Valley and know I spent my boyhood there, say to me, as if speaking of a bright child at school: 'My word, Muswellbrook has done well.' They mean it has doubled its population.

At the beginning of 1974, after driving from Griffith to Bathurst, we were questioned by a professional man on how many shoppers there were in the streets of the main towns. West Wyalong, Grenfell, Cowra – he wanted specific reactions to the shopping situation in each town. They were in the hinterland of his professional practice. He knew the answers – things looked good – but he wanted to hear it again. There was money in it. Shopkeepers and professional men are the backbone of country town patriotism.

They see not only the migration of the smallest factory to their town in terms of new customers; in the new style they recognize possibilities in the 'knowledge industries'; they see the setting up of a college of advanced education as bringing new money into the town. Astute principals of colleges of advanced education play up to this. One explained that he used a special pitch to townspeople on the new money he was bringing into the town: so much temporary money in building; so much permanent money in staff and subsidized students; multiplier effects; add it all up.

In Wonthaggi in Victoria, where the town's main business used to be the State Coal Mine (now commemorated in the Historical Park and the Miner's Rest Motor Inn) the Wonthaggi Hospital, with a wage payout in 1975 of $750,000, is the town's biggest individual industry. Given the bias in the voting system in favour of country areas, the placing of employment-producing institutions in country towns is one of the most important bread and butter functions of Australian governments. All over Australia the country towns, so anxious to preserve their individualism, are thinking of what the government can do for them next.

There is a Tick Gate in the Morori State Forest on the north coast of New South Wales – half a dozen white weatherboard houses beside a checkpoint that is part of the system of trying to control the migration of ticks. 'She'll be right', says the tick inspector, and your car passes from Summerland, the tourist promotion name for the Richmond River district, into The Big River Country, the tourist promotion name for the Clarence River district. On the other side of Grafton, there is another Tick Gate. ('How are you today?' from the inspector.) You pass from the timber of The Big River Country to the banana farms of Hibiscusland. Tourist promotion has become one of the main development hopes of some of the country towns: they combine together to form tourist associations, give their areas names that are often ludicrous, then plan festivals of no local significance whatsoever. Ballarat, scene of the Eureka Stockade, calls itself 'the Begonia City' because in the autumn it has a festival 'set against the fresh, bright, vibrant colours of nature's most impressive begonias'; the idea began in the 1950s and it bears the peculiar marks of flatness and insipidity of that decade. Goulburn, in New South Wales, calls itself 'the lilac city' because it has a lilac festival over the Eight-Hour Day holiday weekend: unfortunately it is a bad season for lilacs, so they import some from Adelaide, and use plastic lilacs for their decorations. In the town of Cobram, centre of a soldier settlement area on the River Murray which specializes in fruit and dairying, they have a Peaches and Cream Festival.

But there are other ambitions. In an advertisement in the Melbourne *Weekly Times* the Wangaratta Development Committee, as well as boasting of the development of their town, pride of Victoria's North-east, also boasts that Wangaratta's 'new arts centre will increase Wangaratta's cultural facilities to a standard usually found only in our major coastal cities', with a theatre, committee rooms, coffee shops, display area, musical recital chamber, bookshop. Wangaratta already knows the renown of its Centre for Continuing Education, a self-generating, locally-initiated activity, set up in an old high school building in 1962 and now providing seminars, night classes, workshops, public lectures, recitals, screenings, as well as acting as a home for the Wangaratta Art Group, the Film Society, the Historical Society, the Wangaratta Players and the horticulture, chess, geranium, radio, gemstone and judo groups.

'The Centre' idea has spread twenty-five miles down the Hume Highway to Benalla, where government offices are as important for employment as private manufacturing is in Wangaratta. Benalla sees itself as the North-east's rival town of cultural enlightenment; its new arts centre has already gone up (off-white, cost $500,000, vaguely Sydney Opera House roof), to house Benalla's painting collections and a creative workshop. Down the street, among 500 native trees and shrubs planted by the Rotary Club, the first stage of the Civic Centre is up, 'a delightful setting for small conferences and discussion workshops'; the planned extensions will include a library and an historical museum. At the Benalla educational centre, FORUM (started 1965), their courses include dressmaking, Indonesian, shorthand, transactional analysis, horse riding, the generation gap, copper enamelling, ballroom dancing, Chinese cookery, cake decorating, yoga, creative drama, gardening, crochet, philosophy and social change, weaving. At the arts centre they have been concerned that the building should seem an integral part of the garden, with 'grass mounds which will create the impression that the area was excavated.' One part of the jogging track nearby has been arranged to 'enable tourists to photograph the art gallery, town bridges and aquatic life prevailing in this area.' There are also two miles of 'nature track' for joggers, winding among large river gums behind the Civic Centre. A visiting Victorian Little Athletics Coach said this section of the track is 'unique, as no jogging track in the metropolitan area has the natural bush atmosphere passed through in this location.'

In a bistro in Albury, where the bar is in buttoned imitation leather and the barbecue has an imitation copper hood, a guitarist plays to people who sit under red strip lighting at plain black lacquer tables waiting for their oyster mornay and chicken *cacciatore*. In a bistro at Bathurst young people in jeans cluster around the dark entrance bar: in the restaurant the red-and-gold-patterned wallpaper, cane-bottomed chairs, red carpet, black ceiling and blackboard menu could be anywhere. At Bendigo, a motel restaurant is at the back of a dark dance floor where the bar glows with wide columns of blue and red light: then a high pitched roof is flung up like the top of a huge tent; one side wall flourishes silk canopies and Persian sphinxes with glaring red eyes; the other is festooned with beads; on the far side a glass wall reveals a walled garden that is lit up as the night comes on. There seems hardly a country town that hasn't followed new vogues: in West Wyalong the Chinese restaurant is next to the craft centre; in Millicent there is a Clockwork Orange Amusement Centre; all over the continent in the air-conditioned pharmacies there is likely to be the same commercial promotion. (When I last tested this, it was for three kinds of foot spray – foot deodorants, foot anti-perspirants, foot freshness.) In the cafe at Wentworth juke boxes flash purple, crimson, emerald. In the restaurant bar at the Renmark hotel the smorgasbord is at one end, the barbecue at the other. There are gas barbecues in the Banjo Paterson Park; red lights and brick walls in the Winewheel Restaurant at Griffith. In the Prineas Cafe, Holbrook, there are clinker brick walls, natural wood veneers, mosaic tiles.

Occasionally you might think you are back in the real thing, with its sincere crumminess. Moulamein, in the Riverina, seems to be the middle of nothing except large sheep stations: its broad main street has more gum trees than shops and in its Wattle Cafe you can sit at a slightly uncertain table on extremely uncertain chairs and look at a wall where there is still an old tarnished mirror with 'Grills at all Hours' set elegantly in its middle in gold leaf. Beside it, a sign over the frying section announces fish and chips, hamburgers, dim sims, chicken rolls, steak sandwiches. But even in Moulamein there is contemporary good taste: if you go to the police station you find a stylish modern building where a door in the dark brick wall reveals a courtyard garden. It is the kind of place that in Bendigo they could turn into a restaurant.

What do the tourists think of as they pass through the country towns? They arrive at their motels in the afternoons and unpack their suitcases and their plastic food boxes. In rooms where there is little communication with the outside except for the silent passage of food through a small panel door, they can spend their nights in fantasy – in plain colonial rooms, with cement blocks painted as stone; in Levantine brothels, among mauve and violet carpets and golden curtains; in simple fishermen's huts, with fish-nets beside the plate-glass picture windows; in medieval castles, with quiet alcoves of glazed tiles and long slender tables; in rooms of fine design, bringing together simple wood and honest brick; in dark blockhouses with walls so thick they could withstand a long seige. Next morning, they assemble around their cars and stow away the suitcases and the foam-plastic food boxes, like men in the courtyard of a country inn a hundred years ago loading their drays for the long journey ahead.

CHAPTER NINE

The Mysteries of Water

Not much more than a hundred years ago it was predicted that Australia would become a great maritime power – not merely an important trading nation (which it now is) but a big shipbuilder and owner of a large merchant navy. The flags of thirty shipping lines flying over Sydney were seen as part of the heritage from British sea-dogs. The idea of 'overseas' has always had a powerful hold on Australians' imaginations: it was where Australia's raw materials went, sustaining the nation, and back over the sea came stocks of commodities and manufactures – and the newspapers, magazines and books that told Australians what to think. When the arrival of a mail ship was signalled, fast boats went out to unload the packets of newspapers and magazines before the ship docked, and they were rushed to the newspaper desks where scissors and paste stood ready. Even now some Australian intellectuals wait for the airmail *Times* or *Observer* or *New Statesman* before they decide what were really the great events of the previous week.

Ships provided successive examples of modernity: the clippers, with their fine lines, seemed to sweep into a new age; then came the steamers, exemplifying human mastery of nature; the liners, offering sophistication; the tankers, confidence; the container ships, ingenuity. Shipping routes implanted maps on the mind: the Cape, the Great Circle, the Roaring Forties, the Suez Canal, and now the routes to Japan, and 'the cruise' circling in a course charted by overtime and long service leave. There was the hope of emigrant ships, bringing people to Australia, and the sadness of troop-ships, sending them back to Europe again. Terms like 'first class' and 'steerage' became grand metaphors for comparative prestige or division within society. Australians can choose an identity by a choice of ocean: they can imagine themselves a

Pacific power, opening out in friendship, or an Indian Ocean power, closed in by threat.

It was the ocean that provided Australia with its first ideas of a frontier of hope and opportunity. The land at the little settlement of Sydney Cove was too capricious: the few patches of good soil found among the sands and clays tended to be on river flats, where farming communities could be washed away. From the beginning *the seaport*, above all Sydney, was vital to Australia; but my example will be the small South Australian town of Robe, now a holiday place, but last century South Australia's second busiest port. On the sea front, facing Guichen Bay, named after a French admiral in 1802 by the French explorer Nicolas Baudin, is a small traffic roundabout called Royal Circus. Behind Royal Circus is the tiny Customs House, pink with red facings, neat, assured, cleaned, restored, painted, classified by the National Trust. Inside the roundabout are Robe's relics and monuments: a stone seat commemorates the passage of Matthew Flinders in the *Investigator*: a cannon from the *Konig Willem de Sweede*, found in 1857, and now painted battleship grey, signifies the hundred or so ships wrecked along the coast; an inscribed plate on a boulder commemorates the 16,500 Chinese gold-seekers who landed at Robe in the 1850s to avoid the Victorian poll tax, and then walked 300 miles to the diggings; a German mine, washed up in 1941, warns of doom. The cannon from the *Konig Willem de Sweede* rises in salute to a little harbour of fishing and pleasure boats: down the hill, a row of Norfolk pines denotes the swimming beach.

The oceans were the bearers of exports and bringers of vital supplies. They were also 'aquatic playgrounds': you had a 'dip' in the surf, or you went out for a bit of fishing, or you played with the water in some other way. Oceans had their sternness – there were capsizes, sharks, rips, undertows, and for a while the cult of the surf lifesaver was important in building national character ('the bronzed Anzac') – but the beach was predominantly a distinctively Australian place where you could go to have a good time (although what 'beach' meant could contrast very greatly from one part of Australia to the next: compare Rosebud, Bronte, Cottesloe, Glenelg). The good-time nature of the beach was condemned by moralists as heathen and by strategists as a softener of the natural will to survive. The surfer stretched out at Bondi getting his suntan was a lotus-eater ignoring the doom beyond the horizon. Across the ocean the unseen enemy was mustering his forces – Australia slept.

When I was a boy the beach seemed one of the surest things there was. We would hire a cottage at Cronulla every summer and spend four weeks there, as much of them as we could on the beach: in a confident world of blue sky, yellow sand, blue and white sea, brown stone headlands and pale grey cement, the lifesavers looked after us with their flags and their public address system. Now half the Cronulla beach has been destroyed; the sand has been washed off the rocks that lay beneath it. At the northern end of Maroubra, a beach we used to visit on one-day trips, all the sand has gone and only boulders remain; at Bondi, where, as I got older, we stayed instead of Cronulla, the sand is shifting, baring old stumps of ferro-concrete, leftovers from an earlier pier, and there are scares about the sewerage. The beach is now becoming a symbol of challenge to the environmentalists.

The land-grabbers all followed rivers: in the Riverina squatters moved along the Lachlan, the Murrumbidgee, the Billabong, the Murray, seizing runs by the simple process of taking the first available space to the west of the occupied area. To them water meant *the river*. Behind the runs fronting the rivers were the 'backblocks', used, if they were used at all, as winter runs. Then, as the backblocks were divided into holdings,water was also available from a *tank* or *dam*, water storage holes scooped out of the earth, at first by teams of bullocks pulling scoops, then by machines. To many Australians water still means a tank (see the chapter in Patrick White's *Eye of the Storm* where Sir Basil Hunter goes for a paddle and cuts his toe). The C.S.I.R.O. has produced an insoluble chemical, hexadecanol, which spreads as a film over the water of these small dams and slows down evaporation.

If you want to play the game of finding national metaphor in rivers, the Murray-Darling river system provides the opportunity. One part of it rising in snow streams, another part in the tropics, it is one of the longest river systems in the world, but its water runs so shallow that the whole system carries a much smaller volume than many lesser rivers. It seems just another unsubstantiated Australian boast. Some people can become as scornful about the Murray's failure to live up to its length as others about Gough Whitlam's claim that Australia could have its own foreign policy. Yet the

Murray-Darling is not a second-rate imitation of some big river overseas.

Both rivers continually lose direction; they flow sideways into billabongs, anabranches, lakes, over a country so flat and uniform that there is very little compulsion for the water to move at all. Before weirs were built, the Darling regularly degenerated into an empty trench across a flat, wide, broken down plain. Optimism was a string of water-holes. At flood-time there is still an excess of activity as water spreads all over the place: blue lakes form, surrounded by wild flowers; sometimes floodwater just lies and rots. The Murray proceeds with more consistency, although spreading lavishly sideways: the water in quiet billabongs gives perfect reflections of river red gums. The union of the two rivers is unobtrusive: they stretch up close to each other until finally nothing divides them. At the tip of the last piece of land to divide them there is some green grass, almost a small suburban lawn. After the junction the river becomes more ambitious – on one side spreading lagoons reflect the gums, on the other golden cliffs reflect the sun. Finally in the anti-climax of Lake Alexandrina, motionless, dull water spreads over a flat plain rimmed in blue-grey. At its shallow mouth the Murray dribbles laconically over a sand bar into the Southern Ocean.

The idea of *the flood* has continued to be one of the important Australian concepts of water. Australian floods have not been as devastating as floods on the Yellow River or the Ganges Delta or the Mississippi-Missouri River basin, but they have come often and unexpectedly enough for destruction by flood to seem part of the natural order. In flood areas State Emergency Service volunteers get certificates for proficiency as teleprinter operators; there are special manoeuvres, involving all the sections in a region – headquarters, welfare, casualty, signals, rescue; volunteers are enrolled to act as river gauge readers; there is discussion of co-ordination with the Natural Disaster Organization. Embankments and other forms of flood control go up, but so many places are built so unwisely on river banks – even Brisbane, ignominiously flooded in 1974 as if it were just a country town – that their residents boast that it would be cheaper to rebuild the town elsewhere than set up workable flood-control mechanisms.

In the north *the wet*, the season of the monsoonal rains,

institutionalizes flooding: yearly excess is predictable. Rivers spread over plains and wash into the sea; thousands of geese, cockatoos and parrots flood the skies; swamps and lakes fill out with waterfowl; tall coarse grass grows like a weed. The sky shines brilliant against the blackness of 'thunderheads'. When the sun comes out after a grey downpour, the soil steams. From November 1 to April 1, over the Coral Sea or sometimes the Indian Ocean, air sucks into itself, forming a destruction machine of wind and rain; the cyclone may move around waywardly for several weeks, given personality by a code name. On Christmas Day, 1974, when a cyclone destroyed Darwin, Australians were able to enjoy feelings of community and wonder at destruction overcoming ordinariness.

It is however the idea of dryness – the idea of water not being there – that has had the greatest economic and political effects in Australia, prompting some of the largest engineering works, some of 'development's' most emotional dreams and some famous poems and paintings. In its classic cultural form, dryness comes as *the drought*, a judgement on human inadequacy. In a more religious period, drought was seen as a direct message from God, punishing colonial wickedness as wickedness was punished in the Bible; now, for people who wish to see misfortune as something earned, drought can be presented as a punishment of human folly – there is a run of good seasons; farmers overstock; their luck runs out; they are ruined by drought and walk off their properties. The judgement is sometimes too severe; some of the greatest fiascos were first-time overstocking, before farmers had the feel of a particular part of country, but it is true that some farmers still have a tendency to forget that in much of Australia the certainty of drought is part of natural existence. A drought can seem immutable. Nothing can be done about it. Farmers can be given money; for a while they might buy feed for their stock, or lease out pasture land; but there is nothing anyone can do about the drought. In a flood, or a bushfire, one of the natural conclusions of dryness, people can take action, even if they fail, but you can't build up embankments or make firebreaks against no rain.

Drought and bushfire (sometimes burning through several million hectares of land) are part of the imagination of most Australians, however vicariously experienced, but more dominant in politics and art has been the more general idea of aridity as an

Australian condition. It has had a disproportionate effect on writers and artists – while two thirds or more of Australia is arid or semi-arid, more than two thirds of Australians live in well-watered areas near the sea. (Although there can be water restrictions in the suburbs and bushfires in the parks.) The emphasis on explorers in school history texts extended that disproportion. It is true, as the explorer Giles said of one of his journeys: 'To the traveller in such a wilderness, when he once turns his back upon water, the ever recurring question presents itself, of when and where shall I obtain more?' But practically the only parts of the explorers' diaries that are ever recalled, apart from a few spurts of Mitchell's enthusiasm, are the dramas of aridity. Other explorers than Mitchell were enthusiastic, but the stress is usually on failure – the land being travelled over is worthless, its rivers disappear in reedy swamps and strings of waterholes, large forest trees droop in the heat, emus gasp with thirst, the skin is burnt off the feet of dogs, screws fall out of boxes, lead drops out of pencils. It can be with the pride of a record-breaker that people recall Eyre's discovery that 'there is not a single water-course to be found in the south east of Australia for 1,500 miles.'

The fascination of dryness and failure produced its most extraordinary episode in Melbourne's reaction to the gallant incompetence that led to the death of the explorers Burke and Wills. Their bodies were brought back to Melbourne and lay in state for twenty days while a hundred thousand mourners filed past. On the day of the funeral, buildings were shrouded in purple and black. Enormous crowds watched the procession, a mile and a half long, that followed the large ceremonial hearse. Guns were fired at sixty-second intervals. Later a bronze statue went up, double life size, to be featured in school history texts for a couple of generations and suggesting that one of the important values in life was bold inexperience. At the La Trobe Library you can still buy facsimiles of the last notes of Burke and Wills.

Some Australians can look at the map and become angry to the point of pleasure that so much of Australia is coloured yellow for dryness, or white for barrenness. It is as if it were the fault of the land itself: if only it tried, it could turn blue and green. They make direct comparisons between deserts of climate and deserts of the mind or speak pointedly of the great cradles of civilization, none of which were in Australia.* The white and yellow are particularly irritating because the maps also show so many fine lines for rivers, but some of the river systems represented by the lines exist only in wet seasons and others for years are stretches of salt sand.

The C.S.I.R.O. is noted for its research in rain-making. Some people hope for a regeneration of Australia from experiments in taking the salt out of sea-water. In the nineteenth century some farmers were inspired by the myth that trees brought rain, a theory held world-wide and given special interest in South Australia in 1878 when the new Conservator of Forests proclaimed that the only reason the interior of Australia was arid was that it didn't have any trees. The most disastrous myth was that 'rain follows the plough.' Usually associated with 'where grass grows, wheat will grow', this was the belief that pushed the South Australian wheat farmers to their frontier of failure. With it went the myth that 'water follows the flocks and herds.' An article in the *Sydney University Review* in 1882 supported this theory, explaining that when stock trampled a mud-hole it would become the nucleus of a pond and that the tracks of sheep and cattle would become drains for water to run into clay hollows. 'Often the mere trampling of the stock, spread from creek to creek, and from valley to valley, aids to reclaim the wilderness to man's use.'

Other enthusiasms had sense. In the 1880s, as more and more successful bores were sunk in the search for artesian water, the prophecy of 'an unlimited supply of good water' spread. The *Sydney University Review* saw how, with artesian water, 'the arid deserts of Australia's interior (as they are still termed in school books)', could become 'her most profitable region for human enterprise'. It wasn't as good as that, but the Great Australian Basin proved by far the largest artesian basin in the world and, with the other ten artesian basins that were tapped, provides water for thousands of artesian bores. To some Australians water is *the bore*, a pipe sunk down into subterranean water, its end sticking up out of the red soil, bubbling.

'Gold will eventually become exhausted, while water will

*The present archaeological work on Australian pre-history is, however, giving interest in the past of the Aborigines as part of the general story of the cultural development of the human species.

continue as long as the world lasts.' 'The triumphant march of water . . . bringing life to the grass and flower, to the loaded tree . . . No price is too high for the promise of such progress.' The rhetoric of the late nineteenth-century irrigation creed brought together the obsession with water, the belief in machines and the craving for a civilizing influence. Irrigation was seen as the beginning of human civilization and now Yankee technological skill, with pumping stations, concrete and pipes had produced *scientific irrigation.* No one believed in this more than Alfred Deakin, in 1884 Victorian Minister for Water Supply: he went off to see what they were doing on irrigation projects in the United States, Italy, Egypt, India. In California he met George and William Chaffey, founders of the first Californian irrigation settlement to be watered by a cement pipeline system, and persuaded them to come to Victoria; they picked the site of the failed Mildura cattle station, in the red sand of the mallee, for an irrigation colony and floated a company. The South Australian government also signed an agreement with the Chaffeys, and they started a second irrigation colony at Renmark. Victoria and South Australia were to ride into eternal prosperity on a great flow of water.

If Australia recognized its national heroes and people still made movies celebrating achievement, there could be one on William Chaffey in Mildura. At an early stage you would establish the 'Chaffey pump', designed by George Chaffey, being careful to establish the noise connected with its working. (It has to be the kind of noise you can wake and hear in the morning.) The movie runs through scenes of success. Then disasters: Murray River crayfish burrow into the banks of the irrigation canals and the banks cave in; salt deposits in the subsoil rise with the water and stifle the vines; there is an economic depression; the Chaffeys are ruined; George goes back to the United States. One morning people wake up: that's strange, no pump noises. They hurry to the river. The men have gone, says the pump foreman: no wages, no pump men. Fear, hatred, doubt register on the faces in the crowd: then – slowly – dawning hope. They'll do it themselves! Shots of the people working their own pump. The vineyards flourish. William Chaffey flourishes. Close in on statue of Mayor William Chaffey (affectionately known as 'the Boss'), binoculars in one hand, walking stick in the other, in Deakin Avenue, Mildura. Roll the credits.

Deakin Avenue is a long, splendid boulevard, its centre gardens of grass, flowers and trees watered with the wastefulness of irrigationists. Instead of Victorian Renaissance-style buildings, Mildura uses boulevardes and trees to show itself a going concern: water spouts out of sprinklers on to the gardens that divide its avenues. It has none of the diffidence of most Australian country towns: it seems somewhere else, Mussolini's North Africa, perhaps, with the excitement of trees, plants and imperial ambition in an oasis city. You get the same feeling in Griffith, in the Murrumbidgee Irrigation Area. In true extravagant irrigation style its main avenue is two miles long, with four lanes of traffic and trees and grass down the middle. At one end of the avenue, in a circle surrounded by four rings of roads and initiating eight radial spokes are its prestige buildings. Griffith speaks of itself as 'Griffith of the Four Faces' – Agriculture, Industry, Culture, Sport – as if it were a nineteenth-century baroque allegorical fountain.

Tourists in air-conditioned coaches with glass in the windows darkened against the sun-dazzle inspect the strangeness of irrigation towns and leave with colour slides of the boundaries where red bareness juts on to green vineyards. The irrigation districts are materialized fragments of the dream of a large dry country transformed by water to become small-scale and European. Long, straight canals carry the brown water banked up behind diversion weirs on rivers; further back, reservoirs of blue-grey water are stored behind great walls of reinforced concrete, celebrations of meticulous engineering and rushes of hope; it was not until after engineers had started the Hume Weir on the Murray that politicians started working out in detail what to do with the water that would be stored in it; when Harold Holt offhandedly announced the Ord River scheme in northern Australia, because he needed a northern dam to round out an election policy, no one had shown that it might be an economic proposition.

The Ord River may be the last of the great dams: more Australians are now aware of how much these high ambitions cost. The agricultural economist B. R. Davidson points out that Australia, unlike the countries it has imitated, has no permanent snowfield and a small population, therefore reservoir costs have been higher and there hasn't been a big enough market for the high-priced fruit and vegetables that would have made economic sense of irrigation. The genius of the Australian countryside was to provide a good return on a small amount of labour: the creation of irrigation areas increased the proportions of labour. The result, according to Davidson, is that irrigation agriculture gives a lower return to capital than any other form of agriculture in Australia.

The most expensive national monument is contained in the sixteen reservoirs, seven power stations, 150 kilometres of tunnels, 130 kilometres of aqueducts and 1,600 kilometres of roads of the $800 million Snowy River Scheme, one of the world's remarkable engineering works and a tribute to the love of water, both as creator of small farms and as maker of electric power. The idea of water as *power* was common in Tasmania, whose main lakes lie several thousand feet up in the mountains and seemed fit only for engineers until the 1970s, when the conservationists put in counter-claims to Lake Pedder, as of value in itself. The idea of water as power moved to the mainland in the late 1940s, as strikes were making coal-mining seem out of fashion; it was attached to the idea of water as irrigation and manifested itself in the Snowy River Scheme plans for inundating old paddocks and townships with new lakes, tunnelling through granite, stringing up steel wires. Now tourists go in buses to worship this concrete, water and steel. Whether it represents a rational allocation of resources is doubtful, but even the launching rhetoric signalled that this was not the only test: '. . . the greatest single project in our history . . . A plan for a whole nation . . .' As each new stage of the Scheme was declared open, the Blowering Reservoir, Tumut No. 2 Power Station, Murray Station I, national leaders assembled and bent their heads reverently over microphones. Their words showed an itch to seek out the spirit of ferro-concrete, as medieval cathedral-builders sought out the spirit of stone and cast it into something that men would remember.

CHAPTER TEN

The Secular Faith of 'Development'

Development for its own sake

The sense of transcendent mission associated with 'development' has been a most pervasive impulse in Australia, prompting action and giving it meaning, a secular faith so widely accepted and pursued with such elevated intensity that Cardinal Moran, the Catholic Archbishop of Sydney, could boast in 1883: 'From being a wild, uncultured waste, so poor and barren that the first explorers shrank back aghast . . . Australia has become a civilized land, clothed with loveliness as a garden, rich with unlocked treasures of gold and silver, and with priceless mines, almost beyond parallel in the world's history.' When A. W. Jose wrote his *Short History of Australia* in 1899 he didn't seem to know how to end the story – no final flourish of 'purpose' was produced to give Australia meaning – but in the 1909 edition he had found a purpose:

> To this point, then, the course of Australian history has led us – that we hold a whole continent of valuable land, using it very imperfectly, but free for the moment from outside interference. This free moment we must use, if we want to retain our hold; we must use it to take seriously in hand the developing of the country's natural resources by cultivating its richer soils, irrigating its drier, exploiting the fisheries along its coasts, opening up and thoroughly working the mines hidden below its surface. These things in the past have been done, for the most part, in a haphazard, unscientific sort of way. To do them methodically, scientifically, is Australia's task for the future; and young Australians cannot serve their country better than by preparing themselves with zealous study to take their share in the task directly they become men.

When 'business' and 'the firm' were being established as the most efficient and real ideas in modern life, it became popular to see the development of Australia as if Australia were a go-ahead business company. In the 1919 election it was said 'You are all shareholders in the great company of Australia Unlimited, the greatest firm in the world.' In the 1928 election Bruce spoke of himself as 'the managing director of the greatest company in Australia, the Commonwealth Government, and its duty is to develop Australia'. The same kind of rhetoric was used by the early medicine-men of free enterprise in the Menzies era. But this language of economic calculation was misleading. The ideas of 'development' in their grander and more theological aspects have never been concerned only with aiding the economy but with other calculations as well: great fears and hopes of geopolitical strategy, dreams of a purer and more civilized existence, ideas of justice, a craving for bigness and a kind of patriotism in which the soil of Australia, not its people, becomes the real Australia, so that development becomes not merely development for exports, or strategic safety, or human betterment, but *development as a good thing in its own right*. For the next few pages I will suggest some of the ideas that surround this religion of 'development' that makes no pretence of being concerned mainly with economic considerations, and that sometimes makes no pretence of being concerned with economic considerations at all.

At the beginning of the century Deakin was speaking of Australia as an outpost of white civilization among teeming millions of coloured races who grew more powerful and more ominous year by year: its fertile eastern seaboard was the envy of every nation; only a wall of immigrant flesh and blood could keep out the hordes. In the 1910 election it was suggested that if airships dropped parties of Chinese on certain parts of Australia it would be months before anyone knew they were there. The new Liberal leader, Joseph Cook, said before the 1913 election that Australia must get its kith and kin from overseas to settle the vast spaces of its interior: it must either people the continent or perish. Between the two world wars Hughes made the 'populate or perish' campaign his own. Australia was a paradise of fools; its whole future depended on developing and populating the great continent. After the Second World War Labor's Dr Evatt was sure that to maintain a regular army and a highly-trained and efficient navy and air force, Australia's population must be greatly increased. In 1963, Labor's new leader Arthur Calwell was saying, 'Either we must fill this country or we lose it. It is as simple as that.' In 1966 John McEwen was brooding over 'this lonely continent'.

To the simple fear of advancing Asiatic hordes was added the moral feeling that it was unjust to hold a continent without developing it: development was necessary to earn the right of occupation. If Australia didn't do its duty and develop the continent, someone would come and take it away in punishment. A conservative political leader said in the 1917 elections that the argument against a small population holding a large continent was precisely the argument against land monopoly: democracy desired that nobody be allowed to hold large tracts of country without using them. Hughes asked in the 1922 election how Australia, with a land capable of supporting anything from fifty million to 100 million could resist world opinion and maintain a dog-in-the-manger policy. Menzies said in 1950 that Australia owed it to the world to develop the resources which God had given into their hands; in 1963 Calwell said too little was being done to justify possession by a comparative handful of people of a vast continent containing such unusual wealth. Hopes of using unharnessed resources were combined with fears about Asian jealousy in the 'Develop the North' campaigns which had a season in the 1960s. 'The value of Northern development cannot be measured in terms of profit alone', said Calwell. 'It must be assessed according to the needs of national security and the welfare of the Australian people.' The monument commemorating this 'Develop the North' campaign was the Department of Northern Development, set up by Whitlam in 1972, but with hardly any power because by then the idea of developing the North had gone out of fashion.

As well as signifying defencelessness, the blankness of the north and the other blanks on population maps also affronted yearnings for an independent yeomanry. The unevenness of shadings on population maps was a reminder of the evils of the cities and of the failure, in Moran's terms, to 'civilize' the continent uniformly. Justifying possession of Australia demanded a bigger population, spread more evenly. To Calwell, part of the moral justification for holding Australia demanded decentralizing its people: 'By no means can it be said that we truly inhabit this continent when two-thirds of our people live in six capital cities, and when forty per cent of the continent is "occupied" by four per cent of our people – it is barely peopled at all.'

The simple drive to go on getting bigger – an impulse natural in a colony's early stage – now seemed the main reason for the existence of a nation. In Bartholomew and Cramp's *Australian School Atlas* a series of exploration maps showed the settlement of Australia in shades of black and yellow. The first map in the series showed a black shape with a tiny yellow blob for the early settlement at Sydney. In succeeding maps other blobs appeared and spread, finally taking over all the black. The European conquest of Australia was marked by more disappointments than was expansion in the United States, but the idea of never-ending expansion was nearly as strong a part of the Australian imagination. With the map successfully turned from black to yellow, the urge to get bigger had now to find new outlets: one of them was found in tables of population growth. It was not just that bigness aided survival, or improved the way people lived. Bigness was good in itself. A politician in the first Federal election campaign said: 'Our population at the present moment is about the same as England in the time of Queen Elizabeth but I anticipate that before the end of the century the population of Australia will be equal to that of Great Britain today.' Hughes could see Australia as 'a mighty nation'; it would 'follow in the footsteps of the great Republic of America, while avoiding its errors'; it was 'richer than the U.S. in mineral, agricultural and pastoral possibility', 'capable of almost indefinite expansion'. In the arguments about what population Australia could 'sustain', it was as if people were crops and their maximum number could be calculated in terms of soil fertility and rainfall statistics, but that within these limits it was within the power of Australians themselves to determine what size it would be and how important it should become. It is one of the colonial characteristics of Australians that they imagine that by immigration programmes they can choose to change their nature.

Australian disciples of the cult of development were not alone in their love of public works. Throughout the modern industrial age, great public works have been depicted as splendid national achievements. As Dr H. C. Coombs said at a Political Science Summer School in 1944:

. . . in a very real sense public works contribute to a fullness in the national life by adding a sense of achievement and a consciousness of growth to the life of an individual . . . National development, therefore, by providing a consciousness of national achievement and a sense of individual participation in growth is capable of satisfying a very real demand.

Where Australians were unique in the world rhetoric of national progress was in the range of emotions stirred by calling Australia a 'continent'. 'A continent for a nation and a nation for a continent', the phrase popularized by Edmund Barton, the first Prime Minister, had the long life sometimes achieved by phrases quite without meaning. It was last seen alive in 1963, used by Arthur Calwell who served as a folk-memory of ancient faiths. In his book *Labor's Role in Modern Society*, Calwell said that developing the continent was the true Australian nationalism:

To no other nation in the world has the opportunity been granted for the sole possession and development of a sea-girt land-mass by a single people. To no other nation has it been given to unite their will and destiny upon an empty land of such vast extent as it has been to us. Ours, therefore, is a unique nationalism . . . The only conquests we seek are conquests over the caprice of nature and over the uncertainties of a country with large intractable areas.

What Calwell had to say about faith in development had value for the very reason that he was being more explicit than was at the time fashionable:

The economic and security arguments do not together provide the full explanation for the unanimity that exists on the need for national development . . . The reasons for that unanimity lie deeper, and are bound up with national sentiment . . . all Australians feel that if the number of their fellow Australians could be greatly increased, then that would be a good thing in itself. This feeling owes little to the hard, factual idea of the economists or the strategists; it is a sentiment, and the best and most honest name for it is nationalism . . . Fortunately for us, there is a continent awaiting our conquest, and its name is Australia.

Pride in the continent's size and in its development again became explicit in the new nationalism of the 1960s mineral boom. Like Calwell's, it was the nationalism of the large land mass. Thousands of speeches buried in research libraries and newspaper files still summon Australians to the nationalism of being a continent – in worship (praising size and potential), and in good works (filling up valleys with water, scooping out minerals, inducing soil particles to nourish plants, planning great achievements in engineering).

A sense of failure was also part of the story, as it is in any religion. In Sydney's Botanic gardens, where a statue of the goddess of agriculture helps support the statue of Governor Phillip and also helps support the ideas of hope and growth, was the site of Australia's first farm, which was a failure. It was here that they sowed the first European grains and found that the seeds didn't mature. Australia had no first harvest to celebrate as the Pilgrim Fathers did on their Thanksgiving Day. Except for Phillip himself there was an almost universal expectation of failure in the first settlement – indeed some of the officers seemed determined on it – and throughout Australian history, even after optimism developed, there continued to be counter-impulses of a fear that fiasco might be the normal human condition. This has been true of the faith in development. There might be no scepticism among the developers themselves at their great moments of creation, whether in ferro-concrete or rhetoric, but there has been a strong counter-faith that Australia is a singularly hopeless country to get anything out of. Just as the title of the book *The Lucky Country* was taken over as a generally useful phrase during the minerals boom in the 1960s, the title of another book, *The Myth of the Open Spaces* had a significant use in the 1940s. It was published only a year after Russell Drysdale, in his Riverina paintings, painted dead trees that looked like Henry Moore sculptures, portraying a hostile environment of limited potential to which the appropriate reaction was acceptance; an attitude, as the art historian Bernard Smith has pointed out, that had been developed fifty years before, by Lawson and others, in the literary tradition. At that time the resources of Australia were seen by some intellectuals as a great deal more limited than they had previously been imagined by politicians, if not by short story writers. 'There seems little prospect of the Australian population growing to more than nine million by the end of the century, even with substantial immigration', said the demographer W. D. Borrie at a Political Science Summer School in 1947; in the same year Dr H. C. Coombs said in a contribution to Hartley Grattan's

Australia: 'The hard facts of comparative geography make it clear that not even the fullest development of resources can gain for Australia the standard of living which now seems within reach of the favoured populations of more generously endowed countries.'

The trinity of men, money and markets

In the 1913 election the Adelaide *Advertiser* had been able to say:

Wisely it is recognized that no party can live on a policy of negation. Movement, progress, advancement in some direction or other are the universal role in things political. This is true in Russia; it is even true in China . . . Liberalism . . . recognizes that no party can stand in the way of political and social achievement and hope to obtain the support of the Australian people.

But in 1926, at an Imperial Conference in London, when Bruce, one of development's greatest rhetoricians, boosted the phrase 'men, money and markets' he was defining the belief of an era in which the ideas of 'movement, progress, advancement in some direction or other' could be narrowed down to the idea of advancement in men, money and markets. These became the trinity of the secular faith of 'development'. After Bruce this mood largely prevailed. It had already had a long history.

Men: *In the verses inscribed on the pedestal of New York's Statue of Liberty the call goes out: 'Give me your tired, your poor, your huddled masses yearning to breathe free, the wretched refuse of your teeming shore.' In the United States a rhetoric of idealism survived even the greatest disappointments of mass immigration but in Australia, apart from the long desire to restrict immigration to kith and kin of the British race and, later, the minority desire to find moral good in multi-racialism, it is hard to find any sustained attempt to attach idealism to immigration policies. If welcoming words were to be inscribed on Pinchgut Island in Sydney Harbour they should simply be 'Give me your skilled and semi-skilled

*It will be noted that, in the literal meaning of his words, Bruce didn't call for female immigrants, only 'men'. But women were also brought to Australia, as unpaid farm labourers, breeders of young Australians, etc.

tradesmen.' Ever since the poorhouses of Great Britain and Ireland were scoured in the 1830s, Australian governments have bought immigrants as labour fodder (or as baby-producers) without making many apologies: whether as worker or mother, the immigrant's function was to help 'develop Australia' as part of a general economic calculation, at times presented so enthusiastically in mathematical terms that it seemed the population figures themselves would do the developing. The idea that immigrants should have skill as well as muscle is new; in the 1830s squatters saw the ideal immigrant (according to a critic) as 'an able-bodied single man from an agricultural country – humble, ignorant and strong'; almost a hundred years later the Country Party was speaking of ideal immigrants as 'agriculturalists, farm labourers and domestic servants'; in the liberalizations of immigration policy in the late 1940s, when for the first time there was an active seeking-out of continental Europeans as well as British kith and kin, there was a preference for pick-and-shovel men. Words regularly associated with the immigration programme were often the solid, down-to-development kind of words that were also often associated with concrete constructions: *markets*, *growth*, *resources*, *industry*, *land*, *expansion*, *production*.

Money: When John Gunther was in Sydney, Frank Packer gave a lunch for him. Gunther asked guests what they had to say about foreign investment. He had expected the usual range of responses he got in other countries – from hatred to an apologetic, pragmatic acceptance. What he got was a sense of almost sexual eagerness for the feel of foreign money and an anxious snapping against anyone who wanted to take it away. When he said he had never before heard such answers this was taken as a congratulation. Packer's friends saw foreign money not only as essential to development, but also as something that, by association, bestowed honour and bigness. It was the real thing (especially U.S. dollars). Foreign money has been seen as essential to the development of Australia since the 1860s, when Australia was seen as a place where the British could do well out of investment; just as some Australians believed prestige and importance came from loyalty to Great Britain, others, in their economic dependence, were proud of their loyalty to foreign money. In the cult of development, foreign money was as fundamental as a new railway branch line, or an expensive reservoir. And *money talked*: louder even than national prejudices. In the boom decades after the Second World War, prejudice against non-white money weakened sooner than the prejudice against non-white persons: Japanese businessmen were still being insulted by visa delays when they were coming to help Australians make more money. When the Shah of Iran came to Australia in 1974 even the most racist Australian wanted his money.

For an ungenerous period Australia applied a double standard, in which it claimed to merit other people's money because it was 'developing resources' and denied poor nations Australian financial aid because Australia itself was a developing nation. External Affairs Minister Garfield Barwick said in 1964:

> We stand mid-stream between the 'haves' and the 'have nots' as a developing country. Our national income and our gross national product, our standard of literacy and education facilities put us vis-a-vis less developed countries in the 'haves'. But in European or American terms, and in particular in relation to our untapped resources, we are an under-developed country, still needing constant infusion of foreign capital for our development.

By this argument Australia itself became a deserving mendicant who couldn't help others: 'Because we are a developing country the amount of capital aid we can provide is almost minimal in its effect.' The self-pitying idea of a neglected Australia was dear to the heart of Bruce. In announcing a Developing and Migration Commission in 1926, he spoke of Australia as ' one of the least developed countries of the world '.

Markets: There has been an emphasis on *men* since the 1830s, on *money* since the 1860s; by Bruce's time, the word *markets* was developing a new and more expensive meaning. There was no longer merely the old concern with finding something to sell that had begun with the clubbing of seals and the chopping down of cedar. Creating sturdy Australian yeomen out of government-sponsored group settlement schemes meant finding someone to buy whatever was produced by those yeomen who didn't abandon their farms. With Bruce, ambitions went beyond ideas of Australian national interest to the interests of the Empire as a whole – he said in 1925, 'the position not only of Australia but also of the whole Empire depends upon a redistribution of its white people' – but even those who were merely concerned with peopling Australia knew that for Australia to absorb more immigrants, markets had to be found for Australian produce. The answer was in subsidizing not only development: exports had to be subsidized as well. Persuading the British to buy cheap food became an important part of Australian foreign policy. The idea of markets developed a righteousness of its own: anything farmers 'produced' had a right to be sold. This became one of the new fundamentals of political imaginations. What was seen as its success – measured by volume without concern for costs – was caught splendidly in the cadences of a triumphal ode by Earle Page, the Country Party leader, in the 1937 election:

For every 2 lb of butter we sold to Britain 10 years ago, we now sell 5 lb; for every 1 lb of cheese we now sell 2 lb; for every egg, three eggs; for every tin of canned fruit, 3 tins; for every 2 lb of dried fruit, 3 lb; for every barrel of wine, 3 barrels; for every bushel of wheat, 3 bushels; and for every 4 bales of wool, 5 bales.

Between the wars, when there was still all that red on the map, the British were 'our best customers' and 'our principal trading partners' as they were 'our race' and 'our only means of defence'. It was an easy over-the-counter relationship: we all spoke the same language, and some Australians felt Australia was only a branch shop anyway. But after the Second World War, markets developed a skittish, cosmopolitan look. There was moral shock in the early 1960s when faithless Britain tried to get into the European Economic Community, but by the time the British made their second and successful application, Japan had become 'our best customer', the United States had become 'our principal trading partner' and for a decade China, a nation not diplomatically recognized by Australia, had been 'a good customer'.

The shopkeepers' language of 'customers' and 'trading partners' may have caused more fundamental changes in some Australians' views of the world than changes brought about by alterations in strategic power. To many, Japan becoming our best customer and China a good customer may finally have made credible what others had seen when Singapore fell thirty years before. For a nation to which some of the most honoured words were those of trade, export figures could have the seriousness that primitive peoples found in the ceremonial exchange of gifts.

Just as pessimism, as well as hope, is in Australian attitudes to development, hating foreign money and despising immigrants are there as well as craving them. Some Australians have hated the ideas of importing men and money as much as others have longed for them.

The distrust of immigrants was one of the strongest of the convict colony's many early prejudices and since 'shared vision of an enemy' is seen as one of the incentives towards group definition, it may have provided the first impulse towards claims to a unique Australian identity. Ticket-of-leave men and pardoned convicts could hate free settlers ('the self-imported devils'): the Australian-born ('the natives') could hate 'the Bloody Emigrants'. Increasingly, all except the rich who wanted cheap labour hated the importing of convicts: if there was ever a prospect of a republican break from England it probably came closest in the middle of the nineteenth century in protest movements against convict transportation. By then it was established that nasty people came in ships (although, since the Australian-born began to make up a majority of the population only in the 1890s it is possible that for most of the nineteenth century the principal among many ethnocentric prejudices in Australia was the immigrant's against the Australian-born). For a time the motto of the *Bulletin* was 'Australia for the Australians – the cheap Chinaman, the cheap nigger and cheap European pauper to be absolutely excluded' – but prejudices went further than hatred of coloureds and Continentals: it extended to the Irish, who were seen as 'alien, enemies of the English crown and English laws', 'ignorant, turbulent, mentally debased and totally unqualified for the elective franchise'; even English kith and kin could be despised. In particular, until the immigration programme after the Second World War, trade union distrust of immigrants was almost continuous: they were job stealers who lowered working conditions.

When the 'quality of life' slogan became popular in the late 1960s some educated middle-class people, believing the immigration programme responsible for newly-defined inadequacies in urban planning, saw immigrants as people whose children crowded out the schools, whose cars caused traffic blocks and whose excrement, through sewerage inadequacies, fouled Bondi Beach. (They did not also see immigrants as a main source of labour for building schools, roads and sewers.) A new fashion in progressivism demanded a small Scandinavian-type welfare state, and immigration seemed to threaten this. This new classification of immigrants as anti-progressive conflicted with the 1960s progressive idea (still held by some people, including me, and likely to be held till death) that Australia's path to moral regeneration was to become a multi-racial nation. There was no model of a Scandinavian-type welfare state 'overseas' that was also multi-racial. One possible compromise was to abolish discrimination in immigration policy, and then abolish immigration.

Hatred of foreign money developed later than hatred of immigrants, but by the twentieth century, attacks on foreign trusts, combines, rings, vends, cartels, combinations and diabolical monopolies were, for a time, an obligatory part of political oratory. 'Trusts and combines dominate the industrial and economic world of today', said Hughes in the 1913 election.

> The cost of living is going up. What causes it? . . . the dominant cause of the increase is the control and manipulation of the market by trusts and combines . . . The trusts of America today have a world power, compared to which that of king or czar is as a grain of mustard seed to a mighty oak. They govern America and help to govern the world.

This concern was most characteristic of the Labor Party, but there were outbursts from non-Labor parties, especially against investment by 'Yanks', whose money was seen by some as coming from the same corrupting source as 'the muck and filth' of Hollywood and other forms of Americanization. The 1930s depression was attributed by many Labor men to an international conspiracy of financial manipulators. Scullin, the Labor leader, said the Depression was 'the deliberate policy or conspiracy by the great moneymakers of the world to bring down prices'. In 1946, Eddie Ward, a minister in the Chifley Labor government, in attacking the Bretton Woods agreement could still say:

> I am convinced that the agreement will enthrone a world dictatorship of private finance, more complete and terrible than any Hitlerite dream. It

offers no solution of world problems but quite blatantly sets up controls which will reduce the smaller nations to vassal States, and make every Government the mouthpiece and tool of international finance.

When Whitlam began his run for office, to a background of McEwen's already-established rhetoric about selling off the farm, the key word had become 'multinational'. By 1973 Australia could afford a revulsion against foreign money: in fact, since the money was flowing in too quickly, with an inflationary effect, Australia could not, for that year anyway, afford any more foreign money. Whitlam shut it off in a way that was seen as good for the economy by almost all economists, if only as a temporary measure, but his political opponents seemed to see foreign money as such an absolute good that it should never be refused.

Rex Connor seeking Executive Council approval on 13 December 1974, for a $4 billion petrodollar loan should be seen as one of the epiphanies of Australian economic idealism. It deserves a large painting. For hope, light up the face of the centre figure, the old Minister for Minerals and Energy, lost in great dreams – dreams of how pipelines, uranium enrichment, coal hydrogenation, and rail electrification would serve the cult of 'development' (*Give me men to match my mountains, give me men to match my plains, men with freedom in their vision, and creation in their brains*, as he said in the House of Representatives); but there is a special patriotism to these dreams because all the projects will be nationally owned, in a way unknown to 'the little men of the opposition, who prefer control by foreigners'; there is also the dream of a panacea, the easy answer Labor had looked for, over the decades, in so many places – this time, ironically, to be found in a new form of foreign money. For hope also light up the faces of the other ministers. Then by some trick of darkness in the background, offset the hopes with a feeling of apprehension, to catch the mood of the viewer of the painting, who knows that what the ministers are planning isn't going to come off.

The cult of naturalness

In the New South Wales north coast town of Nimbin, spread out up and down some little hills beside the Goolmangar Creek, some shops are plain Australian country town in style, others are painted psychedelic-bright: in one, above the windows, a bottle of tomato sauce is portrayed in the moment of orgasm. A craft shop, with temple bells at its door instead of a push button, and painted yellow with gleaming suns, is next to an Electrical Appliances Store, faded, with old cardboard packages of electrical goods in its window. A farmer in red-checked shirt, short-back-and-sides and wide-brimmed hat, walks past a long-haired hippie in tartan poncho, bare feet and high-crowned unisex hat. Sitting beside the grass near the war memorial a hippie girl in caftan nurses her baby and writes a poem. In the general store there is a conventional milk bar; in the hippie cafe, people sit at low tables on floor rugs. The hippies are contented with the local swimming hole; the townspeople are raising money for an olympic swimming pool. Along a nearby valley a dozen old cars parked in the road announce a commune farm, with a geodesic dome, a purple-painted farm house and a yellow tent; on the way to the coast, there is a plantation of newly-fashionable macadamia nuts; in a tiny village on the side of a hill, one of the only two shops is a craft shop; on the coast, at Byron Bay, named by Captain Cook after the poet's grandfather, across from the new bistro there is an 'alternative society' restaurant, The Whole Meal, where instead of chicken *cacciatore* and *crêpes suzette*, there are sesame rissoles with beanshoot salad and pancakes filled with banana, pawpaw and honey.

This is one example of the new cult of naturalness, now challenging some of the old wisdoms of development. Another can be found in Newcastle. Spread out around its flat, silting harbour, with a skyline of steelworks and docks, blast furnaces, cranes and colliers, Newcastle can seem dirty and ugly; it has no monuments to self-importance; its shopping streets straggle into exhaustion; its civic square is dispirited postwar modern; the colonial Customs House turns its back on the town and looks at the harbour. It retains some sense of a past – a bogy hole swimming pool cut out of cliff rock for a colonial commandant to bathe in, old terraces and a few colonial buildings between the headland and the railway station, hilly streets of old houses where the rich used to live, the Newcastle Club with its cobbled wall; but much of its visible past is insubstantial – suburbs of weatherboard houses, mean streets – and some of its memories are of a kind for which Australians have not yet created adequate forms of commemoration – chain-gangs of convicts living on the beaches where they burned sea shells to make lime for Sydney; a commandant rowing up the Hunter River with a whipping triangle in the bow of his boat to encourage the cedar gangs; the robber baronies of coal-owners; colonial troops sent from Sydney with a field gun to intimidate striking miners. But when, during the Great War, Australia's first significant steelworks opened at Newcastle, there began a grave recognition that whatever else might be said about it, as the birthplace of Australian heavy industry Newcastle had a duty to expand. It seemed a routine expression of this belief that as part of an industrial development programme in which an oil refinery and a new steelworks would go up, the three mangrove-fringed islands in the Hunter estuary opposite the steelworks should be linked by dredged-up muck dumped between them. But the mud flats between the islands are winter feeding grounds for 10,000 or so wader birds migrating each year from Japan, Siberia and Mongolia, and in 1974 Japan and Australia signed a Bilateral Treaty on Migratory Birds. According to the *Sydney Morning Herald* writer, Gavin Souter, the appropriate authorities all agreed to preserve part of the islands for wild life, but they were divided on which part, and on this depended the fate of the waders' feeding ground. The New South Wales Department of Public Works took one side; its opponents, according to Gavin Souter, were the Director of the State Pollution Control Commission, the National Parks and Wildlife Service, the Chief Secretary's Department, the Fisheries Branch, the Australian Littoral Society and the Newcastle Flora and Fauna Protection Society.

Another anecdote dates from 1974, when concern for the environment was holding up an alumina project in Western Australia and a petro-chemical complex in South Australia, and when concern for Aboriginal rights was holding up uranium mining development in the Northern Territory: a lunchtime champagne party was given by the Crafts Board of the Australian Council for the Arts at Kim Bonython's gallery in Paddington. Its purpose was to launch a book, *Crafts of Australia*, produced by the Crafts Council to celebrate the tenth year of the international craft movement. Margaret Whitlam made the launching speech. The book celebrated work done in, amongst other things, moss agate, crocheted hemp and sisal, wool tops, yellow gold, silver and amethysts, stoneware, eucalyptus wood, stained glass, steel, natural jute, manilla ropes, porcelain, bullock-hide, frayed canvas, linen wrap and handspun wool weft. The text was in English, French, Japanese and Pitjantjatjara, an Aboriginal language. The paper used for the cover was handmade from the paperbark of coastal Melaleuca trees that had grown in Cleveland Bay, Queensland, and from recycled manilla envelopes.

A number of styles of protest have arisen since the certainties of the Age of the Holden gave way to presentiments of disaster – protest marches, sit-ins, freedom rides, vigils, talk-ins, alternative societies, resident action, green bans. Some have been connected with economic activity only at second or third hand but in those with a direct connection, there has been recurrent concern for a greater reverence for resources and this represents a suspicion, even a hatred, of cults of 'development'. Concern with pollution, scarce resources, the environment, and doubts about economic growth, have challenged whole landscapes of opinion of what life in Australia is supposed to be. Reality is found in the unadorned – in honest wood, plain materials, freedom from certain types of clothes, outspokenness, purer food, more natural expression of the body – or in the sending-up of adornment in old clothes, eccentric revivals, junk, bright paint. Some people are returning to ideas of community and interdependence, co-operation rather than competition, ecology rather than economics. In extreme cases there is preference for the mystic over the scientific, involvement over objectivity, and there is a search for non-verbal communication. In discussion on world resources there are changes in world visions of both doom and hope. To some, there are new ideals of instinctive goodness; to others, new proofs of human evil; to others, new hopes for rationality; to many, all three.

Approaching South Australia's development unit of 'the South-east' the place-names seem Australian enough – Fish Holes Road, Boiler Swamp, Grassy Flats Swamp, Drik Drik, Lake Bong Bong. There is a sign up saying WATCH FOR KANGAROOS. But it is very un-Australian country with its pine forests – plantations of *pinus radiata*, a tree that had almost been chopped out of existence on the central Californian coast where it came from (its wood was too weak and soft for commercial use). In Australia, after it was introduced by the botanist Frederick von Mueller in 1857, it grew hard and sturdy, as it did also in New Zealand and South Africa – and in South Australia in particular, where something like half Australia's *pinus radiata* grow, it can seem a symbol of the rationality and calculation of planned development.

But because it is not an Australian tree, *pinus radiata* can now also seem an affront to the environment. The managers of State Forests worry about the image of the *pinus radiata*. In the Koetong pine plantation in Victoria's North-east, at the entrance to the scenic drive to the Alpine Lookout, a sign says 'Native plants and wild life are protected in this forest': in front of the pines, along the scenic drive, they have put in young native trees. When the trees grow up, the miles of *pinus radiata* will be partly obscured by a thin line of silver gum, candlebark gum, red-flowering yellow gum, manna gum, mahogany gum, blue gum, alpine ash.

I was at a Unesco seminar in the Academy of Science building in Canberra in 1974 – part of a worldwide Unesco programme on Man and the Biosphere – and *pinus radiata*, as an introduced species, challenger of the eucalypts and the acacias, became one of the villains threatening the environment. A poet read a defence of the gum tree in defiance of *pinus radiata* and other foreigners. A scientist hit back: *pinus radiata* was still to him part of a useful, civilizing process that would have been appreciated by an eighteenth-century nobleman-improver. The forest complex in 'the South-east' produces paper and building products, he explained; their processing is powered by electricity produced from the burning of wood residues; any surplus electricity is fed into the State grid: this 'integrated wood processing system' is a neat economic use of resources. With the same volume of enthusiasm the poet showed for the gum, but with less honour, the scientist then spoke about 'the photosynthetic potential' of Australia, as if it were a spiritual quality that could be unlocked by appropriate thought. The discussion touched on great schemes for releasing the solar energy locked in the cellulose of plants and trees. Australia north of the Tropic of Capricorn was the 'only large, politically stable and unpopulated tropical area of the world'; what it needed was a sound method for using its water . . . He was still planning.

CHAPTER ELEVEN

The Civilizing Virtues of Manufacturing

In 1974, when the outgoing president of the Associated Chamber of Manufactures wanted one last insult for an Australian government that had gone so far as to reduce tariffs by 25 per cent, he found it in the word 'feudal'. The government was turning Australia, he said, into a 'feudal state of peasant farmers, miners and cottage industry workers'. Whitlam's insouciant across-the-board 25 per cent tariff cut in 1973 could have been one of the most historically significant of all his government's measures. That such a complicated mess of furtive retreats and bold subterfuges were later necessary to abandon this reform suggests what a strong thrust it might have had, if initially there had been a bit more thought about it.

'Feudal', as used by the Chamber of Manufactures' president, was an echo of the nineteenth-century origins of tariffs in Australia, and the belief that a concentration on manufacturing was a necessary part of social progress and high civilization. Attacking free trade, the nineteenth-century New South Wales progressive Edward O'Sullivan unmasked it as 'a denial of the efficacy of art and science – an abdication of the intellectual gifts'; praising tariff protection, he pictured it as 'the application of intelligence to politics', so that man might 'both aid and control nature'. To David Syme, nineteenth-century prophet of the greatness of the colony of Victoria, the civilizing influence of manufacturing was also obvious: without tariff protection the people of Australia would be 'as utter strangers to all scientific skill and practical dexterity in the arts and manufactures of highly civilized nations as are the Bedouins of Barbary, or the Tartars of Central Asia'. In the world of his rhetoric, protection would produce 'a nice-balanced industrial community, composite, stable and progressive; a self-contained, self-supporting nation' employing 'the great industrial arts' and 'the civilizing and enriching skill which is part of our national inheritance'.

In the early national elections, free trade versus protection was made to appear one of those great issues which determine the success or failure of nations. Even after protection won, the sacredness of the cause still gave it fire. This long debate raised many questions other than economic calculation, as did 'development' generally: sometimes economic calculation was altogether forgotten. Irrespective of economic considerations, manufacturing was considered necessary to provide employment for the immigrants who were seen as essential to the survival of Australia. Increase in population was 'essential alike for the proper utilization and effective defence of our enormous territory', said the Adelaide *Advertiser* in the 1906 election. Manufacturing would not only increase Australia's population and prosperity, it would 'make Australia great' – 'no nation could become great unless prepared to give men and women with brains the opportunity of developing their genius', said the Melbourne *Argus* in the same election. By the 1919 election Hughes saw 'no real reason why Australia should not be one of the greatest manufacturing nations in the world'.

As well as bringing greatness, manufacturing would 'make Australia a self-contained country'; it would 'make Australia more independent of the outside world than it has ever previously been' said the *Age* in the 1917 elections. The desire for independence merged into xenophobic hatreds and fears: free-traders were 'traitorous Australians who live by selling their country to the foreign enemy camped in our midst . . . agents of syndicates in London', said the *Bulletin*, in the 1901 election. George Reid, free-trade leader, was 'the political pimp and parasite of the big English and German importing firms'. 'Australia, using the dumped goods of other countries, had occupied for too long the position of the small boy who had to wear all his big brother's clothes', said a Victorian protectionist in the 1906 elections. The 'enormous flood of foreign goods that were being dumped into the country' were nasty as well as cheap: they were 'goods made by prison labour, by cheap labour, by underpaid white labour, by cheap alien labour' said the Attorney-General in the 1901 election. Seventy-three years later, in December 1974, when 4,000 motor vehicle workers held a protest meeting against dismissal outside their factory in

Melbourne, some of them attacked a small Japanese car, smashing its windscreen and kicking in its sides.

There were yearnings for those civilized feelings of balance and diversity that had also marked support for the complexities of small-scale agriculture against the barbarous simplicities of large-scale pastoral holdings. In fact agriculture and manufacturing could be seen as supporting each other: 'a highly diversified agricultural system requires a home market for success'; on the land, said a Liberal in the 1910 election, there would be 'a thriving people, producing the natural products from the soil' and in the towns 'a body of healthy manufacturers', and each would use the other's products. Along with the idea of healthy balance went the idea of healthy diversity. 'No country could be progressive and prosperous unless its industries were flourishing and diverse', said the Mayor of South Melbourne in the 1901 election; he demonstrated this by showing the successful diversity of South Melbourne as 'a busy, thriving manufacturing centre', with its 'engineering workshops, copper-smithies, brass foundries, jam manufactures . . . soap and candle works, rice mills and biscuit factories'.

'The experience of the civilized world was in favour of protection,' said the Minister for Trade and Customs in the 1901 election. 'Never was there such a thing as a civilized free trade country,' said the Victorian Minister for Railways. A former Victorian cabinet minister asked if the Australian was to be 'a low type of humanity, in not being fit for producing anything beyond raw materials for other countries' manufactures'; a New South Wales protectionist asked if it was to be said 'that the people of New South Wales were to be the hewers of wood and drawers of water for the world'. At cries of 'no' from the audience he said 'Our destiny is higher than that . . . It is wrong to send the artisan on to the land, of which he knows nothing, instead of assisting to plant the country with industries.' Another former Victorian cabinet minister said: 'Civilization is founded on certainty . . . We no longer live the lives of mere animals. We have reason, and try to make a path for ourselves.'

During the First World War, and between the two wars, Australia was becoming a manufacturing country. When B.H.P.'s blast furnaces and mills, built on drained swamps beside Newcastle harbour, were opened in 1915, this was one of the first steelworks to be constructed outside Europe, Japan and the United States; with another steelworks at Port Kembla taken over in the 1930s, B.H.P. was producing some of the cheapest steel in the world. Other plants began to sprout. Motor vehicle assembly lines, glassworks, textile mills, factories for making rubber products joined the earlier-established industries; the latter also expanded. But as the drab buildings housing the new machines went up, the hope for their civilizing mission grew less. Now that they were there, it seemed hard to believe in them. Honour went back to wool, to 'primary industries' and exports.

Exhilaration in the idea of manufacturing was regained in the improvisations of the Second World War. For the men who ran the show it could be great fun producing guns, ammunition, tanks, motor vehicles, destroyers, corvettes, frigates, merchant ships, naval small craft, radio gear, optical glass instruments, chemicals, nine types of aircraft, 140 specialist steels. For the first time machine tools (then the beginning of industrial sophistication) were made in considerable numbers and variety; tens of thousands of skilled tradesmen were mass-produced. In a war marked on the military side by so many fiascos, the expansion in secondary industry could seem something to hold on to. When the excitement was over and the improvised wartime factories had been taken over by civilian firms, steel frames went up in suburban paddocks (where costs were less) for new factories built in new styles. Later, whole new industrial areas were opened out behind fences of chain wiring. Factories now made electrical equipment for people to buy for their homes; oil refineries gave skylines a new seriousness: works went up to process metals, chemicals, plastics, glass, rubber; and other works went up to make objects out of these processed commodities.

For a one-town, two-paragraph example, take Geelong; apt because it has tried so hard since those days in the 1850s when, having established itself as a centre for squatters' exports, it proclaimed itself 'the Commercial Capital', the 'pivot' of Victoria's expansion, hoping to leave Melbourne as the mere political capital. There were humiliations later in the nineteenth century when Ballarat and Bendigo surpassed it, but Geelong was accumulating new treasures – as well as wool stores it put up flour mills, a rope works, tanneries, woollen textile mills, a meat-freezing works, a soap and candle works, a salt works, a butter and cheese factory, a boot factory, a paper mill, a cement works; at the beginning of the twentieth century its population picked up: in the early 1920s it passed Bendigo, then Ballarat. Its great days arrive. Famous trade names enter its commercial directory. Bigger woollen mills are set up, and Cresco Fertilizers, the Ford Motor Company, the Phosphate Co-operative of Australia, the Corio Distillery, Pilkington Safety Glass, International Harvester and, after the Second World War, a new cement works, a number of light industries, the Shell Oil Refinery and, along the bay from the beds of the old salt works, among the yellow grass and cows, the Alcoa aluminium plant. Geelong's population doubles.

Now flowers hang in baskets from its parking meters. It finds a new pride in its old buildings, classified by the National Trust. Grandeur asserts itself in the civic group at one end of Johnston Park – City Hall, Art Gallery, Peace Hall, classical, light grey, with George V staring out from the courtyard across the green grass to the bandstand. Down near the bay Edward VII looks at the Sailors' Rest Home and the stocky assuredness of the wool stores: behind him are the new certainties of the bulk wheat pier, the phosphate wharf, the refinery pier, the aluminium wharf. In the Pancake Kitchen there is an emphasis on honest wood and sincerity in rough brick. Down a lane from Long John's Beef House the Innsbruck Chalet Restaurant is next to the My Gourmet Delicatessen. In the pedestrian mall in Little Malop Street the Rohan Delacombe Fountain, presented by the Geelong Waterworks and Sewerage Trust, celebrates a hundred years of reticulated water. Along the bay, in a shabby world of weeds, yellow grass, flat sand, shrieking seagulls, cyclone fencing, you can stand beside the bilious green of the phosphate works and look across at the white spheres and slender chimneys, the graceful pipes and gleaming tanks of the oil refinery, reminiscent of the white domes of Corot's *View of the Quay of the Schiavoni* in the Victorian Arts Centre.

Above all, after the Second World War, there was a boom in making motor cars. If all the plants, big and small, were added up, motor vehicle manufacture and maintenance was now Australia's single biggest secondary industry. One brand of car, the Holden, the first wholly designed and built in Australia and for a while taking up more than half of the market, became a symbol of national achievement like a Davis Cup champion or a record-breaking batsman. It was a General Motors car, but it was MADE IN AUSTRALIA, riding confidently into the advertisements as 'Australia's Own Car'. The first Holden model was launched at the end of 1948 in a ceremony of mixed styles and cultures. In a company theatrette decorated with flowers and graced by Ben Chifley, the Labor Prime Minister, who had flown to Melbourne from Canberra, silver lamé curtains were pulled back to show a slowly revolving stage covered in black velvet: a spotlight shone on the ivory-coloured sedan while the Brahms waltz in A flat was played *pianissimo* by a ten-piece orchestra. Hundreds of bottles of champagne were drunk. 'She's a beauty', said the Prime Minister. The Holden's success was a success for most of the hopes for manufacturing (themselves part of the more general ambitions of 'development'), although it now seems odd that at the launching the Premier of Victoria saw the Holden as 'another link between the British Commonwealth and the United States of America upon whose mutual friendship and understanding world peace and the future of our civilization depend' and that Chifley should find in the large painted metal object resting on black velvet a sign of how 'world peace depended almost entirely upon the English-speaking peoples'. But as well as repeating wartime pieties these two politicians were signalling the hope that Australian manufacturing would float on English-speaking money, just as at that time it was hoped that most of the immigrant factory hands would still be predominantly English-speaking. The rest was familiar. *National prestige* was served: 'a milestone in our industrial and manufacturing history', said the *Sydney Morning Herald*. The *civilizing influence* was noted by Chifley: 'With Australia on the threshold of the most marvellous opportunities ever within the reach of a young country it is hoped that new trends in education will bring about a better outlook and more understanding between employers and employees.' The importance to *defence* was obvious: manufacture of the Holden was 'important not only economically but from a national defence point of view' (Chifley); it would 'add materially to the ability of Australia to defend its soil and its people in time of war' (the *Age*); 'from a defence viewpoint, an established motor vehicle manufacturing industry will be of major value' (*Sydney Morning Herald*). It played its part in *decentralization*: the engines and gear-boxes were made at the new General Motors-Holden factory at Fishermen's Bend in Victoria; chassis and bodies at the Adelaide works of G.M.H.; general assembly would take place in several States. It was useful for *import replacement* – statistical tables could give materials for promising curves; if the curves wobbled, new tariffs could smooth them out – and in the *diversification of exports*: as part of its world marketing strategy, General Motors sold Holdens in South-east Asian and southern African countries; amongst all the raw material exports, motor cars gave the tables a more sophisticated look. It helped the *population build-up*: a large number of Holden employees were immigrants who took jobs in the assembly lines before they could find something better. That is why it makes sense to call the 1950s in Australia the Age of the Holden.

The success of Rothmans King Size Filter cigarettes, like the Holden's success, catches some of the significant spirit of manufacturing in the 1950s (in this case the late 1950s). The Rothman cigarette was launched in a crusade of novelty: the idea of a filter tip itself was new – Rothmans was the first filter-tipped cigarette to catch on in Australia; so was the new flip-top box; so was king-size length. Off it went with these three revolutionary ideas and its battle slogan (Better Tobacco, Finer Filter, True King Size Flavour – Rothmans King Size *Really* Satisfies); it scattered and defeated the old reactionary brands and like the Holden captured more than half its market. When newsreels and newspapers told of airlifts of cigarette-making machines needed to catch up with unexpected demand Rothmans became a manufacturing as well as a cigarette story. In television commercials associating it with the nation-building competitive sports (an association that for a while it pre-empted), it appeared uniquely Australian in spite of its South African origin, so that it seemed a great Australian cigarette that had achieved a unique manufacturing success: some people saw the success of the Rothmans companies in other parts of the world as an extension of the Australian company, an idea that could seem to be supported by the slogan 'First in Australia, First in the world'; Rothmans picked up an export award from the Department of Trade, Rothmans King Size Filter was not as essential to the defence effort as the Holden, but it was a highly patriotic cigarette.

Its factory was in what had been a wasteland between some suburbs, now taken over by hopeful companies whose factory estates stretched across the flat landscape, their bright, image-establishing colours giving an impression of a meeting of feudal magnates in elaborately coloured tents. The office block of the Rothmans factory was done out in the house colours. Behind and beside it were the air-conditioned halls where women operators watched machines manufacture cigarettes, the parking lots, the tobacco storage areas, the areas for despatch. Inside, in the central reception area, enlarged reproductions of the packs of the company's brands were framed and displayed on the walls like old masters, as part of the general atmosphere of high prestige. By the time I visited it, although the company was still making good profits from other brands, Rothmans King Size Filter itself had lost its pre-eminent position, first to Peter Stuyvesant, a brand started by the same company, and then to the opposition companies who pulled themselves together and launched new offensives, in particular the Benson and Hedges promotion. The last time I was there, the then managing director had just created a crisis of identity in the administration block: he had come back from South Africa with a new view of human nature which, he had explained in a blackboard lecture to his executives, could be divided into those who sought security, those who sought illusion, those who sought conquest and those who sought prestige. There was concern that Rothmans King Size Filter, which was supposed to be a prestige brand, had big streaks of conquest in its television commercials and, in its magazine advertising, suggestions of security. Later, privately discussing what might be done about this, he became restless, changed the subject and boasted about brands that might be launched in the future: he produced a specimen pack of one of these proposed brands and, like a sorcerer calling on spirits, conjured up its image. He was again restless. He told us how he would change the office furniture of the administration block, because it projected the wrong personality for the company in its present marketing position. It would all have to go. This had something to do with modern furniture and antique furniture, but I have forgotten which was to replace which.

'Great industrial arts' . . . 'civilizing and enriching skills' . . . the hope-rhetoric of the late nineteenth-century and early twentieth-century propagandists of the faith of manufacturing was matched by the scare-rhetoric of the free-traders. In the 1901 election George Reid could speak of 'the dark records of the factory system in greater and older nations . . . Surely we should do all we can when imitating the experience of other countries to avoid those things which were worst and most painful in them.' Like an environmentalist of the 1970s he warned against following the example of New York. After a long exile, doubts like these are again getting a big hearing. Following new fashions, more Australians see manufacturing as uncivilized, in their own country anyway; the mark of a sophisticated nationhood now is not to be highly industrialized, but to have the capital and expertise to set up plants in poorer countries, thereby giving them jobs and exporting your pollution.

As an example of this turnabout, go back to the two examples I chose of what seemed to be success in the 1950s – the commercial victories of the Holden car and the Rothmans King Size Filter Cigarette. Cars and cigarettes; symbols of disease, maiming and killing. Death from heart attacks, intestinal ulcers, stomach cancers, come from nicotine. Death from cancer of the lungs, larynx, the throat, the tongue, come from tobacco tars. Death from chronic bronchitis, emphysema and other diseases come from smoke particles absorbed in the lining of the respiratory system. Motor cars have become an even greater symbol of a civilization questioning itself. In the chariot races of the roads they are one of our main causes of torture and death; the muck their exhausts throw out makes them a principal poisoner of the lower atmosphere. As polluters they join the factories: some of the same film cameramen who in the 1950s and early 1960s celebrated factory openings by filming them now celebrate the filthiness of the same factories by filming the pollution of rivers by factory wastes, fats, salts, acids, oils, tars, grease, and the pollution of the air by factory ash, grit, fluorides, hydrocarbons, sulphur oxides, ammonia, organic acids. And the tedium of assembly-line work and other repetitive jobs is seen as a pollution of the mind.

Because the *Age* was such an apostle of manufacturing, I shall quote from it on the disgrace of the Holden, now for many a symbol of the general failure of policies of manufacturing-at-any-cost.

When General Motors-Holden threatened retrenchments in December 1974, Claude Forell, an *Age* columnist, threw a whole book of new faith at it.

. . . we should seriously ponder whether we need a motor manufacturing industry at all. Like the horse-drawn coach, the steam locomotive and the canal barge, the contemporary motor car is a means of mobility that is sure to be superseded. It is dangerous to life and limb, destructive to our urban environment, wasteful in its use of energy and resources and increasingly extravagant in its demands upon society. The sooner we find something better the happier we shall be. Its mass manufacture is no longer the status symbol of a technically advanced society, but is much better suited to a country with plenty of relatively cheap, low-skilled labour, and a pliant government.

On pollution of the mind, he wrote:

Its methods of mass production require assembly lines of unskilled and semi-skilled human robots whose monotonous and mindless toil typifies man's subjection to the machine. As in America, the Australian motor industry has relied on shipload after shipload of immigrants, most of whom stayed only until they realized they could find better jobs elsewhere.

Overall Forell concluded that:

Australians should recognize the folly of successive Liberal-CP Governments in encouraging such a costly, inefficient and vulnerable industry to develop to an extent where it can easily hold us all to ransom . . . Our leaders have been too obsessed with a belief in industrial development at any price and too deluded with a faith that growth can be unlimited . . .

These insults to manufacturing were part of a general questioning, or revulsion, that came over intellectuals and others in the industrialized nations in the 1970s. To what extent has the industrialization of Australia been, as David Syme had hoped in the nineteenth century, a display of the great industrial arts and the civilizing and enriching skills? To what extent has it produced modern expertness, sophisticated techniques, extensions of the intelligence? One answer is that for ordinary workers in factories where there is extreme specialization of labour, the work can be an insult to even an undemanding intelligence.

But if one moves observation from workers on the factory

floor (acknowledging on the way that many skilled tradesmen also work in manufacturing) to their bosses – it seems hard to doubt the benefit in having Australians who are trained, and in the contemporary sense 'intelligent' enough to make modern decisions. But does this have to mean, as Claude Forell put it, the production in the 'grossly inefficient, fragmented and labour-intensive' car industry with its 'costly short runs' of a 'proliferation of superficially attractive models tricked out with a variety of expensive options', 'subordinated to whatever marketing psychologists believe consumers want or can be persuaded to buy'? And, given Australia's low performance in high-technology manufacturing, where brilliant management is needed in Australia is not predominantly in manufacturing but in urban planning, environment control, public transport, education, cultural facilities, community services, recreation amenities, national parks and museums. In 'production' in the narrower sense, the best results may come from research, extension work and management in mining, farming, forestry and fishing, and in the processing of these primary products.

In manufacturing, there have been some special weaknesses in the Australian experience: so much of it has been foreign-dominated, or at least derived from foreign examples. Manufacturing has been the least innovative sector of Australian industry. Its principle, as distinguished from the research-based and invention-based primary industries, has been that of *copying*. In manufacturing, other countries have done Australia's thinking for it. Australia might be thought of as a country that was 'industrialized' so far as the attitudes of the mass of the workers were concerned, but was not so completely 'modernized' at the top. Two of the great symbols of the Menzies era, the Holden car and the Rothmans King Size Filter Cigarette, were in reality symbols of derivativeness.

On the south tympanum of Melbourne's Shrine of Remembrance, in the group representing the soldier's homecoming to the fruits of victory, the woman who stands for agriculture is a recognizable symbol, but the best that could be done for manufacturing was to represent it by an ancient Greek making a pot: the Greeks didn't have a goddess of factories. The forms of honour paid to manufacturing, despite its importance, have not come as easily as those given to farming. Hargrave, the pioneer in aeronautical design, gets his head on the twenty-dollar note, but not as convincingly or recognizably as Farrer and Macarthur, the wheat and wool improvers on the two-dollar notes: Hargrave experimented with cellular kites and curved wing surfaces in the 1890s and his earlier construction of a rotary aeroplane engine were first of their kind, but they did not lead to productive action in Australia (although the Germans used his work). Manufacturers were accepted into the gentlemen's clubs more readily than the rich men who ran department stores and, like the department store magnates, some of them received knighthoods, but more in their general capacity as 'businessmen' who were part of the big money game than as honoured makers of useful objects. Exhibitions of manufactured goods do not have the same dignity as the agricultural shows; manufacturing has had practically no mention in postage stamps and none on coins; manufacturers have a poor showing in public statues, although on retirement their portraits are likely to be painted and privately hung in boardrooms. Not many manufacturers have become national heroes; the few given exemplary qualities tended to be noted either for their association with bigness (Essington Lewis and B.H.P.) or for their toughness, shrewdness and suspected sharpness ('Gunboat' Smith, who put together the glass combine) rather than for their manufacturing achievements.

The principal monuments to manufacturing have been the factory buildings themselves and the machines within, just as temples, as the principal place of negotiation with deities, are the prime monuments to religions. The main honour paid to manufacturing has come from manufacturers and their ideologues, principally by using the key phrases and sentiments of the almost universally accepted cult of development, in the dominant form it took after the Second World War ('growth and jobs') or, more contentiously, by drawing on the key phrases and sentiments of the cult of 'free enterprise', one of the most persuasive and long-lasting fountains of party-political rhetoric in Australia. Free enterprise extends much more widely than manufacturing, but over the period when making objects in factories seemed of particular importance, the manufacturers seemed prime examples of the virtues of free enterprise.

Whereas, until recognition of the 'environment crisis' the secular faith of development transcended political parties, the secular faith of free enterprise has been one of the main 'product differences' between the parties (see chapter 15). When Adam Smith published *The Wealth of Nations* in 1776, he offered a marriage of self-interest and rational order: the basis of individual decisions was selfish, but the interactions between individuals meeting buyers and sellers in the market place ensured 'as if by an invisible hand' that social harmony and economic progress came out of these individual conflicts. These doctrines gave meaning to a muddle of actions in British provincial towns in the late-eighteenth century, when a few men invented machines and a few hundred promoters made a killing building factories where the energy released in burning coal changed water into steam, which pushed pistons, that turned wheels, that made iron engines do the work of many hands. Adam Smith's doctrines have gone on being related to factories as if his ideas themselves worked the machines. As interpreted by manufacturers in Australia they mean (with a qualification to be discussed in a moment) that the prosperity of Australia depends on the freedom from government intervention of the men who run the factories. As W. H. Anderson, Federal president of the Liberal Party put it in 1952, Australia needed 'healthy competitive economic conditions, with abounding opportunities for the adventurous to prosper, for the industrialist to reap his just reward, and for the enterprising to pursue his plans for the future unshackled by the need for government approval or official sponsorship.' Anderson detected an 'Australian tradition, a story of pioneer courage, determination and enterprise which produced the Australian type who leans not on government, but stands on his own two feet.' But an essential part of the cult of 'free enterprise' in Australia also contains the belief that manufacturing business should stand on the government's two feet: as well as the tradition of the free market there is an equally strong tradition in Australian manufacturing, derived in the first place from Germany and the United States, that it should be helped by government tariffs and by other means. Ironically, Adam Smith's arguments were directed principally against the very systems of tariffs that are seen by Australian manufacturers as the basis of their business. When the new idea of using machines in factories spread from Britain to Germany and the United States, tariffs were seen in these countries as essential for encouraging the growth of machines: at about the same time belief in protection became part of economic revelation in the colony of Victoria and, later, all Australia. The cult of free enterprise in Australia means that governments should protect manufacturers with tariffs, import controls, taxation incentives, credit rates, public utilities, special public works, or whatever else manufacturers declare necessary and can bribe, coax, or blackmail governments into providing; but governments should not intervene in ways the manufacturers see as unnecessary. A few purists say otherwise. Anderson, who was head of a sausage and smallgoods firm, wanted protection only for 'Australian defence and development' but other than that, 'free market prices, both internally and externally, must become the measure of industry's worth and efficiency'. He was a freak: normally, supporters of free enterprise oppose free market prices or interpret the needs of 'defence and development' to include whatever it is they make. Part of the 'socialism' for which the Whitlam government was attacked in 1975 was closer to the ideals of Adam Smith than the policies of the manufacturers who attacked it – it was a policy of lowering tariffs and of breaking up collusive agreements. It was the 'socialists' who wanted to restore some of the market operations that in theory the free enterprise men supported, but in practice feared.

When Opposition Leader Bill Snedden came back from the United States in December 1974, part of his airport press conference was given over to a defence of his statement in New York that 'Australia was faced with the clear choice between socialism and free enterprise', but another part of it was given over to the assertion that 'the government must immediately implement a strong economic programme to protect Australian industries from overseas competition'. For him there was no conflict between supporting free enterprise and protecting industries against competition. Support of free enterprise means government support for individual manufacturing firms so that they can go on existing in the way they choose. Speaking in contradiction is a normal part of the traditions of political rhetoric: this particular contradiction is a normal part of Australian political rhetoric.

Gorton put it directly during the 1969 election, without pretence about 'free enterprise':

> The government believes it is essential to ensure that its policies adequately reflect the important role manufacturing industry plays in the nation's economy . . . Industry cannot expect to achieve the full development of its efficiency and skills alone. In today's world, industry needs the support of effective government policies.

Even in yesterday's world, the matter could sometimes be stated bluntly. J. B. Brigden, Professor of Economics in the University of Tasmania, said in 1928:

> . . . development has always been a leading subject of Australian policy. In no other country has the tradition become so firmly established that it is the duty of governments to lead in the development of every resource that may enlarge production.

With manufacturers relying on government assistance, 'economic rationality' in its classic sense came to mean the doctrines of non-manufacturers – government officials, politicians, economists, journalists – who wanted to restore certain market conditions that they thought would lead to a more rational allocation of resources. (Whitlam was one of these 'economic rationalists'.) This was opposed by free-enterprise men because although they too were rationalists, they were not trying to be rational about an 'efficient' economy, but about a 'fixed' economy fixed to suit them. For men who saw free enterprise as the right to stay in business, a free market would be too much of a risk.

When I called Australia a lucky country, I had in mind that Australia was sufficiently like the innovative industrial societies to be able to take over their ideas into a high-cost system protected by tariffs, and this came so relatively easily that Australia industrialized without developing some of the social characteristics of an industrial society. There was only a very small relation between invention and manufacturing, for example, although there was considerable improvisation. Australia was strong in engineers, but weaker than almost any other industrialized country in industrial design. Overall, if with exceptions, there was a scepticism towards original talent, even a hatred of it. The smart thing was to get the design of a proven success from overseas and then follow the instructions on the back of the packet.

Some of the big men in manufacturing might have lunch at the Melbourne Club, pouring their sherries from decanters laid out on the polished antique table in the Reading Room; others might lunch at the American Club, buying their whisky sours in the Polynesian Bar, listening to Hawaiian Muzak as they looked out through the large windows at a view of Sydney Harbour superb enough to be the observation post view of a conqueror. Whatever foreign milieu they might draw some of their sense of importance from, they would also feel entitled to the honour due to an industrial innovator. It was their enterprise, they might think, on which everybody else's prosperity depended. But usually they were simple imitators. They claimed the dignity of enterprise, but at the best their enterprise was in improvising adaptions: their personal success often lay less on enterprise than on conniving – working the rackets within the company game. The era of Australia's internationally notorious crumminess was also the era of its industrialization.

CHAPTER TWELVE

The Secular Faith of 'Growth and Jobs'

When Billy Hughes was writing a series of articles (put together as a book in 1910) for the Sydney *Daily Telegraph* he had, as a Labor man, a blunt explanation of unemployment:

> The unemployed man is a deliberate creation of the capitalist. In order that he may take advantage of these periodic revivals of trade, for which unregulated production is responsible, it is essential that an army of men trained to do his work, and unfit or unable to get work elsewhere, should be available. A man by necessity, chance, inclination, or what you will, is attached to an industry, and in the vast majority of cases he becomes and continues its helpless appendage . . . Every industry trains many more men than it normally requires. These unhappy wretches, by virtue of their training useless for anything else, are the veritable slaves of the industry. In order that for one year, month or week out of every two or three, employers may have an abundant supply of labour, millions of hapless men are daily sacrificed.

The word 'employee' established itself in the third quarter of the nineteenth century; it was part of the new tendency for more people to earn their living by working for a 'firm'. A generation later 'unemployment' and 'the unemployed' came into use as respectable terms, with the realization that individual laziness or some theory of tragic necessity were not adequate explanations for joblessness. As 'the unemployed', the workless sounded more dignified than when they were spoken of as 'paupers', 'beggars', 'vagrants', 'tramps', 'the destitute', or one of the other words with which they had been insulted by history. Similarly 'unemployment' was a more comprehensive term than the older 'destitution' or 'distress': defined as a *social problem*, unemployment was a situation that something might be done about. This view was spreading when Hughes wrote his articles for the *Daily Telegraph*.

'The unemployed man is everywhere. He is the disease of modern civilization', Hughes said in one of these articles. 'Unemployment is the modern riddle of the Sphinx, which society must solve, and that speedily, or perish.' The governments of the Australian colonies had avoided poor rates and workhouses: they had been happy to make no special arrangements about periods of worklessness, passing them off as aberrations for which some temporary expedient could be patched together. If the workless numbered enough to arrange protest meetings, marches, torchlight processions, deputations to the Premier, a government might provide work by deciding to clear bush for a new suburban road, or dig a new sewer, or get on with some other plan. More usually a government merely handed out rail passes for workers to get out of town into the country, where there were usually plenty of jobs. In the 1890s the New South Wales government assisted 27,000 men out of work to go fossicking in abandoned gold diggings. Sometimes a government handed out a temporary grant to private charities that ran the night refuges and soup kitchens, then took it away when food queues shortened.

Governments began to be more imaginative after the 1890s depression, the disasters of which were given extra drama by bank crashes, political and business scandals, unprecedented strikes, the eight-year-long Great Drought, epidemics of typhoid fever and other infectious diseases, and the struggle against employing 'nigger labour' in the north. The annual statistical register of New South Wales, called, in a splendid expression of late colonial optimism, *Wealth and Progress in New South Wales*, had been in the habit of leaving in print, year after year the sentence, 'No poor rate is levied in the colonies, nor is such needed', but, as T. H. Kewley points out in his book *Social Security in Australia*, the words 'nor is such needed' were dropped after the early economic fiascos in the 1890s. The idea of setting up labour exchanges was copied from New Zealand, and from 1910 onwards (for thirty-four years) there was talk about starting a national unemployment insurance scheme. When the Labor Parties developed they believed that legislation 'to burst up the big estates' was an essential weapon against unemployment. Right from its start protection had also been seen as an anti-unemployment device. As C. H. Pearson, Victoria's most widely known intellectual, said in an article, 'One natural and legitimate object [of protection] is to keep employment constant and wages high.'

Manufacturers benefiting from protection might believe, as Hughes claimed, that a pool of unemployed made business easier and kept unionists in their place. Self-congratulatory belief in self-reliance and free enterprise, with the pleasurable doctrine that a rich man had always earned his success, had extra savour with a threat of privation, although starvation was now coming to be considered over-dramatic. But once the Labor Party became protectionist it saw protection as the most fundamental of all supports for employment. Inconstant in so many of its other faiths, it held steadfastly to the rhetoric of the campaign against unemployment.

In the 1922 election Matt Charlton, fighting his first election as Labor leader, tried to make unemployment the main election issue. The alternative was the belief that Hughes should be Prime Minister of Australia forever because Germany had lost the war. Charlton presented his opponents as tools of vested interests determined to reduce wages and lengthen working hours by bringing in enough immigrants to create a pool of unemployment. 'Never before in the history of the country has there been so much misery,' he said. 'Fifty thousand starving unemployed daily seek work. The Nationalist government takes no effective action to remedy the evil. Instead it is swamping the labour market with immigrants.' In the 1925 election Bruce defined the 'paramount issue' as 'the maintenance of law and order . . . the maintenance of our free institutions, our advanced civilization, and our prestige within the Empire and abroad', but Charlton again tried to stress unemployment. Although still attacking the policy of bringing in immigrants when Australians were out of work, and hoping 'to break up large estates' to relieve unemployment, this time he put his main emphasis on protection. The government had allowed 'the country to be flooded with imported goods, whilst its own industries languished'.

In 1928 Scullin, the new Labor leader, countered Bruce's attempt to fight yet another election on the issues of law, order and loyalty to the Empire by claiming that

> the real issues, which vitally affect the welfare of the country, are the tightness of the money market, and the appalling amount of unemployment

> . . . Men are searching hopelessly for work, but no one wants them . . . the trade depression is worse and unemployment more acute than I have ever known it in Australia . . . Men everywhere are carrying their swags, including large numbers of migrants who were brought here by alluring promises.

The government's failure to provide adequate protection meant that 'the country was being flooded with products of cheap-labour countries'.

> In this great land of Australia there should be no such thing as want in the midst of plenty . . . The object should be to protect manufacturers from importations from other parts of the world; to keep men and women employed; to create and maintain a higher standard of living and remove the appalling tragedy of unemployment.

In the 1929 election, Bruce urged abolition of the Federal arbitration system and Scullin was happy to accept this as the issue but the unemployment theme was still there. 'On Mr Bruce's admission we have an unprecedented volume of unemployment . . . The Labor Government will bend its energies to straightening out our finances, and to opening up new avenues of work.' By the 1931 election Scullin, having presided as Prime Minister over a collapse to a level of almost one third unemployed, called for a revival of faith in protection. Lack of protection had caused unemployment and the Depression; lowering tariffs now, as called for by the 'pseudo-protectionists and rank-free traders' of the Opposition, would make things worse.

> In years of drift to the verge of bankruptcy, overseas manufacturers with depressed markets were permitted to dump their goods into the Commonwealth, thus piling up an adverse trade balance, crippling Australian industries and throwing thousands out of employment . . . The tariff wall which has been erected must be maintained . . . If the floodgates are again opened to importations, if our industries are again to be crushed by outside competition, every effort made for the unemployed will be nullified.

Jack Beasley, leader of the breakaway New South Wales Labor Party had an even simpler solution to unemployment: he would nationalize banking. 'A National Commonwealth Bank would see that the real wealth of the people as measured in goods, was covered with sufficient credit to allow trade, commerce and employment to continue.' By the 1934 election, Scullin was inclined to believe that easy credit rather than protection would cure unemployment. There were reminders that in the 1920s under Labor's rivals 'the nation was flooded with imported goods, and the adverse trade balance brought Australia to the brink of bankruptcy', but the main emphasis was on how the 'money masters' and 'captains of industry' had, with policies of deflation, forced 'a million human beings in Australia to the border of starvation'.

The present monetary system has failed. Another has to take its place. Control of monetary machinery for private profits has to give way to national control for the benefit of all . . . All around are idle machines, factories and workshops wonderfully equipped to produce very much more than the people are able to buy because, though needing so much more, they have not the purchasing power . . . In this enlightened, progressive age we remain slaves to an obsolete banking system. The nation's economic energies are bound with financial ligatures stagnating the life blood of industry.

The 1937 election appeared to be fought on questions of defence policy (which Labor's opponents wanted to make a question of loyalty to the Empire); but John Curtin, now the Labor leader, also managed to bring unemployment into it by offering 'defence against war and defence against poverty'.

Instead of advancement in Australia there is malnutrition and too much compulsory idleness. It cannot be disputed that a Government could, if it so desired, absorb manpower in a campaign on national construction works. Governments use manpower in war to destroy assets. The Labor Party declares that its Government would use manpower to create assets.

In the two wartime elections, 1940 and 1943, Curtin, while urging that Labor could conduct the war more efficiently than its opponents, also tried to secure for Labor a monopoly of the idea that after the war there would be a 'new social and economic order', in which 'full employment' was essential – 'full development of resources, full employment of manpower and full provision for social securitv'.

In the 1946 election Ben Chifley promised to 'safeguard the

nation against inflation and the miseries and hardships of a depression: provide full employment for all our people and develop and expand our country to its true greatness by a careful programme embracing all aspects of financial policy.' In an eve-of-poll advertisement it was affirmed that 'Australia will vote LABOR because full employment is in the foreground of Labor's policy and because Menzies and Fadden have NO plan to ensure continuous and productive employment.' In the 1949 election, with Menzies campaigning for free enterprise and against communism, Chifley came out more strongly for full employment in a style worth a few sentences since it is so typical of the Labor approach at that time.

> The Labor Government has shaped all its financial and economic measures towards maintaining full employment . . . So far as it can humanly contrive, never again will dole queues be seen in this country. Never again will competent workmen stand idle for months and years while limitless work remains to be done. Never again will young men drift hopelessly from town to town and from State to State, searching for jobs.

Chifley returned to a modified version of Hughes' theme of 1910:

> This policy of full employment is being criticized and derided. It is blamed for shortages, blamed for rising prices, blamed for strikes. You cannot have discipline and efficiency, so critics say, unless you have a degree of unemployment. Not too much unemployment of course – that would be bad for business. Just a nice six or eight per cent of unemployment, just a quarter of a million or so out of work to keep the fear of the sack in the hearts of all the rest. The Labor Government rejects this barbarous and intolerant view and dismisses as absurd the arguments used to support it.

He recalled the Depression when 'hundreds of thousands of bread winners' were 'thrown on to a pitiful dole. Farmers were sold up, and shopkeepers closed their doors, and insecurity, misery and want were forced upon our people. We are determined with all the power at our command that shall not happen again.'

The 1951 election, which Menzies saw as about communism, Chifley tried to turn into an election about inflation, offering 'stabilization of the economy' compared with the catastrophic level of inflation of 'the Menzies do-nothing Government'. Since at that time it was not possible to campaign against both inflation and unemployment, he didn't have much to say about employment, but by the 1953 Senate election, Evatt, now leader of the Labor Party, was able to come back to it.

> It is plain that the Commonwealth Bank, under Government direction, could finance employment up to the limit of available men and resources . . . full employment can be maintained and assured without causing or contributing to inflation such as has been experienced during the three years of the Menzies-Fadden Government.

He made a definitive statement of a prevailing belief: 'The basic condition of full employment is that total purchasing power should always be high enough to set up a demand for the products of industry which can be satisfied only if the full available labour force is used.'

In the 1954 election Evatt made so many promises that full employment was merely one on a long list ('Labor believes that a primary need for the development of Australia is an adequate supply of cheap credit'); full employment almost disappeared in his policy speech in the 1955 election but it was strongly in his 1958 policy speech, with a return to Hughes' theme of 1910:

> The Menzies Government has led Australia to the absurd economic orthodoxy of the depression years . . . Economists all over the world now declare that Central Bank credit exists to be used when the economy is depressed or stagnant and men are unemployed. But the Menzies Government sits back tired and very lazy and leaves things to take their course . . . We are back to the early depression days when anti-Labor Governments said it was the unemployed man's own fault that he had no job – that he was unemployable. The Government's lip service to the idea of full employment has been conveniently forgotten because it is more profitable for big business to have pools of unemployed to draw upon. The secret objective of the Government's backers now appears to have been achieved – they have a permanent unemployment pool.

The recession of 1961 seemed exactly the situation that so many Labor speeches had been preparing for. In his policy speech in that year Calwell, now Labor leader, offered full employment within twelve months. 'The choice is between Labor's policy of protection for Australian industries and the Menzies Government's free trade policies which are drying up the springs of growth. Without Labor there can be no full employment, prosperity, development or security. Let Labor put Australia back on the rails of progress.' In the 1963 election, Calwell used most of the phrases by then seen as distinguishing competence from incompetence in economic affairs: *stop and go, credit squeeze plan, growth.*

We will plan Australia's way out of the disastrous cycle of stop and go . . . Are we to set all the energies, assets and talents of our nation to work in vigorous sustained efforts for continued, uninterrupted growth? Or are we to continue the weary round of boom and bursts that has been a characteristic of stop-go economic policies under the Menzies Government? . . . We cannot afford another credit squeeze with all its waste and hardship.

Old themes were still there too:

The Government deliberately decided to abandon the policy of full employment in an effort to cure economic troubles which were of their own creation. Cost stability was more important to them than full employment and the avoidance of the preventable misery and distress that followed unemployment and many business failures . . . The credit squeeze is the one economic weapon this Government knows how to wield, and they have wielded it three times in a decade, with disastrous results on each occasion. The credit squeeze is the weapon of people who think of the economy in terms of finance and profits, and not in terms of the employment of men and women, the production of goods and services for human use and benefit, and the progress and development of the nation.

I have quoted so many speeches because the political speech was the cultural form with the longest continuous life in expressing hatred of unemployment. Attitudes towards unemployment received no official commemoration – no statues or stamps or school history texts commemorated its struggles – and other forms of expression did not last. It is hard to think of the 1890s depression without the sacred angry phrases in the trade union journals, the black and white drawings showing the fat, greedy rich, the skinny poor, the deserving mothers pulling thin shawls across their shoulders against the cold and the protest ballads (*See the army of the rebels marching on for evermore. We are countless as the pebbles that are strewn along the shore*). It is difficult to recall the 1930s depression without the realist novels and paintings, the front line wit of Lennie Lower, the harsh photographs. But none of these forms lasted. What did last were the mouths of the politicians and union leaders, open at public meetings. So many mouths. Prime Ministers' mouths. Union secretaries' mouths. Backbenchers' mouths. Premiers' mouths. Job delegates' mouths. The mouths of great labour ideologues. The mouths of Leaders of the Opposition. Communist mouths. Jack Lang's mouth, widest of them all, showing those strong, terrifying teeth beneath the moustache. When the mouth had almost done its work there would come the great crisis moment of the speech, the reference to the dole queues, the closed factories, the evicted farmers, the hungry children. The call that it must never happen again. The audience stirs. It sees both its humanity and its predicament, and the great line that divides good from evil. But what mouth opens after Arthur Calwell's? By the time unemployment came again, the rhetoric for seeing it as the basic priority was dead.

Associated with the political speech about unemployment was another great folk creation that died as a political form with Calwell; memories of the 1930s depression. For a time many people who wrote or talked about Australia believed this to have been one of the great founding dramas of the Australian imagination, comparable to the Great War, the shocks of land settlement and other ravaging experiences. In 1945 Alan Walker, writing his book *Coaltown*, a social survey of Cessnock in the Hunter Valley, New South Wales, talked to miners who earlier, for eight years, nine years, ten years, had been 'doleys', living in tin huts or bag humpies, relying on relief work or the dole. He found 'deep pessimism' hanging 'like a thick fog over the whole town'. 'No one is confident enough to assert that the district has a future.' 'They must wait with a grim and hopeless expectation for the post-war depression which they regard as inevitable.' I would guess that it was probably somewhere in the 1950s – after the advent in suburban backyards of the Hills hoist and the electric mower but before the arrival of the barbecue and the patio – that people began to believe that perhaps there didn't have to be another depression: by 1967, in a survey of a group of electors, people of 'the Depression generation' did not appear to be distinctively different from those of other generations in their broad outlook on politics and society. Nevertheless, the Depression had been a folk nightmare of such impact that to have been alive then – even for that majority of Australians who did not lose their jobs – was to have gone through a disaster in which things seemed sharper and more 'real', with a feeling that people had shared a crucial experience together.

As in other such dramas, there were stylized scenes of the Depression that appeared to say it all or, when it was over, bring it all back. In Sydney the shanty towns of the evicted were almost instantly turned to this use – not only as symbols of failure but to the apologists as symbols of reassurance: the *Sydney Morning Herald* said the Happy Valley shanty town at La Perouse was an example of 'self help and orderly conduct', of 'complete self-government with an absence of bickering': when the Governor's wife visited it she said she had seen one little house in which she would not mind living herself. The idea of men queueing for 'susso' (sustenance) seemed to have special imaginative impact in Melbourne, as did the very word 'susso'. The image of relief workers breaking stones was a strong symbol, as were the abandoned farm, the derelict shop, the dole ticket, the packet of sewing needles or mothballs offered by the door-knocking salesman, the swaggie, hitting the track or jumping the rattler, the run on the bank, community singing, the tariff wall, the plan for recovery, the slogan, the soup kitchens.

Younger people got sick of hearing about the Depression, just as they got sick of hearing their fathers talk about the war. Within the Labor Party an obsession with unemployment, instead of being an essential element of party rhetoric, was seen by younger members as one of those old-fashioned habits that was holding the party back – 'the Depression mentality'. In the first edition of *The Lucky Country* (1964), I spoke about the Labor Party being 'petrified' in its attitudes. 'The Labor Party is a collection of memories, of how things used to appear to be.' 'The 1930s depression – a driving idea for the older men of Labor – can mean nothing to more than half the politically effective age groups.' But by the last edition (1970) these sentences had been dropped and there is a new paragraph which begins

After leading his party into its eighth successive defeat, Arthur Calwell retired. His successor, Mr Gough Whitlam, a generation younger than Calwell, gave promise for the future. He seemed to understand that not only the Labor Party, but Australia as a whole, needed a psychological reorientation, a new tone and style to make it adaptable in the modern world.

It seemed to be one of the great talents of Whitlam that he had dispersed the 'Depression mentality': it seemed as if unemployment would never be such a problem again.

When the demand for 'development' in Australia has led to extravagantly fanciful decisions, this has not been just because of the demands of the profit-makers, or the strategists who seek size and strength, or the romantics whose imagination is touched by the dream of Australia as a continent, or the men who enjoy playing with big projects, or the automata whose imaginations are limited to what they see as the economic. The consensus on 'national development' also came from the labour movement's demand for jobs. At first this was to be satisfied through land reform, then through tariff reform, then through credit reform, then by general economic growth. But some non-Labor politicians (although not those who really believed in the hygienic properties of a pool of employment) could accept much of the same aims. Jobs, growth – these two words defined a most important idea of where the centre of Australian politics might be, or at least where one of its centres might be. In this particular version of a 'centre', differences in Australian politics were defined by margins of precedence: was the emphasis 'growth and jobs' or 'jobs and growth'?

In each State, after the economic collapse of the early 1930s, the voters, as soon as they had a chance, dismissed the government in power and put the other lot in. The victory of the Liberal Country League in 1933 in South Australia and the election of Labor in 1934 in Tasmania resulted in regimes that lasted for decades. Here were two politically opposed regimes, yet on the question of jobs and growth what was the difference between them? Each was driven by demands for economic growth to provide jobs that would ensure survival, and they both went about it by way of state socialism. T. J. Mitchell, in an article in the *Australian Journal of Politics and History* suggests the prime mover in South Australia may have been J. W. Wainwright, newly appointed as Auditor-General. Wainwright's argument for encouraging employment didn't rely on humanitarian appeal, it was an accountant's argument – employment saved money: 'Given reasonable encouragement by the State, the public, traders and the press,' he wrote in 1935, 'some thousands of persons now unemployed and a burden upon the State could become again independent people with money to spend, which would bring about still more employment and prosperity to all, and more revenue to the State, less expenditure on rations and reductions in taxation.' But his methods were the same as those of supporters of 'the mixed economy' (as it was later known). In 1938 he wrote:

> In all countries individual initiative must be relied upon for the production of primary and secondary products. The part the State should take in supporting individual initiatives in primary production has been developed in detail in most countries, but the State's part in secondary production has not, except in totalitarian countries. It seems obvious that the State can combat unemployment only by the development of a sound secondary industry policy.

In Tasmania nearly a third of government revenue went into development projects. There was a special fascination in the use of the high lakes for hydro-electric schemes. In the central highlands, Hydro Electricity Commission road signs became one of the most important forms of human communication; visitors' galleries were put into the power stations and near the spillways to ensure wonder; in the language of Hydro-Electricity Commission patriotism, Tasmania was the 'All Electric Island'; incantations of success praised Tasmania's per capita electricity consumption as four times that of the mainland, three times Great Britain's, almost equal to Norway's. The lure of cheap electricity brought mineral processing plants, newsprint mills, textile mills. In South Australia the 'free enterprise' government nationalized the savings bank and the electricity utilities. The South Australian government went into the housing business, to keep rents, and therefore wages, down and it became a developer of cheaply serviced industrial sites; governments offered special credit to new industries; there were tax incentives, extensions of technical education. New industries came – metals, cars, chemicals, textiles, timber. Some of the special difficulties of the unemployment crisis of 1974-5 came from the political need to keep some of these South Australian industries going.

I will now give another, shorter selection of policy speeches and eve-of-poll pronouncements, this time from the Liberal Country League premiers of South Australia and the Labor premiers of Tasmania. In the late 1930s Premier Butler of South Australia boasted of the great reduction in unemployment ('Today 93.5 per cent of the State's trade unionists are employed . . . Could any other Government do better?'), and of his government's general concern for 'the workers on the lowest rung of the ladder'. An alkali industry was established at Port Adelaide, a blast furnace at Whyalla. 'The permanent absorption of the unemployed in private industry is the true solution.' Premier Ogilvie of Tasmania, where the State Labor Party had as a plank for some years 'Justice for Tasmania or secession with Dominion status', boasted of transmission lines, highways, 'almost unlimited mineral wealth', 'a comprehensive mining policy' and, by 1937, 'an annual production increase to a figure which was a record for the past 30 years'. By the end of the 1940s Premier Playford of South Australia, with successful campaigns behind him for 'a phenomenal growth of secondary industry' (a superphosphate industry, steel tube mills, shipbuilding yards, cotton spinning factories, cellulose mills) and 'extensive electrification of many of our country districts', boasted of 'the continuation of progressive policy' in which, with 'assured employment', factory workers had increased by 60 per cent. (He did add that individual citizens had also shown initiative and enterprise, 'qualities on which the Empire had been built'.) In Tasmania Premier Cosgrove knew that, with a 'record number of persons employed in industrial development', 'no other State had such good prospects for healthy economic development.' He displayed factory employment figures, capital investment figures, figures for the gross value of secondary industry, figures of increase in hydro-electric horsepower, positive programmes for the maintenance of full employment, heavy industrial plant. In the 1950s Playford went on speaking of 'the State's amazing industrial development': 'During the term of my Government, production per head of the population in this State has risen from the lowest in Australia to the highest' (1956): 'South Australia's unemployment rate has been consistently the lowest in the Commonwealth as a result of a policy which has stressed development' (1959); 'The development of new industries is a vital factor in maintaining full employment' (1962). Cosgrove had a similar vision of the 1950s, made up of aluminium production, the shipbuilding industry, a 25 per cent increase in population, the rayon industry, a sulphate of ammonia plant, more electric power for expanded production of zinc, newsprint, copper, carbide, cement. In 1956 he reported that in the previous financial year there were 3,789 new electricity consumers. I shall leave the last word for E. E. Reece, in his first policy speech as Premier of Tasmania in the election of 1959: 'Tasmania maintains its position as supplier of more electric power per head of population than any country in the British Commonwealth and it is second in the world.'

I went to Canberra as a diplomatic cadet in 1944. Among the lecturers in the two-year course were government officials who took time off from their departments to lecture us on marginal utility or the constitution of the Chinese Republic, or listen to our tutorial papers on Sorel's influence on fascism or the rise of nationalism in Australian literature. We soon knew that what really mattered in the administration was 'the White Paper'. Some of our lecturers were directly connected with its drafting; others were connected with people who were connected with it. Drafting the White Paper was not just a matter of words: it could seem what really mattered in Canberra under a Labor government. Men would stay up until after midnight arguing about a rumour that a particular paragraph in the White Paper was to be changed. The full draft was ready by December, but a re-drafting went on and there were six more drafts before it went to cabinet in April of the next year. There was gossip about compromises and inadequacies; when the politicians got to it and did some more re-drafting, some of its earliest supporters felt the true spirit of the White Paper had been betrayed; but after the White Paper (now entitled *Full Employment in Australia*) had been presented to parliament on 30 May 1945, as a 'unique and historic prospectus' and 'a charter of a new social order', it became magic. It no longer mattered what was in it. What was important was that it was there, like the A.N.Z.U.S. Pact which later acquired similar properties for the Liberals.

The White Paper was an official assertion that there actually could be full employment. It had taken Australia thirty-three years to follow British initiatives, begun by Lloyd George in 1911, towards providing unemployment benefits. This time there was a gap of only two and a half years in following a British initiative: the Beveridge Report in Britain had been released in November 1942; in May 1945 Australia had the White Paper. In fact the White Paper went one better: it represented a government policy and that made Australia the first country in the world to make such a commitment by such means. The government was also trying to spread the good news amongst other nations: a part of Australian diplomacy much boasted about in 1943, 1944, 1945 – at the Hot Springs conference, the Bretton Woods conference, the San Francisco conference – was its attempt to make full employment an international obligation. Perhaps the problem that Hughes had seen as the modern riddle of the sphinx was about to be solved by Australia.

If you were to put a figure on it, in the mid-1940s faith in full employment meant keeping unemployment down to no more than five per cent. This seemed impossible, or at the best remarkably difficult. 'A great deal of really terrific work will have to be done in relation to the financial and economic structure of Australia,' Menzies said in 1945, 'if we are to keep unemployment down to five per cent.' (Sixteen years later he almost lost an election because unemployment had risen above two per cent.) Even if it was possible, to some it seemed undesirable, as it was to F. W. Eggleston, author of *State Socialism in Victoria:*

When employers are actually bidding against each other for men, they realize that they cannot be sacked and that no preference can be given for skill and harder work. Under the circumstances I think it is clear that full employment actually means a definite decline in production per man.

With such a pleasurable prospect as up to nineteen workers out of twenty having a job, there was considerable use of the puritan language of self-denial. There might be full employment, but people needn't think they were going to enjoy it. It was not just a question of human happiness, but of seeing to it that everybody *worked for a living*. Nor was it a matter of meeting 'consumer wants': to maintain full employment there must be an emphasis on 'capital projects . . . projects which will not produce immediate satisfaction or enjoyment . . . To do this we must forgo expenditure on current enjoyment,' said Dr Coombs at a Political Science Summer School in 1945. 'After the war,' said Professor T. Hytten at the same summer school, 'it may be a choice not between guns and butter but between machines and butter'; Professor D. B. Copland looked to the puritanism of Russia:

> We will be seeking to devote a greater proportion of our total effort than normal to the production of capital goods, just as we did to the production of war goods . . . This was the policy pursued by Russia in the years before the war . . . As everybody knows it was done at the expense of controlling consumption and at great sacrifice, even though the standard of living of the people was slowly rising.

The phrase 'the milk bar economy' was coined as a term of contempt for the frivolous habit of merely producing what the people wanted. There was a continuing concern that while people drank their caramel malteds 'vital sectors' were being 'starved'. By this emphasis on production for production, the humane concern that people should have jobs developed into plans indistinguishable from the policies of those who pursued 'national development' for other reasons.

Supporters of the new policies were steadfast disciples of faith in economic growth, perhaps the most widespread secular faith in the world after the Second World War, affecting communist and Third World countries as well as the capitalist industrialized countries. New methods of statistical measurement had produced new goals which were at first reflected in the phrase 'national income' and then in the phrase 'gross national product'. To those concerned with human welfare as much as those concerned with national strategic strength, estimates of gross national product, usually referred to in the abbreviated (and more sacred) form, G.N.P., seemed a simple test of failure or success. To students of the importance of a confident repetition of initials, G.N.P. might seem as significant in its time as S.P.Q.R. was to the Romans and A.M.D.G. to the Christians. To the magic of letters was added the magic of numbers: human activities that by G.N.P. statistical conventions could be given a number were what mattered in life: those that couldn't be measured were not to be taken into account. They weren't part of the economy. Even among those who knew what the numbers meant, this limitation could be forgotten; laymen, whose use of the numbers could be largely incantatory didn't always know about this limitation. There were many examples of a sense of Australian failure in the 1960s when a year's

G.N.P. figures pointed in the wrong direction. I shall take my commemorative example from Arthur Calwell's book *Labor's Role in Modern Society* because it represents so many features of the Australian version of faith in economic growth.

> If one measures Australia's production performance against that of other countries with which we trade, our record is quite mediocre. Japan and Germany, both devastated by war, have doubled Australia's rate of growth . . . Per capita income has grown no faster in Australia than in the United Kingdom – a country with a particularly stagnant economy. In the world growth-tables we are well down the list. Compared with such countries as Germany, France, Italy and Japan, our record in economic growth is not fast enough.

If Adam Smith was the ideologue of free enterprise at its most unlikely, members of the new faith in a 'mixed economy' could look to the extremely lucid and convincing writings of J. M. Keynes; these made everything seem easy, for a generation and a half. In the economics course I took as a diplomatic cadet, we were run through this and that in the first year, then in second year when we sat down to Keynes's *General Theory of Employment, Interest and Money* we knew it was the main meal. Keynes's was a different rationality from Adam Smith's. It didn't find a natural rationality in events, to be discovered only if things were left alone; it looked instead for ways to impose a rationality that events might lack if left to themselves. What went on in an economy depended on what was spent by consumers, businesses and governments and it was up to governments to take the initiative and make both their own spending and that of the others more rational; to keep total spending up if consumers or businessmen cut down their spending, governments could spend more themselves and, in several different ways, encourage consumers or businesses to start spending again. It was 'the responsibility of Commonwealth and State Governments', said the White Paper, 'to provide the general framework of a full employment economy within which the operations of individuals and businesses can be carried on.' This approach pleased both old Labor hands with their belief that the panacea of cheap credit would relieve unemployment, and new university-educated men coming into government departments, who were looking for more sensible ways of running things. All it lacked was the depression it was designed for: as it turned out, by the late 1940s unemployment was down to 0.5 per cent, not 5 per cent.

Confidence grew that there wouldn't be another depression. Threat of a depression was one form of economic crisis that economists could always do something about. The tools were in the shed, waiting. Keynesian faith developed into the idea of 'fine tuning'. Economists could be imagined as being at the instruments console of an automated factory, watching indicators, making calculations, turning knobs. Taxation policy and banking policy could be moved around to meet whatever minor economic crisis turned up next. Sometimes there was a slightly uncomfortable jolt, especially when, by accident, a change of policy developed more force than was intended (like doctors, economists could cause a significant proportion of the total diseases they purported to cure) but compared with the past, fine tuning appeared to work well; or at least it didn't seem to do much harm. Among what were thought of as 'comparable countries', only Germany was significantly lower than Australia in unemployment, and few of these countries had lower rates of inflation. There was a comfortable feeling when one thought of the world that the rules of the economy were known or were there for the knowing. If things went wrong in economic policy, in the form of 'stop-go' it would be seen simply as a mistake in diagnosis: the methods were there; the government's officials would do better next time. For the Labor Party of the late 1960s the economic problem almost seemed to disappear: it was a matter of 'achieving general welfare through full employment without inflation'. The shadow Treasurer, Frank Crean, read a number of books and did a bit of writing himself: he was getting ready for the job. Then when Labor was at the instruments console, with the 1974 inflation-unemployment crisis things came apart in their hands.

By the end of the 1960s, when so many of the certainties of the rich, industrial countries began to be challenged, there had been reports in Australian newspapers of the phenomenon of 'stagflation', of inflation and slowness in economic growth happening together, a conjunction not allowed for in fine tuning. Briefly, this didn't seem to have much to do with Australia, but by 1971 Australia was quickly becoming like the rest of the rich industrial world and showed signs of 'slumpflation', of inflation and unemployment happening together. Amongst those who knew that Gough Whitlam had not caused the world economic crisis there began to grow an uncomfortable feeling, shared in all the other affluent countries that, after all, the rules of the economy were not known, or that there were some new rules but no one could find out what they were. Keynesian economics seemed busted. A substitute form of confidence had not arrived.

This was the real economic crisis that began to threaten the Whitlam government in 1974. What had happened was a crisis in faith: all over the world people seemed to be losing one economic faith without agreeing that they had found another; they didn't know what to believe next. When Whitlam realized that the old faith on which his programme of steady amelioration depended was not working, he seemed to retreat into sulks: in fact what was happening was that he was recovering from culture-shock. He was changing from a concept of inflation being primarily caused by demand (too much money chasing too few goods) to a concept of inflation being primarily caused by the push of wages and prices, which somehow had got a momentum of their own. Snedden had learned some of the language of this distinction before Whitlam did. He spoke it during the 1974 election but he was unable to talk about it as if he meant it or in a way that made people think they understood. Then for a while unemployment became the major scandal; briefly the crisis in faith seemed to ease – unemployment was a familiar problem; there were plenty of books on it, and Jim Cairns, then the Treasurer, had read them. But the crisis was still there. In 1975 there were new fashions, with great concentration on limiting the budget deficit to a sacred number and worrying about the money supply.

In the period of lost faith, I cannot believe that in terms of inflation and unemployment it made much difference whether the Labor Party or the Liberal and Country Parties governed Australia. The Liberals may have taken a different direction from Labor's but they would probably have ended in a similar situation. If one looks at inflation from the traditional view, one can see it as being, in the first place, 'imported' into Australia, in the forms of higher export incomes and higher import prices. Liberal addiction to foreign money and Country Party dislike of upvaluing the Australian currency might have heightened inflation in 1973, as Labor policies did by other means. The Liberals might then have followed Treasury advice earlier than Labor and tried to deflate in the traditional manner, but this might have produced higher unemployment earlier, with no drop in inflation, and a panic attempt to increase employment, costing just as much money as Labor's, even if some would have gone to different people. The inflation rate would then have been pushed up. The unique magnifier of inflation in Australia may have been the arbitration system, and this would have produced much the same results whoever was governing.

But the real crisis was a conceptual crisis, a crisis of intellect and faith, accompanying a collapse in the economic order of the affluent age. The system wasn't working any more. There was no longer an effective belief (one that seemed to get results) that certain kinds of events were the prime ' causes ' of inflation and that therefore they were the events to change. This loss of faith was evident throughout the capitalist industrial nations. Each of these nations seemed able to produce its own ' causes ' for reaching a situation common to all of them. With the rules apparently gone, all policies ended in unexpected distortions. Everywhere there was inflation and unemployment. The optimism of the full employment era had gone. What was needed was some way of running things in which there could be both sustenance and honour in *not* working, or at least in not working at what was thought of as a ' job ' in the Keynesian era. Instead, the phrase ' dole bludgers ' was used in 1975 and 1976 to describe the unemployed, as if there were still jobs to have, and it was their fault they didn't have them.

In an article I wrote in *Newsweek International,* I recalled how, some 900 kilometres west of Sydney, driving across the red-sand plain we saw a sign beside the road saying SUNSET STRIP. We drove off the highway along a sand track between recently planted trees and behind the trees we found a long street lined with a couple of hundred houses, tennis courts, gardens, speedboats. There was a lake for boating on one side, and a golf-course on the other. Outside the recreation hut a notice-board said SUNSET STRIP PROGRESS ASSOCIATION. A man who proved to be the oldest inhabitant explained to us that Sunset Strip, which had started eight years before, was a ' retirement area '. The economic significance of this oasis of suburban optimism in a red-sand wilderness was that its only economic activity consisted of pension and superannuation payments and unemployment-relief schemes. In that sense, it represents what some people see as a spring of optimism for the future – the notion that the affluent societies, even if they have lost the trick of maintaining conventional full employment without hyper-inflation, will find new ways, quite different from our present techniques of job creation, to maintain welfare without destroying dignity. (Not all of them necessarily government handouts: new economic forms – collectives, co-operatives, communes – might also develop.) Left, right and centre, political parties have tended to base employment and welfare policies on the expected growth of manufacturing. But it is the decline in the dynamics of manufacturing that is part of the present crisis. Perhaps we need a patriotism of not earning wages, or a new principle of sustenance such as a universal minimum income scheme. The search for a 'new Keynes', an economist who would light up some new path, may be a march in the wrong direction. It may not be economic policy we are looking for, but changes in political policy and political idealism, and in social morality – and in the structure of social and economic power. It may simply have been an oddity of history that for a while we could make a prophet out of an economist.

There is a well-known photograph of an early New South Wales labour exchange. A clerk in a stiff collar and waistcoat sits behind a dark desk. Papers are carefully arranged in piles. The applicant beside him is arranged as carefully as the papers. Opposite them, at another but smaller desk, a senior typist works at her machine. Behind her, at an appropriate-sized desk, sits a junior typist. All of it is a decorous reminder of the strong substance of the state. For a modern comparison, I walked up to the employment office at Bondi Junction. Brown flecked carpet and natural woods run together in the unobtrusive taste of a well-designed motel. Bright posters are on the walls. Fourteen unemployed men (shorts, jeans, beards) and women (mini-skirts, jeans, long skirts) are arranged so casually that even the queue looks as if they just happen to be standing there.

In both these scenes there are women – employed women, unemployed women. Yet the great secular faith of 'growth and jobs' has been one in which the image of 'jobs' has been of jobs held by men. It was *men*, money and markets that Bruce wanted for Australia's national development; it was the unemployed *man*

Hughes was concerned about. The whole mythologized view of 'the worker' is that of a man. All those clenched fists are hairy. Working women are not seen as a significant part of the economy. If they lose their jobs many women, for technical reasons are not even defined as unemployed.

Although the virtues of work are an accepted part of the faith of almost every Australian institution, nevertheless for women to work has often been seen, and still can be seen, as a social problem. At the time when girls began to prefer jobs in pickle factories to jobs as servants a rearguard action was fought by the guardians of propriety to promote the virtues of domestic service over the debilitations of factory work. The very freedoms offered to girls in factory life were seen as evil. In *Gentle Invaders*, Edna Ryan and Anne Conlon describe how in a 1911 Royal Commission in New South Wales the chairman was obsessed with the dangers of moral depravity in factories, in particular the 'pernicious influence' and possible stimulation of the sexual system that came from crowding men and women together. Even when the employment of unmarried women became more widely accepted, the employment of married women was still seen as a danger to breeding, likely to lead to the race suicide of birth control or to barrenness. Now it is presented as the problem of 'latchkey children', neglected while their mothers work.

What is most remarkable about this resistance to women working is that it has been one of the few regular public acknowledgements that women *do* work. In most other discussions about employment there is often not much sign – sometimes there is none – that there are any women there at all.

Until very recently, most women workers have come cheap. The cheapness of women's labour has been part of the profit-basis of Australian business. And, along with immigrants, they have been particularly useful in stocking some of the factories that offer the dullest jobs. For most of the period in which there have been rules about wages, women's wages could be as little as half those of men. The idea that women's wages should be three quarters those of men began to acquire reality in the late 1940s. It was not until the bold intervention of Whitlam's newly elected government in 1972 that the move towards true equal pay received unqualified government support. This was one of the many reforms introduced by Whitlam that seemed to be lost among the sensations. When historians add them up they may be so impressed that they will not write up the melodramas that occupied most people's imaginations at the time.

With an irony usual in matters of reform, this discrimination against women was, in Australia, to some extent concealed, or even made honourable, by what appeared to be a great advance in human welfare: the idea of a 'family man' or a 'living wage' sufficient to support worker, wife and family. The 'living wage' was a hoax in that it was not sufficient to support a family unit of the size predicated and that its payment was not in fact related to family size at all, being available to married men without children, and to unmarried men while it was not available to women who had dependants; if they had to support families they had to do it on a wage that might be half the 'living wage'. A more accurate name for the 'living wage' would have been 'the male wage'.

At present a large part of the traditional women's battle for equal pay seems on the way to being fully won, but there is a lot of battling ahead for women to gain equal access to the more highly paid and responsible jobs and for the moment almost no progress for the more radical idea that a man does not necessarily have to be the 'breadwinner' in a family; that this is a position he can share with his wife, or one that she might altogether take over from him. Only the success of these aspirations would finally destroy the 'maleness' of the economy. One should remember that they were aspirations developed in the Indian summer of affluence when all things could seem easy. Some of the *élan* of women's emancipation has come from the apparently ever-expanding job markets of the era when manufacturing was still working as a central dynamic. What happens if the dynamic of manufacturing is now running down? If, in the future, there is more battling for jobs, the struggle for women's rights may take forms not imagined in the 1960s.

CHAPTER THIRTEEN

Keeping up with the Machines

'Love me, love my Holden. I laid that on the line with the missus before we were spliced.' In his novel *My Love Has A Black Speed Stripe*, Henry Williams presents a narrator who works in a Holden assembly line with a 'never-ending line of car bodies forever inching out of the oven', and who tries to assemble his own life to serve the Holden Monaro that in an orgiastic moment he honoured with a V-shaped black speed stripe to match its black vinyl roof and black hub caps. In his world of air filters and oil checks, reality comes with the feel of the brake pedal; to find evil is to look under the bonnet and see a mess of dirty oil and grease; virtue comes with a bucket of warm soapy water and a big clean-up around the engine block; life develops meaning 'humming along the Pacific Highway, the big powerful gliding machine a joy to handle, the four coil suspension making it like the wheels were encased in velvet gloves, the V8 cylinder murmuring like a song beneath the bonnet.' When he watches the television series *Homicide* what he likes best are the cars:

> . . . there's usually a pretty big car chase in every episode . . . the cops, of course, are always in their Holden chasing Falcon or Valiant or Renault. One episode, I remember, when the crooks . . . tried to get away in a Mercedes Benz, but the cops in the old Holden still caught up with them.

When his wife quarrels with him for buying new hub caps instead of the dress he had promised her, he starts sleeping in the carport. ('I've always liked the smell of oil and the sight of tools lying around.') When he decides to kill her, he does it with his car. He cuts through the brake lines so that the brake fluid will spill out when the car is speeding; he weakens the steering wheel, loosens the wheel nuts and, along with two neighbours who have not paid due honour to his car, his wife is sent off in a Monaro meticulously tuned to death, but with a spotless engine block. The novel is a parable of the significance of machines to Australians.

The roads that lead into Australian capital cities would give a visitor from the Middle Ages the idea that the whole city is *en fête*; flags, symbols, signs, pennants, streamers, bright colours, all celebrate the festival of the motor car – along with caravan sale-yards, accessory stores, drive-in cinemas, motels, car sale-yards, service stations, regional shopping centres, new road systems, towaway trucks, ambulances. One machine, the internal combustion engine, is in itself enough to account for what some now see as the devastation of the cities but that until the day before yesterday most thought a democratization of them. Add to the internal combustion engines of motor cars those of diesel engines pulling trains out into the countryside, and of aircraft flying so low over the suburbs that in 1973 the threat of a new airport in Sydney was thought strong enough to affect a by-election.

And then add machines driven by electricity. One of the significant tales of modern life began when Edison, having invented the electric incandescent lamp in 1879, decided to sell electricity. He had to plan a source for the electricity, how to supply it safely to households, how to measure its consumption, how to fix lamps and turn them on and off. He studied a map of New York, chose a suitable district, designed dynamos, cables, switch boxes, fittings, sockets, wall switches, fuse boxes, meters; he bought a four-storey building and installed eight steam boilers in it with eight steam engines and eight of the dynamos he had designed; workmen dug trenches for the cable conduits. On 4 September 1882, when his generating station was brought into operation, he said 'I shall enter into competition with the gasworks.'

In Australia by that time people were already using machines in their homes: the small hand-operated lawnmower, the small hoses with their sprinklers and sprays and the more manoeuvrable wheelbarrow had changed gardening, Singer sewing machines had changed clothes-making, the new kitchen ranges had changed cooking. The age of the gadget had begun, with vegetable cutters, jelly strainers, egg beaters and other novelties; the phonograph had been invented. Now electricity was to come into people's houses and make these machines work more efficiently. Electricity was still to leave some initiatives to the gasworks – new gas machines were invented to match some of the electric machines – but electricity as well as giving power to cookers, room heaters, vacuum cleaners, irons, dish-washing and clothes-washing machines, refrigerators, was to work machines that Edison had not imagined: radio, television, cinema. It is not a hundred years since Edison lit up a neighbourhood south of Wall Street with electricity, but now it seems so ordinary that Australians should live in houses where work is done by machines that I have recalled Edison's achievement as a reminder of some of its extraordinariness. Add the machines that created city 'office life' – the typewriter, the telephone, the lift. Add the mechanization of hospitals, the cremation of corpses.

There was a steam engine in Sydney Town in 1815, used along with the windmills and watermills for flour milling: Buenos Aires did not get its first steam engine until 1845. This is one of the many significant differences between Argentina and Australia, one of the ways in which two nations with many similar geographic characteristics and apparently similar economic potential in fact developed so divergently: coming from a machine-inventing society, Australians were able to become machine-users much more easily than Argentinians. By 1845 two Australians had designed a machine to strip grain, the first of thousands of significant innovations in farm machinery that were to come from Australia, some modifications of foreign ideas, some world advances. After a rather slow, stupid start, Australia was quicker than most other countries to use new machines on farms; in other industries it was not so innovative, but it was one of the few countries where industries were mechanized with practically no social disorder, although physical disorder could come from the filth of the machines. The combination of the early speed with which machines moved into farming and their later remarkably peaceful penetration of other parts of Australian industrial life makes Australia, by the standards of such matters, one of the most successful of the 'machine civilizations'. The machine, whether Australian-invented or, more usually, derived, is one of the central cultural forms in Australia. One could write a book about Australians by writing about Australian machines.

Of course many other nations are also 'machine civilizations', but it has been the placid acceptance of the machine in Australia that has been remarkable: personal machines (motor cars and domestic equipment) can be seen as giving life much of its value, even worshipped, and for some people they provide the main part of conversation, but industrial machines are, on the whole, simply taken as part of the natural order, part of our cargo of luck. There has not been much of a cult of the industrial machine in art or rhetoric, as there was in the United States, for instance, or the Soviet Union. Industrial machines are accepted as gravely important expressions of power, but nothing to make a fuss about.

When I was a boy on holidays in Sydney one of my uncles would sometimes drive us along the Princes Highway: after the old terrace houses of Newtown (where my grandmother had lived before she married) between St Peter's railway station and the Cook's River Bridge, there was a stretch of dirty factory buildings, some with walls of galvanized iron, some wood, a few cement, all with corrugated iron roofs, and usually painted black, the paint fading and peeling. It seemed an un-Australian part of the Princes Highway; we were passing some ugly old thing left over from England, threatening our memories of a day's sunbaking and surfing at Bondi, or a picnic at the Botanic Gardens, or a day at the zoo; we didn't get back to Australia until the other side of the river when we were among the brick cottages of Arncliffe, one of the earliest of Australia's suburbs (where my grandparents moved to their first house after they left Newtown). Because it is rich in brickworks and abandoned railway workshops, some of this part of the highway still seems much as it was in the 1930s: but there are also many new buildings, more substantially built in various contemporary styles – some in cement, painted mulberry purple or cornflower blue or lime green; others in clinker brick, pale white brick, brick veneer or green-glazed tiles. They bear sensitively-designed logotypes of their trade names.

But these are only small manufactories. In the same area – next to a huge brewery that breathes out white smoke and hop fumes, a reminder of one of the first of Australia's industries, and, in its accretions, a museum of outmoded factory styles – are the twenty-six hectares where Leyland Australia's great dreams of profit were neatly set out in clean, confidently-designed buildings of metal and glass, connected by overhead bridges: all of it busted in 1974, in one of the early dramas of economic crisis, when Leyland's favourite model failed. The confident design and the twenty-six hectares are now taken over by the government as a defence store.

Large factories at their most ambitious are more often out of town where space can be wasted more cheaply: broad sweeps of grass set off rationally-planned buildings; glass-fronted administrative blocks dominate landscaped gardens; there may be a fountain set with good taste among natural rock and native shrubs; great spaces of asphalt are there for the workers' cars. The whole estate, set beside a highway, is seen as a good investment for the company's image. At what used to be the market town of Dandenong, on the outskirts of Melbourne, they still have a market (273 stalls, 'a memory', says a guide book hopefully, 'of Dandenong's origin') and for good measure a Myer store, built like a fort, with no windows. But what seems to give real meaning to Dandenong are factories put up since the Second World War, most notably the General Motors-Holden plant, next to the Heinz factory, with a monogram on the wall of one building as if it were an expensive handkerchief. Its slender, dreaming chimney stacks and glass-walled buildings, as rational as the Crystal Palace, stand as a memory of the hopes of the 1950s and 1960s. Sixty-five kilometres down the South Gippsland and Bass Highways, the G.M.H. proving-ground, its privacy protected by clumps of bush and cyclone wiring, was once seen as one of the most important of the alchemist's laboratories ensuring Australia's prosperity.

A factory is itself a machine. It is an attempt to arrange other machines together to make one big machine. Humans needed in factories also have to be arranged like machines. With about a quarter of the work force in factories (by comparison, fewer than seven per cent of employed or self-employed people work on farms, and of employees alone only about three per cent work on farms) the factory is one of the dominant work forms in Australia. Its paradox is that it both cuts down on jobs and gives people work. One of the special anxieties of economic growth was the need to pile up new factories to provide jobs because old factories, by becoming more efficient, might provide fewer jobs. Increasingly, companies were tolerated not because they provided goods but because they provided jobs; yet it was also demanded of companies that, for the sake of efficiency, they provided as few jobs as possible.

To the extent that in the national repertoire of types people are defined by what they do for a living, factories are a prime definer of Australians. Words like 'shift-worker', 'foreman', 'manager' are an important part of Australians' imaginations. Factory workers were emerging as 'types' at the end of the last century, but to give some idea of the changes since then I shall refer to two novels written about factory life – *Fact'ry 'ands*, by Edward Dyson, a collection of pieces first written for the *Bulletin* and published in 1906, and *The Unknown Industrial Prisoner*, the novel by David Ireland published in 1971.

Dyson, working from observations of 'jam, pickle, lollie and biscuit factories, shirt factories, rope works and paper mills', saw himself as an initiator who had uncovered 'true types of a pronounced Australian class not previously exploited for the purpose of the writer of popular fiction'.

> You may find my factory hands, decked in their best, patrolling the chief thoroughfares of the workingmen's suburbs on fine Saturday nights, the girls in twos and threes, the boys in small parties, the 'donahs' grimacing and giggling, the lads 'wording'em' with the laboured jocularities peculiar to their class.

With the laboured jocularities peculiar to his literary style, Dyson wrote about a small stationery factory, its floors connected by a lift worked by pulling a rope, where he portrayed a self-identifying community for whom only a few work terms were needed: *the proprietor*, *the fat ledger keeper*, *the clerk*, *the office boy*, *the town traveller*, *the packer*, *the hands*, *the foreman*, *the forewoman*, working together in a place evoked by words as simple as *the clerk's high stool*, *the packer's bench*, *the trestle table*, *the cellar*, *the paste pot*.

When David Ireland wrote about a 350-acre oil refinery he needed more words than that. He uses place-words like *locker-room*, *mobile canteen*, *control panel desk*, *amenities room*, *company bus*, *toilet facilities*, *mess hall*, *staff dining room*, *employees' car park*; notice-board words like 'Personnel to use this facility only during authorised breaks'; bosses' words like *head office*, *top company executive*, *middle management*, *Administration Block Operations Division*, *Engineers Division*, *Personnel Department*, *Industrial Relations Officer*, *Training Officer*, *memo*, *Education Officer*, *Public Relations Officer*, *expense sheet*; little people's words like *staff man, safety officers, shift superintendents, tea lady, supervisors, foremen, welders and fitters, storemen and packers, electricians, riggers, drivers, gardeners, maintenance men, day workers, shift workers, cleaners*; policy words like *job applicants, operations manning figures, pension fund, redundancy classifications, redundancy payments*.

What is most likely to be forgotten about the growth of factories in Australia is how essential to them was the flow of cheaply paid women. To Dyson, 'fact'ry 'ands' were as likely to be girls as much as boys; in the factory he writes about in his book, the forewoman and the female 'hands' were as much part of the scene as the fat ledger keeper and the paste pot. At the time he was writing, at the beginning of the century, something like a third of all factory hands were women; in the 1920s the proportion rose almost to half; in Victoria women made up almost two thirds of all the factory workers. The proportion of women workers has declined since then, but something like one in four factory workers is a woman.

The basic idea of the factory – of putting together a number of disparate machines and humans to work like one big machine – extends beyond manufacturing plants. In its rationality, office life can be seen as a factory – all those items of machinery, furniture and humanity are arranged, or are thought of as being arranged, in some reasoned order, with an idea of rational *flow*, as if the people and furniture and office machines were continuing equations. Sometimes an organizational chart is produced, making the various sections of an office look like the parts of a machine. Government departments can also be thought of as factories – great machines of people organized to produce marks on pieces of paper; so can the transport industries, the big construction industries, the mining industries. Even some education systems have factory aspects. So can farming. In this sense the majority of Australians paid wages for working are 'factory hands'.

The critical issues for the human components of such 'factories' are: *how much is individual judgement still possible?* and *how impersonal is the inert mass to which the individual belongs?* Yet much of the rhetoric of work is about 'individualism', 'risk', 'enterprise', 'independence', 'initiative', as if these were there for the asking. This is one of the greatest elements of humbug in traditional Australian economic faith. The joys of individualism and so on may be available, in theory anyway, to most Australians in their private lives, but they are appropriate only to some jobs, not all, or most. Since most Australians are, in my sense, 'factory hands', if they all began to display initiative, industry would collapse. The doctrine being preached is irrelevant to most people, but can be used to their detriment, denying the legitimacy of those things they *do* want at work: breaks in the monotony, greater companionship, more money, less work.

When Malcolm Fraser, expounding his 'philosophy' to the National Press Club in July 1975, said, 'maximum freedom from dictation and regulation is essential to self-respect and self-fulfilment', he was speaking anarchy. Put those principles into effect among ordinary wage-earners and the businesses run by his fellow-members of the Melbourne Club would go broke. To a 'factory hand', what does it mean to say 'People want self-respect above all. Without freedom there is no self-respect. They want freedom to strive and to achieve and to seek excellence?' If Australians were to take him literally when he said, 'Men gain faith in themselves and their capacity by achieving through their own efforts', Australia as we know it would fall to bits. 'Work' and 'the job' are so important in Australians' lives that if the main idealisms produced about them are inapplicable to most people, there is a crisis in morality. The necessarily factory nature of so many jobs is simply ignored.

Some of the rhetoric of salvation through hard work can also be misapplied. In 'factory' industries – I have already given the example of farming – it is cleverness that is more important than hard work. Sticking to hard work can lead rhetoricians into ludicrous confusions. Australia Day, commemorating the beginning of the colony of New South Wales in 1788, provides annual examples of this. With the Pilgrim Fathers in mind, orators try to seek examples of a Protestant work ethic that didn't exist in the 736 criminals and 211 marines who founded Australia. The *Alpine Observer*, reporting the 1975 Australia Day ceremony at Bright, in Victoria, quotes the guest speaker, Federal M.P. Mac Holten, as anxious to point out how 'hard work' is necessary to 'keep this nation in the forefront'. 'I think there is too much emphasis placed on not working in this country.' Then he did the best he could with the 736 Founding Convicts: 'On this, Australia Day, we naturally think about 1788 when the original pioneers arrived here . . . These were the people who made Australia.' The facts are that on the night before Governor Phillip's proclamation of the colony, while the sailors were getting drunk in their ships, 'some swearing, others quarrelling, others singing', on shore, in the middle of a violent thunder-storm in which five sheep and a pig were killed by lightning, the men convicts got to the women, who had landed that day, and celebrated the landing of the colony in 'debauchery and riot'. This gives poignancy to a misprint in the *Alpine Observer's* report of his speech: 'If it had not been for our forebears being so hard-working and loyal, we would not be enjoying the high standard of loving [sic] we have today.'

In a country where one of the main functions is serving machines, high prestige is attached to the energy that drives the machines, in particular, to electricity. In South Australia, the wine-making Barossa Valley is the valley most often mentioned, and every valley in Tasmania bears such individual pride that parliamentary debates can sound like a battle of the river beds, but for those Victorians who are practical-minded the valley with most prestige is the Latrobe, where Victorians make electricity. The Latrobe Valley isn't short of other boasts. 'Australia's premier highway runs through the Latrobe Valley' is one of the self-congratulations of a brochure produced by the Latrobe Valley Development Committee, and as part of West Gippsland the valley takes for its tourist promotion all that it wants from Gippsland's history of its early settlers: forests of mountain ash were ringbarked and burnt, and grass seeds sown so that by the 1890s a new landscape had been created, fit for cows; with cream separators, refrigeration and co-op factories, Australia's most prosperous dairying district was established. The butter, casein and dried milk factories of this dairying industry are still in the brochures, but the valley's significant claim to difference comes from its great store of brown coal ('the world's greatest deposits of commercially usable brown coal'). The remains of swamps of tens of millions of years ago in which branches and tree trunks slowly decayed are now sliced up and laid out as open-cut mines. 'The world's biggest open cut mine' is a huge dark-walled open space several miles long with roads zig-zagging down the terraced sides of the coal face and railway lines laid across the bottom. Tourists come to see dredges browsing on the coal. Close-up, it is soft and rubbishy-looking, like dried mud.

From this brown coal the valley is able to realize two of Victoria's richest official dreams – the progress of humanity towards electricity, and the proud independence of the State of Victoria demonstrated by self-reliance in a source of energy. The importance of brown coal in expressing Victoria's independence of New South Wales black coal is so great that its inadequacies have at times been hushed up. It is in fact a low-grade fuel, two thirds of it water, and producing electricity from it is economic only if generating plant is beside the open cut, otherwise freight rates would be too high, with trains transporting twice as much water as useful hydrocarbons. It is inferior to the brown coal of Germany, but it was only when they had ordered the boilers and started stringing out power lines from the Latrobe Valley to Melbourne that the engineers found that the coal's moisture content was almost half as much again as they had planned for. They kept quiet about this mistake, and managed to improvise an answer. The coal must be used almost as soon as it is scooped out and special techniques are necessary – it is crushed and partly dried, before being blown into a burning chamber. But these deficiencies can be made seem emotionally attractive. The State Electricity Commission booklet *Power Generation in the Latrobe Valley* says, in language similar to that used to excuse an inferior wine, 'The brown coal of the Latrobe Valley is a young, relatively soft coal . . .'

The briquettes that are made from it, by drying the coal and compressing it, have been advertised as 'Victoria's own fuel'. Briquettes are a patriotic source of energy, a reminder of how Victoria once feared depending too much on the coal miners of New South Wales. 'It seems monstrous,' said the *Morwell Advertiser* in 1888, speaking of energy supplies, 'that . . . we still continue to play second fiddle to New South Wales.' A tourist display at the Yallourn power house proclaims that 'complete reliance on brown coal resources for Victoria's solid fuel need' is 'the declared policy of the State'. When Australians still warmed their houses with fossil fuels in open fires, if people in New South Wales stared reflectively into their fires they stared at the glow of coal and coke, while Victorians stared at the glow of briquettes.

The State Electricity Commission is part of the self-consciousness of Victoria as the Hydro-Electricity Commission is of Tasmania's. But the importance of the S.E.C. and the H.E.C. is not merely in expressing independence: in both States there is also a positive love of electricity, not just because electricity is Victorian or Tasmanian, but because it is electricity. The S.E.C. brochure *Power Generation in the Latrobe Valley* begins with a small poem called 'Power from the Valley':

> Electricity . . . modern industry and our high standard
>   of living would be impossible without it.
> For continued growth, a modern industrial society is
>   dependent on an abundant and ever increasing supply
>   of economically available energy.
> Half a century ago the State Electricity Commission began to
>   develop the Latrobe Valley resources – a development
>   that was to help change Victoria from a rural to a
>   predominantly industrial community.

The Latrobe Valley power-houses are an important tourist attraction – especially for Victorians. When across the plain they see the eight high chimneys of the Hazelwood Power Station, alone in the sky, or approach the open cuts and the generating stations of Yallourn, along a black road sweeping past a splendidly imperial entrance of two huge, wide concave columns, white smoke pluming from their tops, water cascading at their bases, they are near the heartbeat of one version of what it might mean to be a Victorian. They reach this heart in a building four times as high as the one in which Edison started it all, and a quarter of a mile long: a loud demanding hum is trapped in long metal containers that are warm to the touch; behind glass windows men sit at a large semicircular instrument console. When we were there an S.E.C. guide said to a party of tourists 'It's a good day for the S.E.C. when it's wet and cold as it is now. That's when you use more electricity.'

Australia (although behind the United States and Canada) is one of the world's highest per capita energy users, consuming twenty-seven times as much per head as India. It serves its machines well. Its high use of energy makes it one of the most 'modern' of nations; it is also one of the few high energy users able to supply most of its own fossilized hydrocarbons. It was Rex Connor's love for these hydrocarbons and for other forms of energy creation that did so much political damage to Whitlam. Connor's obsession with finding basic truth in the principle of energy led him into a romantic mood that knew no politics. All the reasons he gave for wanting to raise four billion petrodollars were matters of energy: natural gas pipelines, a petrochemical plant, three uranium mining and milling plants, solar energy research, the electrification of heavy freight railway lines to save diesel fuel.

Because he liberates energy to work Australian machines is one of the reasons why *the engineer* has been such an important social type in Australia. When I was a boy there was a physical stereotype of the engineer: he had a manly face, good in all weathers, showing toughness but also the intelligence that was needed in a man who put his brains to the serious use of mastering tables, instruments, calculations; he had a clipped moustache (from the war), a pipe between his teeth, strong hands (the nails carefully pared by a penknife), well-made, sensible clothes (pencils in waistcoat pocket), stout shoes. A famous photograph shows the Victorian Electricity Commissioners at Yallourn before the battle began, the great General Monash among them, men of decision with feet firmly planted in the mud. The teaching of engineering was one of the first tertiary-level subjects to reach thoroughness. It was the engineers who made Australia hang together according to all the best modern plans, and it was they, especially in linking things up, who turned Australia into an efficient machine.

The engineers' Australia can be seen as a transmission system – a nation-factory in which the connections that make everything possible are grids of high-voltage power lines, grids of pipelines, grids of road and rail transport systems, air networks, telephone networks, a nation held together by wires and pipelines, planned by engineers, produced by immigrant navvies. Progress has been an extension of the routes of the transmission systems. Jose saw it that way in his *Short History of Australia:*

> As Macquarie's road-making had brought about the first great increase of settlement, so in these later times the extension of railways was a great factor of progress. West and south from Sydney, north from Newcastle, year by year the lines went further towards the bounds of New South Wales . . .

The 'great Zigzag' that got the railway line through narrow cuttings of dark rock, and across light-brown sandstone viaducts through the savage scenery of the Blue Mountains became 'one of the sights of the colony'.

A recent article by J. B. Hirst in the journal *Historical Studies* makes the point that Australia was first settled at the opening of the great age of modern road- and bridge-building in Britain. Australia's communications have always been good. One might argue that in many cases what has been more important than isolation is the way the parts of the nation-factory have been linked together so efficiently. Some of the colonial roads of the 1810s and 1820s were built on John Loudon Macadam's latest techniques: Mitchell's Victoria Pass, cut out of the Blue Mountains in the 1830s, was commended by Charles Darwin as 'worthy of any line of road in England'; in the 1850s it took only five years after gold was struck at Bendigo for the coach service between it and Melbourne to be running faster than coaches in Britain. Isolation of the kind known earlier in North America was not known to Australia: the great sheep and cattle rushes across the inland plains never carried the squatters beyond the world market economy. Efficient communications meant that from the start there could be highly centralized government from the capital cities. Absorbing industrial machines without much distraction was part of Australia's cargo of luck; so was the efficiency and easiness with which it maintained communication and supply lines within itself, causing distance and diversity to shrink.

Work gangs bringing new railway lines seemed irresistible, and a reasonable person might have expected that railway expansion would go on forever. When the Sydney and Melbourne lines met at Albury there was a banquet in the specially-decorated engine shed; 200 waiters and two Governors came from Melbourne and Sydney, along with 976 guests. To dramatize Albury's cosmopolitanism, the clocks on its railway station gave both Sydney time and Melbourne time. Decades later, when a new-style train was put on the Melbourne-Albury run it was called 'The Spirit of Progress'. Progressiveness could even be measured in policies towards city trams: Sydney could seem newer and better when the old 'toast rack' trams were replaced by 'corridor trams'; even newer and better when all the trams were sold as hen houses, farm sheds, holiday shacks, or just burned off, and replaced by buses. Now new styles of trams may replace the buses. At Melbourne, when a new freeway was put out to a new international airport there were some of the expectations of a country town when the railhead reached it: everything would be all right now. In the Brisbane City Hall (where there is a sign saying 'the only clock face in the Southern Hemisphere where a lift passes through the centre of the clock') they have had a show-off exhibition in the foyer exemplifying Brisbane's progress, with proclamations such as 'The Transport Department runs 635 buses which last year covered $13\frac{3}{4}$ million miles carrying $65\frac{1}{4}$ million passengers.' It was not surprising that when Rex Connor became Minerals and Energy Minister, one of his first steps towards progress was a plan to set up a national pipeline.

The idea of the factory, one of modernity's great cultural forms, rational in efficient layout of machines and in a division of labour that can be meticulous enough to force occupational idiocy on its victims, is progressive in the certainty that if rough things go in at one end unshaped, at the other end they will come out smooth, and *made*. The idea of human improvement is often related to the idea of progress in a factory: like manufactured goods, people can be processed and made better. This is the sense in which schools can be factories: the State Education Departments in Australia, in their most centralized moods, have been huge machines of buildings, techniques and trained operatives for processing rough inputs into smooth outputs. When new educational ideas developed they included new ideas of how to lay out classroom furniture – the layout of machines is the basic rationality in factory production.

Industrial managers must speak of specific targets, by which they can measure progress. Sales managers prepare marketing plans, stated in terms of objectives, strategies, sales drives, tables, charts, graphs. Plans are multilithed as reports with different sections printed in different colours for intelligent reading. Two of the great art forms of business are 'the figures' and 'the graph'. Throughout executive suites, anxious people estimate life's success in arithmetic: the idea of the falling curve in a graph is a stock symbol in illustrated jokes, as popular as the desert island used to be. There is a strong commitment to methods: there are *budgets* and *appropriations, methods engineering, work study, operations research, managerial expertise, flow patterns.*

For a while, roughly at the time when 'productivity' had become a key phrase, there was anxiety about whether Australian managers, compared with managers overseas, had enough brains to understand these organizational techniques. In a Political Science Summer School in 1957, speakers were anxious to assert the need for intelligent thinking in order that the secrets of productivity be revealed. 'More work does not raise productivity . . . Productivity-consciousness . . . is not so much a matter of hard work or longer hours as a systematic concern for the effective use of labour.' But 'Australian managers . . . in general . . . are not productivity-conscious . . . Our rate of increase in productivity over the last twenty years . . . is only about half the rate which has been maintained over the same period in the United States.' Yet 'without progressive and enlightened management we probably will not get much technological change.'

An Administrative Staff College and an Institute of Management were established; courses were introduced at universities and existing courses in the technical colleges were expanded. Management consultants set up in business. Efficient management would be found by education: 'In relation to all the nations with whom we like to compare ourselves we are the worst, or I should say the least educated', said one of the speakers at the 1957 summer school, 'Lack of adequate education, both technical and in the wider sense, is the main hindrance in Australia's development.' Shame at the small proportion of G.N.P. spent by manufacturers on research and development joined shame at the low placing of Australia in international tables of per capita expenditure on education. The very phrases bring back the aspirations of that time . . . *technology, G.N.P., per capita.*

American-owned companies were continually irritated by the inability of some of their Australian staff to get their plans the right way up. Some companies had complete drillbook procedures for preparing plans which their subsidiary companies all over the world had to follow; each stage of a plan had to go to the parent company in the United States, and be approved, or amended, before the next stage was produced. In one company I got to know, there was continuing friction because in the United States the company was running third in its market whereas in Australia it was the leader: this seemed very disorderly. It would have been more in the interests of rational world planning for the Australian subsidiary to drop to third place. In many such cases it was not just that the parent company wanted the Australian company run to suit the parent company's economic interests; it was something more than that – the parent company wanted to impose a particular rationality on the Australian company as part of its world view of what life really was. Things had to be done in a certain kind of way, for its own sake, with a kind of moral imperative.

The enthusiasts of protection had expected the spread of factories to be accompanied by 'the application of intelligence to politics'. It hasn't worked out like that. Earlier expectations of this happening seemed nonsense by the between-wars period, when for a while there was practically no use found in any field for those 'intellectual gifts' expected to 'aid and control nature'. When this changed, the dream of applying intelligence to politics was realized in ideas of national 'planning' that most irritated businessmen, at least in its 1940s expression of a total plan allocating national resources to secure maximum efficiency in achieving national goals. Enthusiasm for this ambition shrank; by the 1960s, dreams of rationality had moved to 'indicative planning', usually based on a French pattern then in fashion, although a few widely-read people preferred the Japanese model. When indicative planning was in season, Calwell explained in *Labor's Role* how simple it was: 'Once the growth-targets were worked out in the basic section of the economy similar targets would be worked out for particular sectors. The planning authorities . . . would ensure that resources of men and materials were available to meet those targets and any inconsistencies and overlapping in plans of the various sectors would be eliminated.' After consultation and discussion the preparation of such four- or five-year plans 'would provide the economy with the dynamic which it clearly lacks at present'. Indicative planning had wider support than did total planning: for a few seasons even some manufacturers talked about it, part of one of those enervating conversations in which educated Australians engage, like characters in a late nineteenth-century Russian play, endlessly discussing if they might put into operation the latest ideas from overseas – filling in the time by talking, waiting for something that didn't happen, then changing the conversation to the next big idea the foreigners had adopted, again talking about something else that wasn't going to happen.

The most generally accepted belief about the application of intelligence – and this time one that was in use, not just talked about – was the 'fine tuning' idea of the economy as a machine. The collapse of this idea is our economic crisis.

To some people progress in Australia has meant, in effect, good engineering – the preparation of apparently sensible programmes and their efficient execution, a cut-and-dried business in which technological potential is known and defines the future. Policy consists in doing what you know you can do. To work the machine you simply follow the instructions. It is through the prospect of a solution that one defines the problem. 'Issues' became those matters for which Australians had, or thought they had, an instruction sheet. It is the style of *the soluble problem*: if you have the answer, you have the question. Important matters are those for which there are apparently efficient techniques.

Such matters can often set most of the political agenda. Australians gave special value and importance to dams, generating plant, factories because they knew how to build them. In some State governments and sometimes even in Federal administrations there was little new political policy not connected, directly or at one remove, with engineering. As Marx has said 'mankind always takes up only such problems as it can solve.' Since Australia is a machine civilization, it seemed normal for most investment to go to machines and what served them. Even education policy became money for new buildings, new equipment; if questions of quality were raised they were expressed in the mechanical question of 'staff-student ratios', a measurable matter, like the exact proportions of metals to be used in making a special steel.

The 'developers' – the men who made fortunes or went broke pulling down old buildings in the cities and suburbs and putting up new ones – were perfect agents of the principle of the machine. They had splendid new technologies – some of their cranes were as tall as the buildings knocked down – so they put them into action. For a while, 'high rise' and then the building complex called a 'centre' seemed as progressive as, in its day, the Bondi corridor tram. When the first objections came, refinement was added with the ideas of 'the plaza' and 'the mall' (with re-designed 'street furniture'), and the city 'strategic plan'. But by then it was becoming fashionable to wonder if a whole part of this ripping down and putting up was not simply making things worse than they were before. Investment had gone into city development as earlier it had gone into dubious dams: the machines and the techniques were there. God had indicated his new intentions by giving Australians the mobile cement-mixer.

The idea of *the soluble problem* could be extended, because of Australia's colonial origin and its earlier veneration for everything British, to become a more general anxiety to catch up with what people were doing overseas. Policy could also consist of trying to 'follow the instructions' of what they were doing overseas. If they had worked out some new technology or some new technique of administration overseas, progress was a matter of applying the same technique in Australia. For some people, if Australia was not fully adopting overseas techniques it was 'backward'. I tried to capture this kind of sense of dissatisfaction in my book, *The Next Australia:*

> ... in the manner of an island people, Australians can lump all the rest of the world into one nation, which they call 'Overseas'. Most islanders (the Japanese, for example, or the British) basically despise 'Overseas', but in Australia it can be admired with a touching innocence. It is 'Overseas' that Australians then become expatriates from. They regret that Australia is not up to the standards of 'Overseas'; if some politician makes more of a fool of himself than usual, they ask, 'What will they think of us "Overseas?"' Having constructed Overseas out of all the nations, one then picks the eyes out of them, so that by comparison Australia becomes the Country Without Qualities, the least of them all, the world's one non-nation. They write better Overseas; look at Dostoevsky. They paint better Overseas; look at Rembrandt. They cook better Overseas; look at the Chinese. They're more liberal; look at Denmark. They're better at social services; look at Sweden. The Japanese can arrange flowers better than Australians; Filipinos are better at batik; Paraguayans are more musical. Does Australia have mosques as good as Pakistan's? Sauna baths as good as Finland's? If there is some way in which Australia seems better than most places – whether in a relaxed style between persons, or in growing wool—this becomes a fault because of its oddity. That's not what they do Overseas. The mineral boom was acceptable. They have those Overseas.

But for others, there was hope that we could match them Overseas. This helped to make Whitlam work: in his build-up to the 1972 election, he raided other countries for social and economic policies as engineers raided them for new techniques, and manufacturers for new licences. He was going to lead us out of our backwardness.

But he was, unfortunately, like the city developers and the dam builders, a man of the machine. His particular machine was his programme. He had turned it into a mystique, arguing that, 'developed between 1967 and 1971 and presented in the policy speech of 1972', it had become a mandate from the people. Once elected all he had to do was to follow the instructions.

In this reform period he was one of those 'technological liberals' who hope to solve human problems by treating government as a machine driven by the energy of economic growth. All that was required from human hands was rational and humane direction. Rationality was to come from a Petroleum and Minerals Authority, an Australian Industry Development Corporation, an Industries Assistance Commission, a National Pipeline Authority, a Trade Practices Commission, a Prices Justification Tribunal, an Interstate Commission, a Ministry of the Environment. Humanitarianism would come from universal health insurance, a National Superannuation scheme, a National Compensation scheme, an Australian Assistance Commission, a Hospitals Commission, a Preschool Commission, a Schools Commission, a Land Development Commission, a National Employment and Training scheme . . . But by the time Whitlam gave the Chifley Memorial Lecture in 1975 he admitted he was wrong in his assumption about economic growth. And no one could find a new instruction sheet.

In F. K. Crowley's *A New History of Australia,* Heather Radi says:

> He liked big projects and liked to present policies which dovetailed neatly into each other. He pursued the logic of the situation, and his analysis of problems was usually sound. But politics is not a neat business. He lacked the ability to extemporize when the ideal solution eluded him. He had no flair for reshuffling the pieces to produce new solutions. If a piece was missing he could only proceed in disregard of it . . . or niggle away at it . . . never getting the hoped-for results.

She was not writing about Gough Whitlam, but about Stanley Melbourne Bruce, the first Australian Prime Minister really to try using the government as a machine to work the economy. In the time of Bruce, engineering backed by governments flourished: the Burrinjuck, the Eildon and the Hume dams were built; railway expansion was still optimistic; Bruce gave money for State governments to be equally lavish with roads; the Riverina was expensively irrigated; Victorian brown coal was expensively turned to electricity; Western Australia established a dairying industry at disastrous cost; the policy of subsidizing exports began; Boards, Commissions and Councils were created. Bruce did not himself take all these initiatives, but he was trying to push the Australian economy along lines he saw as best for it, and State governments were of the same mood. Now when economic rationalists look for examples of thoughtless spending, they are likely to find them in the dams, closer settlement schemes, railway extensions and other bold government innovations introduced in the age of Bruce.

CHAPTER FOURTEEN

Realism and Romance

When I was thinking of writing this book, I decided to liken Australian matter-of-factness to the realist school of the nineteenth-century novel. I had in mind the general switch in nineteenth-century intellectual life which developed such regard for 'facts' that art was seen as a direct expression of a 'reality' waiting to be recorded. Novels came through as slices of life, the *real thing*, cut and dried. But when I looked up a collection of writings on realism I found that Walter Bagehot had beaten me to it. In *The English Constitution*, published more than a hundred years ago, he said that in English-speaking communities of the new world the

> prosaic turn of mind is intensified. In the American mind and in the colonial mind there is . . . a *literalness*, a tendency to say 'The facts are so and so, whatever may be thought or fancied about them' . . . [The Americans] worship visible value; obvious, undeniable, intrusive result . . . The 'new Englands' of all latitudes are bare-minded . . . as compared with the 'old' . . . The *réalisme impitoyable* which good critics find in a most characteristic part of the literature of the nineteenth century, is to be found also in its politics. An ostentatious utility must characterize its creations.

There are various qualifications one could make about this, but many aspects of Australian life seem exactly evoked by the phrases 'prosaic turn of mind', 'literalness', 'bare-minded', 'ostentatious utility', and the idea of a unique definition of 'the facts'.

'The facts' are often seen as necessarily connected with money. But as this book has suggested in several places, to insist on the importance of the economic is no guard against fancifulness. 'Realism' can produce costly and frivolous projects, even if conventional vision misses their fantastic nature because plans are put up in precise figures and are made manifest in metals and cement. The Egyptian pyramids also seemed extremely practical. They were a thoroughly researched and brilliantly engineered device for protecting the souls of dead pharaohs.

What bare-minded seekers after literalness are, in effect, affirming is not a concern for efficiency but the primacy of 'the economic'. What they want to matter in life is 'the economic', and little more. Of course in the human manner they are ambivalent, or at least mixed up and self-contradictory, but the real devotees of practicality can give a 'practical' twist to almost all their other interests. Christianity becomes associated with thrift and hard work. Sport becomes a useful nation-building discipline. Active supporters of a church can spend much of their time raising money and worrying about the maintenance of buildings. Competitive sport provides many opportunities to be practical – forming committees, raising funds, building grandstands, picking teams.

Colonial pragmatism can be thought of as Anglo-Saxon common sense, or as philistinism of the kind described by Matthew Arnold, despising anything that is not clearly part of the economic system. Bagehot saw the colonial pragmatists' prosaic turn of mind as coming from 'the struggle with the wilderness'. 'Physical difficulty is the enemy of early communities,' he said, 'and incessant conflict with it for generations leaves a mark of reality on the mind.' But conflict with wilderness didn't leave the kind of 'mark of reality' on the minds of Latin American colonists (although they were remarkable for their loot and greed). Wildernesses seemed to affect only the minds of English-speaking colonists. A quite different explanation, as presented in Manning Clark's *A History of Australia*, is that 'British philistinism' migrated to Australia, and flourished.

British philistinism (or Anglo-Saxon common sense) is never far from calculations of cost, price and income, but not just because of avarice. 'Aristocrats' and 'Continentals', to take two cartoon opposites of 'British philistines', can be even greedier about money, but without granting it such exclusive respect. They can find validity in other aspects of human existence. It is the refusal to grant validity to anything except the narrowly economic that is one of the marks of philistinism (or of Anglo-Saxon common sense).

Its devotees can even give narrowness to 'production'. In the age of growth-statistics anything which has price on it can look as if it is contributing to national growth, but the extreme production enthusiast believes that even with a price on them the arts, entertainment generally, and even more generally, the 'leisure industries', and most of the service industries do not 'really' contribute to growth. The 'real' products are the processed products of farms, forests, mines, fisheries and factories. To some the real 'product' is simply a manufactured article: what matters in life is the making of objects in factories.

James McAuley catches a domestic aspect of the dryness of the Australian imagination at the end of his poem 'Tabletalk':

> On relatives my parents were agreed:
> Too much association doesn't do,
> And doubly so with the bog-Irish breed –
> They're likely to want something out of you.
>
> On friendship too the doctrine was as cold:
> They're only making use of you you'll find;
> Prudence consists in learning to withhold
> The natural impulse of the sharing mind.
>
> What is the wisdom that a child needs most?
> Ours was distrust, a coating behind the eye
> We took in daily with the mutton roast,
> The corned-beef salad, and the shepherd's pie.

In public policies 'realism' can lead to a daily distrust – a no-bullshit approach which, as well as being stupefying, can be self-destructive. The tininess of vision with which Gough Whitlam was observed – often, shrewd eyes narrowed to see only what didn't matter – shows how dangerous shrewdness can be. When in the mood for a grand style, Whitlam wanted to crystallize changes of national consciousness so that, one view of the nation having dissolved, another would harden. It would seem 'realistic' for a rich, white man's country stuck at the end of the South-east Asian archipelago to shed the remnants of its old imperial ways and change how it saw itself, the quicker the better. But even Whitlam's own supporters were inclined to think this a lot of bullshit: no votes in it. They were wrong about the votes, but even if they were right, a less bare-brained community might think how a nation sees itself and the world to be of practical importance, since this is likely to affect its future actions and might also affect other nations' attitudes towards it. If Australia ever suffers that great catastrophe that some of its prophets take pleasure in regularly proclaiming, it might be because Australians were too shrewd.

When Matthew Arnold used the word 'philistine' he often directed it against the attitudes of the new middle classes towards the arts. The 'aristocrats' loved money as much as, or more than, the 'philistines', but they could also accept the validity of the arts. Part of the assault of the philistines on the aristocracy was to try to invalidate the arts as useless frills. There is use for that view today. Bare-minded Australians showed an agitation about government aid to the arts that was hardly matched by the amount spent in grants: what might have been at stake was their own middle-class self-esteem. It was not a crude democratic protest from the ordinary people; the significant protests came from élites. Was it because their own standards of ostentatious utility appeared challenged? Were they showing fright that some of the old 'aristocratic' uselessness might be revived, affronting standards less prosaic than those which had given them importance?

To consider how there is no necessarily 'economic' objection to the arts, take a far-fetched example: imagine that objects like petrol, cigarettes, soap and detergents, whose product differences depend almost entirely on images that come from reactions to advertising, packaging and retail display, were distributed by the government as cheaply and rationally as possible, although with a small sales tax representing part of the money at present spent on their advertising, packaging and display. The money from this tax would be used to subsidize television programmes. In economic terms, what is the difference? We would get somewhat cheaper petrol, soap and cigarettes. Television programmes would still be subsidized by the sale of consumer goods. Some people in the advertising and marketing business would have to get new jobs (perhaps they would make television programmes).

Take another far-fetched example: with a satisfactory surplus in the balance of payments, tariffs are altogether eliminated on the import of textiles and a few other products on which Australian prices are high and prices of Asian imports low. If necessary, some firms would be subsidized for strategic purposes, and the cost charged to the Defence Department. The others would go. Since the main reason for propping up these inefficient industries was to provide jobs, what policy do we have now? There might be jobs in more efficient industries, some of which might expand. But if job provision is the test, in economic terms it would make sense to charge a small tax on the cheap imports (not bringing them as high as their present price, however) and with the money subsidize art and craft activities. In economic terms what would be the difference? The same number would be getting money. Clothing and some other goods would have become cheaper. Our Asian neighbours would have found better markets in Australia.

These examples may seem ridiculous. But also ridiculous is expensively keeping people in factory jobs making objects that would cost a great deal less if imported. If our present economic crisis goes on, it might become too expensive in inflation rates to keep all these factories going. But by fiddling around with money, we might keep people 'employed' by subsidizing more arts, crafts, general education and community programmes. Australia would become something less of a money civilization and something more of a 'performing' civilization, with works of the imagination an intrinsic part of more people's lives. To continue the fantasy: the immigration programme might also be designed to suit these new purposes, encouraging greater ethnic diversity and general cross-cultural fertilization in the arts and the intellectual sphere. Instead of creating expensive manufacturing industries, art colonies, say, might be subsidized at low rates, with a per capita payment that might work out at less than present unemployment benefits.

There is nothing physically impossible about such ideas. In neutral economic terms they would make more sense than the way we move money around now. They could lower the cost of living and if enthusiasm for performance spread, the need for subsidies might dwindle.

There have been plenty of societies where people spend much of their time engaged in 'the arts'. Many of them have been aristocrats of course, dependent on a large labour force, but our machines already offer us the capacity to be aristocrats if only we had a new way of looking at machines and at each other; but performing cultures are not necessarily aristocratic, as those Australians who manage cheap excursion fare holidays in Bali discover. For that matter, in 'sport' Australia already has a performing culture.

I have put up these far-fetched ideas to dramatize certain aspects of the way Australians live. Such changes now are 'impossible' because of the many vested interests that would work against them, and because of the kinds of values and definitions of reality at present dominating Australians. But in a number of ways we already do have an art-practising civilization – in the special sense of the 'industrialization of fantasy'. The phrase is Andre Malraux's. In *Anti-Memoirs* he says 'In assimilating rationalism to the machine, the West lumped them together in opposition to what is called fantasy. Whereas in fact, in Moscow as in Chicago or Rio or Paris, our age is precisely the age of the industrialization of fantasy.' He was thinking of 'cinema, television, all the disseminating works of the imagination', the entertainment machines from which, 'our civilization gives birth to as many dreams every week as to machines in a year'. He was talking to Nehru and he drew a distinction between 'the make-believe of the Ramayana', whose values 'are the highest values in India', and 'the present day make-believe of the western masses', noting that 'the owners of the dream-factories . . . are not here to help people, but to make money'. There are 'dream-factories' in Sydney and Melbourne and the other Australian cities, and boxes pick up their messages in almost every household in Australia and for that matter in almost every motor car. If it is true of other nations it would also be true of Australia that the 'dream-factories' with the 'new cycle of blood, sex, sentimentality, politics or death', satisfy 'the instincts of the masses in a way they have never been satisfied before' and that, if in the world of the imagination 'our gods are dead, and our demons very much alive and kicking', then the people might 'become more enslaved to instincts and to elementary dreams than almost any civilization the world has ever known'.

The great profits of fantasies and their mass distribution are as much a part of Australia as of other machine civilizations; dream-factories are able to turn any aspect of existence, politics as much as fiction, into easily assimilated entertainments. There is no doubt about the historical uniqueness of such money-making, nor of its industrialized methods, although I don't know whether the result in people's minds is as unique as Malraux says. What is demonstrably unique is what he calls 'the most colossal resurrection the world has ever known' – the resuscitation of works of art from all the dead civilizations 'brought together for the first time in our own', so that for some people 'art' and 'museum' are pretty much the same thing.

I want to extend Malraux's phrase 'the industrialization of fantasy' beyond entertainment machines, to use it to cover all aspects of Australia's selling civilization: the shops, the 'products', the packages, the merchandising and advertising, all the cultural forms of modern commercial life. These works of the imagination are intrinsic to Australians' lives. The main public symbols and other public cultural forms were once those of church or state; now they are those of commerce. One stands in front of an expensive purchase with the awe our predecessors might have given to a religious object. In a department store at Christmas time one can experience the elevated intensity of mass religious hysteria. Some of our most significant images come from contemplating things we buy, or want to buy. It is for the selling of motor cars that a long metropolitan highway is allowed to go *en fête*.

Three examples. The first is an elaboration of the idea of *the fair* in commercial art-practising civilizations. Fairs are not just matters of buying and selling. There is magic about them – for most of their history they had religious connections – with a sense of special occasion and of *display*; they are proclaimers of value. When the 1851 London Exhibition created the culture form for great fairs in the industrial age, the Australian colonies almost immediately prepared their own imitations. Melbourne's Exhibition Building, in 1880 the largest structure in the city, still stands, an intact expression of Victorian grandeur if you look at it from the front, providing one of the domes on the Melbourne skyline, but at the rear vandalized with messy extensions and parking lots. Its murals announced Victoria's entry into the arena of nations with personifications of Painting, Music, Sculpture and Architecture, as well as of Manufacturing, Commerce, Agriculture, Science, Peace, Plenty, Labour, Age and Youth. The two great exhibitions held in the building before great exhibitions went out of fashion included 'useful objects', especially in the exhibits from the United States (which was criticized for it) – sewing machines, lawnmowers, automatic door-closing devices, typewriters – but many objects of art were also displayed amongst the potted ferns: marble sculptures, stained glass, jewellery, musical instruments, hundreds of paintings.

In 1974 I went to the Exhibition Building, to The *Sun* Homes Show, to find out what values were now proclaimed. It still announced progress and novelty – in 'aluminium patio covers with a difference', 'the most advanced venetian blinds', 'the modern Scandinavian eiderdown'. There was the old hope of transformation ('we'll change your old kitchen into a sparkling new kitchen in less than two days') and the coming of colour television was hailed as a new revelation. There was some sense of threat in displays of protective electronic anti-intruder systems, domestic panic buttons, laser beams with early-warning bell, but there were still the old assurances that life could be made easier – with electrically-heated, fully automatic, maintenance-free swimming pools ('manual chlorination is a thing of the past'), a compressor compacting an average week's garbage into one small disposable bag, home radio inter-communication systems, electric slippers, electric char-grill barbecues for outdoor living, electric insectorates for troublesome garden bugs; there were still the appeals to rationality – in Multicube furniture that could be arranged as room dividers or focal points or play areas or toy storage groups or relaxing corners; in Multiplan wall units; in a modular entertainment unit. There were many expressions of contemporary good taste: copper fountains (indoor and outdoor, to enhance home or business), ceramic tiles, imported pebbles, Japanese bridges and wishing wells, homemade furniture in classic style from Italy, symbolic bricks, genuine oregon beams. The clothes hoist, token of suburban banality, had become collapsible so that it could be hidden when not in use. An air-conditioning unit was promoted as 'Environmental Control'. Cocktail bars were offered in Tasman pine, colonial style; to hang behind them there were reproductions of old advertising mirrors. A brand of bricks called Settlers promised 'the old world feeling of early colonial brickwork, at the same time presenting a smart contemporary appearance'. With Bush Haven timber (specially treated pre-sawn logs) you could build your own termite-resistant log cabin.

More than 200,000 people went to this show, reacting to the images of the world it offered, its reassurances (older people could still feel young when they were addressed as 'the Electricity Generation') and its changes ('the Viking Home Sauna – the modern way to relax'). Fairs of this kind are great centres of cultural diffusion: at the kind of inter-tribal ceremonial exchanges that made up the first 'fairs' there might have been a few puzzlingly unfamiliar artefacts to wonder at but here, every year, are hundreds of new visions of the human imagination.

Not only this – the idea of the fair has been extended so that it is available any day of the week. When I was a boy the city department stores, made tall by passenger lifts, had become permanent fairs, reflecting changing cultural forms and values with an intensity that shone out into the suburbs and the country towns. They were not only fairs, they were great display monuments and along with the elaborately contrived cinemas (Sydney's State Theatre offered 'the largest and choicest assemblage of artistic treasures that has ever adorned a theatre') they seemed what mattered in the city. They were controlled by powerful families headed by knights honoured by King George, masters of politics as well as of taste; when you went into a department store you were entering a magnate's palace. Democracy also had its fairs – in bargain basements and cash-and-carries that were spreading into chain stores – and these were also centres for disseminating new artefacts and new values. (One of the important dates in Australian social history was the opening in 1914 of Coles Variety Store in Collingwood, Melbourne, with goods costing threepence, sixpence and a shilling. In 1919 Coles announced the slogan 'Nothing over two and six'. In 1924 'Woolworths stupendous Bargain Basement', offering 'the things people want at rock-bottom prices', opened in Sydney.

But now city department store fairs have also been democratized, in the suburban shopping centre: a great permanent fair is accessible not only on an occasional day in town, but locally. Another date in Australian history was the opening of Roselands, near Bankstown in Sydney, 'the biggest shopping complex in the southern hemisphere', on 13 hectares, with space for 20,000 cars, ten restaurants, more than a hundred shops, a raindrop fountain, its own Theatre Beautiful. It rises above prostrate suburban roof tops like a great mosque.

The example I shall take, however, is not Roselands but the more human-scale Miranda Fair Shoppingtown, on Sydney's southern border. I mention it because I remember the township of Miranda when two punts crossed George's River instead of two bridges.

When we used to pass it on our way to my grandfather's weekender at Yowie Bay there were only a few houses along the road, backed by scrub, and there was a general store where we might stop and buy kerosene, or condensed milk, or rope – country things. Within my lifetime this strange change has occurred: the bush has been flattened out, thousands of houses have gone up and the general store has swollen into Miranda Fair, centre of cultural diffusion in the Shire of Sutherland. When I used to walk along the bush track from Miranda to Yowie Bay, dreaming that the sticks I was treading on were death adders, the department stores of Sydney were a long bus ride and a long electric-train trip away: now four of them bulk out a large part of Miranda Fair Shoppingtown, their logotypes emblazoned on its facade as if announcing that kings were in residence. Around them, in Tudor Court, Camellia Court, and five other 'Courts' shops sell clothes under titles ranging from Speciality Knit Shoppe and The World of Fashion to The Denim Store and Marakesh Indian Gear; you can get food at the Golden Phoenix Licensed Restaurant, the Donut Hole, the Studio Coffee Lounge, the Terrace Restaurant, the Igloo Takeaway Food Service, the Gem Sandwich Bar. Among the shops, some stick to old values and label themselves plainly as chemist or jeweller, photographer or hairdresser; others proclaim new values – Sound Centre, Rings and Things, Toyworld, Girl Talk, The Fruit Bowl, Sportique, Surf Dive 'n' Ski. A tradition of an Australian sacred place is maintained – a wishing well, whose proceeds go to a local charity – but instead of throwing the coins into unhygienic water, you insert them through a slit in a wooden cover over the top of the pseudo wishing well. Along two sides of the three floors of Miranda Fair, and on its roof, empty cars stand waiting for things to be put in their boots. If a volcano arose out of Botany bay and covered Miranda Fair with ash, imagine what a Pompeii it would make.

The idea of the fair is given its greatest impetus at the shopping carnivals – the sales and the seasonal promotions or the special store promotions. At Grace Brothers, Bondi Junction, up the street from where I am writing this, they give us every few weeks a new view of the world and its values. For a while, in the display windows the dummies stand dressed in autumn clothes, surrounded by sheaves of ripened wheat, and we contemplate the virtues of fruition. Then the dummies are stripped and re-dressed more fancily as part of the celebration of the virtues of Englishness: beside them are symbols of tradition – the royal crown, the Speaker's mace, the orb and sceptre, cases of Beefeater gin. The dummies are stripped again; now they are dressed in denims: construction work signs go up around them; for a few weeks we celebrate the chic of plainness. Then the dummies are put into their warmest clothes; the bare branches and fallen leaves put around them signify winter. Before each new promotion is launched – and similar promotions are being held in all the other Grace Brothers stores – special advertisements are prepared, expressing the new theme; special display material is handed out; things are moved around inside each store to bring up the new emphasis; the store spruikers are given a new patter.

The greatest of the buying festivals, of course, are those that celebrate Father's Day, Mother's Day and, above all, Christmas Day. The festivities of Christmas Day itself are as old as feasting, present-giving, family-feeling and institutionalized benevolence: the novelty is in the preceding festival of 'Christmas shopping'. This proclaims Australians' acceptance of shopping as an essential part of the social order; it is an annual re-enactment of belief in shops, money, prices, pursued with a devotion that absorbs weeks of activity. As one of the ways of reaffirming shared priorities and a sense of purpose, it declares that money, buying and selling are necessary to family love, human benevolence and social geniality. The Festival of Christmas Shopping is the greatest of Australia's festivals as an art-practising civilization.

My second example of how to approach the industrialization of fantasy is in the world of the iconographers who design 'products' and their packaging and advertising. I was not sure which word to use. *Necromancer* is good, since there is so much magic in the summoning up of products; *astrologer* might apply to the market research people who attempt to be experts in planning and predicting. But *iconographer* seemed better. It has a sense of craftsmanship as in the making of icons; there is the same concentration on the *image*, not so much on what is, as what appears to be; and there is the same duality in the sacredness both of what is represented (the 'promise') and of the representation itself. Of course people who invent great new things – internal combustion engines, telephones, wireless – are not iconographers, but there are no longer many important inventions in household goods. Most of the basic inventing was finished before the First World War: since then it has been matters of extension, improvement or, increasingly, of looks. Most of the money that goes into designing new models of the motor cars Australians spend so much money and conversation on is spent on the creation of 'personality'. At the two great exhibitions held in the Melbourne Exhibition Buildings in 1880 and 1888, really new machines like lawnmowers or typewriters were displayed; at the 1974 *Sun* Homes Show it was more that things had been got up to look a bit different. At the best there were improvements rather than inventions. In many cases there were simply new advertising claims. It is in the arts of contriving an impression of a product that the skills of the iconographers are tested, whether in the basic product design, or in some cosmetic change, or in changes to its pack or general store presentation, or in advertising and general marketing.

An article in the *Australian Financial Review* discusses the market repositioning of lemonade: 'Throughout its summer TV campaign Cadbury-Schweppes is attempting to reposition its lemonade product as a premium quality family drink, not simply an adjunct to the flavour range. Rolling hillsides, waterfalls and soaring violins take the product well away from its former tinkling-glass aura of sophistication in an attempt to forestall the steadily declining lemonade market – now around 20 per cent and falling, with the cola market up to 35 per cent of the total soft drink market and climbing.' Research suggests lemonade has 'a pre-war image, little prestige, and is attached to values of childhood'.

Another example: a director of the S.P.A.S.M. advertising agency discusses his agency's image in the *Financial Review*: 'Melbourne has a more conservative business climate than Sydney, and the agency that flaunts itself in an arrogant and controversial manner is likely to offend more people than it attracts. So S.P.A.S.M. presents its radicalism in what it hopes is a reasonably subtle and courteous way.' The *Review* then goes on: 'Last February the agency moved into an old bakehouse in South Melbourne, a building that is deliberately designed to look like a set from *The Clockwork Orange*. The interior of the agency looks as businessmen expect agencies to look – candy pink bannister, silver ceilings, giant telephones and Mickey and Minnie Mouse instead of Ladies and Men.'

As another example, I found in my own files recommendations for the 1967 campaign for Egg Creme Shampoo, made by a copywriter in the agency for which I was then a 'Creative Director'.* This agency recommendation points out that with so many shampoos on the market, most basically the same, the question of what the product is may not be as important as the question of what it can be made to appear to be. The report goes on:

> Obviously the product that will really gain attention is the one that cuts loose from the pack; but seeing that all the products really have much the same form, how can this transition be effected? By presentation . . . and by presentation alone! A completely new form of presenting the product will cause terrific *impact* and *interest* even if only because of its uniqueness! To comply with the petulant philosophies of our young moderns we should bait them with *unique moods* intermarried with an au go go basic claim. Our suggestion is a short series of commercials based on a 'Perils of Pauline' format. This would constitute one girl caught up as a heroine in remarkable situations. She shares exciting experiences with the viewer. An all-important ribbon of humour would run tongue in cheek throughout every commercial. Of course her beautiful tresses remain immaculate throughout her hair-raising experiences.

A sample television script follows this recommendation: A girl is shampooing her hair under a safari shower set up in a sand dune: a tiny black girl in pantaloons and turban stands holding a silk cushion with mirror and brush. At the top of the dune a man in authentic 'Riff' costume is watching. Later, when the girl is dressed and brushing her shimmering long blonde tresses she sees in the mirror the Riff mounted on a camel, bearing in waving a long rifle. She nonchalantly fires her silver-plated pearl-handled revolver. Four or five Arabs tumble from their camels under a volley of fire. In the classic hip-firing pose the girl casually snaps off another two shots. Some more spectacular falls of Arabs. The Riff flicks down his cloth mask, revealing a handsome Sean Connery-type smiling

* Here and there in my novel *But What If There Are No Pelicans?* I have tried to give some impressions of advertising agency life, based on experience in one of my strangest forms of exile.

face. The girl looks up, pouts, cants her head, then very deliberately points the gun to the camera, and click-clicks knowingly on empty chambers. The little black girl rolls her eyes and shrugs her shoulders. The girl is seen riding behind the Riff on the camel as it jogs into infinity while the words say: 'Captivate the wildest characters with Egg Creme Shampoo – For girls who get around!'

Just turning over the files, to see a few of the characters summoned into life to sell products in television commercials ten years ago, I found: for a brand of ovenware, 'The mother in this film should be a Rose-Marie type. Not too young, not too old. A warm person capable of translating cold space age facts into everyday language'; for a brand of cigarettes, in an advertisement set against an outback sunrise – 'a new kind of Australian whose personality (individualistic and assured, but companionable) is surrendered only to the splendid physical presence of Australia'; for a mouthwash – 'attractive pert brunette (age 22-25), highly animated face with sexual suggestion, good strong white teeth, seen under the shower'.

In *Steppenwolf* Herman Hesse says of consumer products:

> These playthings were not mere idle trifles invented by manufacturers and dealers for the purpose of gain. They were, on the contrary, a little or, rather, a big world, authoritative and beautiful, many-sided, containing a multiplicity of things, all of which had the one and only aim of serving love, refining the senses, giving life to the dead world around us, endowing it in a magical way with new instruments of love, from powder and scent to dancing shoes, from ring to cigarette-case, from waist-buckle to hand-bag. This bag was no bag, this purse no purse, the flowers no flowers, the fan no fan. All was the plastic material of love, of magic and delight. Each was a messenger, a smuggler, a weapon, a battlecry.

In a third approach to the industrialization of fantasy, one might consider the creation of the social type represented by words like 'the consumer', 'the shopper', 'the customer' or 'the public'. In rhetoric the consumer is held sacred, but privately the necromancers usually see the consumer as the person they must conquer. Marketing can use the language of battle, with targets, campaigns, strategies. Even at their most loving the necromancers must woo the consumer with trickiness, artfulness and determined stratagems of seduction. Yet there is also the fear that the consumer's unfathomable capriciousness can still bring the whole show down – boards of directors, executives' dining rooms, expense accounts, all finished, because of the consumer. However clever the necromancers' contriving, the deceits won't work unless something is moving in people's minds that matches some of this trickiness. Many new products disappear. Ultimately all products will fail.

In the creation of the social type of 'the shopper' there are also created many ideas of 'the woman', especially of the woman as *housewife*: shopping can be seen as the distinctive female contribution to the economic life. It is as huntresses (shoppers) that women matter, mistresses of the handbag, stylists of taste for the home and in this sense upholders of the social order; or as Beverley Kingston puts it in *My Wife, My Daughter and Poor Mary Ann*, women are 'the chief consumers for a capitalist economy'; or as Anne Summers puts it in *Damned Whores and God's Police*,

> Consumerism is a function which involves mainly women. In the era of the affluent society both growth and jobs have depended on constant excitement of consumer demand: the honour is given to women of providing the largest section of that demand. In the role of goddess of the gift, women are even seen as determinants of the tastes of men and the success of whole lines of men's goods, toiletries and electric shavers for example. In the role of goddess of the family their sense of conscience and feelings of inadequacy are charted after expensive market research expeditions looking for exploitable weaknesses. In addition, of course, as goddesses of glamour they are required to change the colours, shapes, feel, smells of various parts of women's bodies and to clothe themselves in various declarations of assertion or compliance. As an auxiliary force in the honouring of the acknowledged public function of women in the economy are the women's magazines.

One reason why I have given these three examples of possible approaches to 'the industrialization of fantasy' is to suggest that it is misleading to see this life, as some critics do, as so empty and flimsy that it is about to fall apart, because it lacks the rituals and beliefs of older civilizations. On the contrary, it is ordered and filled with symbolic associations (what you think of the symbols is a different matter). And it is responsive, adaptable: fashion and change ripple through without destroying it. In fact, given their importance to the survival of commercial firms, fashion and change are essential. This life might be better described as tough and resilient.

As one example of its operation as an agent of change, consider how Australian commercialism adopted 'national' overtones in the early 1970s. When the British television crews came out in 1973 to portray 'Whitlam's new nationalism', the supreme example they found was the already-showing ocker cigarette commercials of Paul Hogan; think of the brand of bricks called Settlers at The *Sun* Homes Show and the timber for the do-it-yourself bush hut. There is such a demand for 'authentic colonial' television commercials that the Australiana Village at Wilberforce near Sydney has a set price for its services. At the time I was writing this there was a long description in the *Australian* of the shooting at Wilberforce of a commercial for a male toiletry line, 'Cobb & Co.', with its 'strong outdoor athletic and ruggedly handsome personality'. No sooner had Gough Whitlam won the 1972 election than Benson and Hedges cigarettes came out with an advertisement with this dialogue:

'You know, we'll be among the very first tourists visiting China,' I said, as the plane circled over Peking airport.

'Where shall we go?' she asked. 'When we're not having to visit communes and things, that is.'

'I personally am going to spend most of my time eating,' I said, offering her a Benson and Hedges.

'You're thinking of all those banquets they gave Nixon, I suppose.'

'I certainly am. I wonder what they'd have given an Australian president?'

'Steak and thousand-year-old eggs, probably,' she smiled.

In a different direction: consider the use of coloured people in advertisements; the change of the household cleaner from Nigger Boy to Bigger Boy.

Although both radicals and conservatives (if for different reasons) may detect effeteness, to the participants there can still seem a great vitality in the commercial art-practising civilization. Shopping can still be filled with promise. Whenever we drive back to Sydney I can feel a sense of hope when I see the first of the signs saying 'Fresh Cut Sandwiches'. What critics find is banality, which is different from effeteness. Ever since the first reactions against modern urbanism and industrialization in Europe in the nineteenth century, there has been a gap between 'high culture' and everybody else's habits and this has provided generations of intellectual despair. In Australia this sense of disturbance is sometimes made worse, on the part of those who learn culture from books, by the contemplation of what is seen as the provincialism of Australians.

What might be the real point is not just the fact that new things have happened (although part of the intellectual crisis comes from the inability of artists to absorb industrialism and suburbanism into their useful experience), but the difficulty for artists and craftsmen of integrity to find a place in the industrialization of fantasy. However great were the lies of the old religions, they usually allowed the existence of artists of great artistic faith: commercialism usually does not. It is characteristic of the kind of commercial art-practising civilization I have tried to evoke that those fashioning the artefacts or determining their fashioning are likely both to despise and to fear those for whom they are doing it: their whole morale is one of lies and bad faith. Has there ever before been an art-practising civilization based so thoroughly on distrust?

CHAPTER FIFTEEN

Workers and Bosses

At Broken Hill, beyond the Memorial oval and trotting track, the caravan park and the Gasworks oval, is the cemetery. On one of the first graves in from the gate a column rises above a tall tombstone, a globe on top, bearing the legend WORKERS OF THE WORLD UNITE. On one side of the tombstone is the heading THE RED FLAG, with the words of the first stanza of the workers' song chipped in underneath. On other sides are various tributes to Percy Brookfield, Broken Hill's greatest hero, whose body lies beneath. These eulogies suggest his memory will live with those who love honesty, truth and justice, that the elements were so mixed in him that Nature might stand up and say 'This was a man', that he was one of the giants who moulded the age, scorned by poor souls with stunted vision, that he lived the part that warms the heart and wakens manhood's pride. At the bottom of the tombstone is the line ERECTED BY THE WORKERS OF AUSTRALIA.

Brookfield's life was given greater poignancy because he had been shot dead trying to take away a gun from a Russian madman who was firing into a crowd at a South Australian railway station. His death was seen as a politically meaningful 'assassination' by the time his body lay in state in the Broken Hill Trades Hall. But his hero status derived more from his career as an independent in the New South Wales Legislative Assembly, where he held the balance of power; the year before he had helped Broken Hill unions win, after a 20-month strike, new conditions that were among the most remarkable in the world.

There was an heroic atmosphere in Broken Hill in 1921. The Trades Hall, its stocky rusticated stone front with fancy facings and a French Renaissance iron roof sticking aggressively into Sulphide Street, could seem the most confident building in town. 'The Big Strike' of 1919-20 was the last of three great battles (the others in

1892 and 1908-09) demonstrating a belief that workers were a separate class of persons, with collective values better than those of others, united against common enemies, and by this opposition defining and proving themselves. More than a generation's conflict had produced a saga of collective memories: union leaders handcuffed and shackled; police from Sydney marching down Argent Street with rifles and bayonets; mounted troopers on patrol; mine managers burned in effigy, mock graves marked with the names of shift bosses; the word 'scab' tarred on to dozens of corrugated iron fences; miners stoning a train of blacklegs; shearers burning a paddle-boat carrying strike-breakers and, in the 1909 strike, miners dynamiting installations; boycotts, pickets, meal coupons, defence committees; the disasters of lead poisoning, collapsed mine workings, underground fires, dust storms and sand drifts threatening a mean, unloved town; memories of the great labour orators, pamphleteers and organizers attracted to Broken Hill because it seemed a place where workers were coming into possession of themselves – and of triumphant mass processions. (In his book *The Rise of Broken Hill*, Geoffrey Blainey describes a mass procession marching behind a banner on which were lettered the words 'Behold, The Workers Think'.)

After the 1921 agreement, a great battle seemed won. Broken Hill saw itself as the guiding star for Australia's workers. The idea of One Big Union died – although the miners in Broken Hill still call their union the 'Industrial Workers Union of Australia (Mining Department)', as if they were waiting for all the other unions to join in – but the Barrier Industrial Council was set up ('United we stand, divided we fall') and through it all the unions in Broken Hill spoke with one remarkable voice. The president of the Barrier Council was seen as 'the uncrowned king of Broken Hill'. By threat of boycott, the Barrier Council could control prices in shops. Firms not advertising in its daily paper, which all unionists were forced to buy, could be declared black. The unions organized sickness fund committees that, with company and employee payments, provided benefits well above what governments provided. There were union-sponsored funds to improve recreation areas, holiday committees, picnic committees (the union picnic remained an important cultural form, with special oasis parks developed in the western dryness). Very largely, access to jobs was 'inherited' by those born in the town. Four times a year, on 'Badge Show Days', all unionists at Broken Hill had to wear that quarter's badge, to display good financial standing. Sometimes there were portraits of union heroes on the badges, sometimes slogans: 'Workers Unite and Win the World'; 'The Union, Your Guiding Star'; 'All for Peace. Workers Unite Against War'; 'Unity Triumphant'; . . . 'Workers! Socialize Industry!'. One of Australia's great heroic themes has been the idea of 'the working-class struggle'; it was particularly lively at Broken Hill, and in coal-mining towns north and south of Sydney, in the neighbourhoods of the docks, and in some other places where people lived and worked close to each other. In weakened and more intermittent form, it was one of the sustaining secular faiths of a large proportion of other Australians, providing an heroic sense of risk and the possibility of sacrifice in a transcendent cause, challenging the prudent, diligent and methodical outlook urged by the ideologues of the money-and-machine ethos.

The working-class movement had a sense of honour different from the 'individualism' of free enterprise. It gave individual honour to working-class heroes and martyrs (if sometimes with suspicion), but more pervasive was the group honour it gave the workers simply because they were workers. They didn't have to *earn* honour; they were born with it. They didn't have to achieve honour by hard work or enterprise, or by becoming successful in some way: by being workers, unless they were 'traitors to their class', honour was theirs for life. So, existing with varying intensities and coherence, one of the major social orders in Australia – one of the major forms of distribution of social honour – has been the group ethos of 'the working class', challenging and being challenged by other social orders, but existing in its own right – perhaps it is the real 'alternative Australia' – with its own values, styles, exemplary characters, sacred phrases and symbols, its own incentives and coercions. Despite its significance to so many people, the honour of the working class is virtually ignored in public life, but not by accident: its symbols would be too powerful an affront to what prevails. Compared with rural virtue it is presented as a sectional minority interest and while the heroism of soldiers and explorers is celebrated all over the country in marble, bronze and granite, apart from a few oddities such as Brookfield's tomb, the heroism of the worker goes without monuments; Labour Days in each State are just another holiday. But to those who see themselves as part of it, 'working-class consciousness' can become all the more real from this lack of general acceptance: a sense of opposition can sharpen belief and a sense of suppression can increase the appetite for belief in the final victory of the workers.

There was, of course, nothing unique in 'working-class consciousness' in Australia. Its development simply meant that Australia was part of the new world of money and machines. The creation of the worker as a social type was part of nineteenth-century industrialization, one of the greatest examples of how social types can be created by economic circumstance; the idea of the wage earner as such rose above all the different ways of earning a living into the abstract concept of *the worker*, which was then matched by the abstract concept of *the employer*, both abstractions made possible by a money civilization which stated a person's value precisely in terms of cash, and a machine civilization which standardized human beings.

However, accretion of the idea of 'mateship' gave Australian working-class consciousness a certain local flavour, although mateship was also extended to legends of the wartime volunteer armies. This accretion strengthened the feeling that 'the working-class movement' was the genuine Australia, the repository of true national styles and ideals. It could also extend to race and ethnic chauvinism (at Broken Hill they say, not unhappily, that they haven't got many migrants), and to sex chauvinism (once a Broken Hill woman married she had three months to stop working). Although in home life 'working class' could mean as much to a woman as to a man, in its public aspects the very term, with its economic emphasis, tended to exalt the importance of men.

Nevertheless, if purged of its sexism and ethnocentricity, there is in Australian forms of working-class consciousness some premonitions of those ideas of the 'goals of complete Australian sovereignty and abolition of obeisance' that could have a 'catalysing and liberating effect on the national life' that the poet Les Murray celebrated in the April 1976 issue of *Quadrant* when he wrote of the vernacular republic discerned as

inherent in our folk tradition, which is to say in that 'folk' Australia, part imaginary and part historical, which is the real matrix of any distinctiveness

> we possess as a nation, and which stands over against all of our establishments and colonial elites. This is the Australia of our deepest common values and identifications, the place of our quiddities and priorities and family jokes . . . It is this stratum which the Whitlam victory touched in 1972, with results that may be irreversible for all that has happened since . . . It [the vernacular republic] is the subsoil of our common life, and to live consciously outside it or in opposition to it, without expatriating oneself, is a crippling strain.

In 1958 the theme for Broken Hill's Badge Show days was 'Workers of the World Unite!' By 1968 it was 'Workers Support the Town Dental Clinic.' Even in Broken Hill, the ideal of the working-class movement as a heroic struggle for a new world gave way to hopes for getting a better cut out of the present one. By the lead bonus scheme in which anyone who worked on the line of the lead-zinc lode received part of the profits according to the world price of lead, employees became, in effect, shareholders; and, as Geoffrey Blainey has pointed out in *The Rise of Broken Hill*, through their union they had more say in the running of the company than most shareholders. When I was in Broken Hill having dinner at the Legion Club, with the poker machines clicking away, the menu offering French dishes with slightly misspelt names and the waitress explaining that she couldn't serve us the bottle of wine we had ordered because drink waiters belonged to a different union from food waitresses, we talked for a while with the president of the Barrier Industrial Council; in the course of a description of how the mine managers drank and ate at clubs like this, just like the miners, he said 'We don't have class consciousness here.'

In effect, Australians are 'working class' only to the extent that they see themselves as such. They do not act on other people's descriptions of their relation to the processes of production, but on how they themselves define themselves and the situation they are in. According to various surveys, a majority won't use the phrase 'working class' in self-description, but about 40 per cent will do so. But what do they mean by this? What priority does it have for them? Even those who think of themselves as working class can also (must also?) think of themselves in other ways.

Australia was one of the first countries to disappoint some of the hopes held for 'the workers': by the end of the nineteenth century it was being proclaimed as a 'working man's paradise', but when people from other countries came to write it up they complained about finding not the ideal toiler worthy of a statue but a 'petty suburban proprietor' sitting on his front verandah, smoking his pipe, reading his newspaper and giving his bourgeois opinions; he might begin his union's annual banquet by toasting Queen Victoria.

Another funeral. Another uncle of mine, dead in 1941 from a burst appendix his doctor had diagnosed as a stomach ache and treated with castor oil; an electrical fitter in the railway workshops at Chullora, then on the outskirts of Sydney, he cycled there every day, six miles each way, from the flimsy, scantily-furnished fibro house, where he lived with his wife and three children. He wasn't a petty suburban proprietor; he rented the house, paying the landlord every Friday. He kept a few silver coins knotted in the corner of a handkerchief and said it was his capital. He saw himself as a worker, a trade unionist, a Labor man. (He had many arguments with my grandfather, a retired railway conductor who saw himself not as a worker but as an *Australian*, and therefore an aristocrat ready to accept as equals those whose great-grandfathers had also chosen to come to New South Wales in the eighteenth century.) When my uncle was buried, there was no red flag on his coffin. Instead there was a lambskin, symbol of purity, and a sprig of rosemary, emblem of immortality; once a week, wearing his dark suit and his black bow tie he had gone off to his Lodge, travelling into the city by electric train carrying a bag holding his Masonic regalia; he had risen to be a Worshipful Master. So poor that the undertaker refused to deliver the coffin until my other uncles paid for it, he was honoured with a big Masonic funeral. To some Australians this used to be the kind of thing they meant by 'equality'.

In the successor volume to this book, I'll try to put up a detailed view of the relationship between how Australians see themselves in the economic order with the complexities of rival perceptions of social order in Australia. I'll try to link this with systems of power and put up a view of Australian political life in these terms. For the moment, I might just add that, as promptings to action, the future shape of Australians' perceptions of themselves as 'working class' is unknown. These promptings might be unlocked; they might be trapped; they might simply dissipate. Nevertheless, the idea of the working class has been one of the most powerful elements in some kinds of political change in the twentieth century. In Australia it has been particularly significant in the Labor parties, although at present they seem to be abandoning it; each of the various communist parties claims itself as the only embodiment of the true interests of the working class. At present the trade unions are the institutions where the idea of 'the working class' is most thoroughly articulated, where public expression of its existence is most steadily maintained, and where its ideals are most likely to be mocked by the inadequacies of action. The traditions of the working-class movement give legitimacy to the office-bearers of the trade unions (and they interpret these traditions variously). With the kind of irony familiar to students of change, out of the inchoate yearnings and moods of many hundreds of thousands of wage earners, out of the visions of their orators and writers and the improvisations of circumstance, certain social formations (trade unions) have arisen and set hard and the inadequacies of these social formations are excused by reference back to the magic of the old ideals that have not yet been put into practice.

At times this legitimation is little more than empty ritual. Imagine a hall with new panelling on its walls, strip lighting, new-looking chairs; some members of the New South Wales Legislative Council are on the platform, a map of Australia behind them and tough-looking microphones in front. In the hall, dinners inside them that have been paid for on expenses, conventionally-dressed men sit quietly, assenting when required. The language of the speakers is officialese: 'terminated the employment', 'an embargo on the importation of these goods', 'the organizations affected are in a position to take action','a flow-on arising from the award', 'the various instrumentalities'. In its general style the meeting could belong to any group of business people sitting in token assembly. All that was distinctive was that as a meeting of the Labor Council of New South Wales there was the ritual use of the word 'comrades' and the addressing of the chairman as 'Comrade Chair'.

In the basements of the trades halls splendid old allegorical union banners fade into dust; old working-class poems and songs are more likely to be remembered in chic wine bars than at union meetings; not many fists are still clenched in salute. But many cultural forms of unionism are still a lively part of Australian economic life: the dramas and personalities of shop committees and shop stewards; the lunchtime meetings and the stop-work meetings; the sense of involvement a unionist can have driving home from work when the secretary of his union comes on a talk-back radio session. The small number of 'activists' are kept busy by the constant obsession with 'getting the numbers' (in quiet unions for a quorum to approve the balance sheet, in a severely factionalized union to stack a meeting); the anxious counting of heads at meetings, committees, councils, conferences, congresses, executives; the great moment of settlement when the results of the postal ballots for the election of officers come in; the mythology of 'the rank and file', as important to unionists as the mythology of 'the consumer' is to the iconographers of marketing; the delights and the perils of 'apathy'. For the in-factions in a union there are the jobs – of secretary, organizer(s), research officer(s), and the (usually) part-time positions of president and other executives and committee members; the out-factions try to find their way in. The in-factions have a professionally printed union journal; the out-factions have cyclostyled leaflets. There is the necessarily aggressive and threatening tone of all union public discourse; and the tough private slang, some of it the nervous language of gangsters. Unions are one of the many institutions in the economy reinforcing its maleness: women make up nearly thirty per cent of all union members but they are likely to provide only three per cent of the delegates to an Australian Council of Trade Unions congress. For officials, there are the delights of office: the greater freedoms and more diverse satisfactions of union work compared with the tedium of a job; for some (especially communists, their sympathizers, and anti-communists), the excitements of supporting their own political faith against a rival faith; the pleasures of meddling with the machines of the Labor Party; possibilities of membership of the A.C.T.U. executive, or a Labor Council executive, or of a seat in a municipal council, perhaps a seat in parliament; the television interview, the overseas trip.

Running through it all are the rituals of the arbitration system: on the one hand the demand for ceaseless public hostility between managements and unions, in the manner of adversary legal systems, with a ritual of exaggerated claims; on the other hand, the pretences of judicial impartiality – when what is really occurring is administrative decision and the most fundamental partiality is towards the preservation of the arbitration system itself. There are the moments of face-to-face private negotiation with company managements; then the greatest of union dramas, tearing apart the ordinary with its sense of power and possible disaster: *the strike*.

In a country like Australia, the strike is one of the most important ritualized methods of combat. It is usually a safe form of violence. It is known and allowed for. Its rules are usually followed. It is similar to the limited and regulated fighting that used to mark life among some of the peoples in the islands to the north and north-east of Australia: provided one side didn't have a full victory, not many people were killed. It is a way of adjusting differences between rival groups. It is a ritual affirmation of shared identity and shared values. It can be enjoyable. If it doesn't become too serious there can be a sense of sport about it: the leaders have the thrill of the chase; their members have a few days off, with a break from routine and perhaps a certain reassurance of their importance. The unofficial strike, conducted against the union's wishes, or the executive's wishes, can add to a sense of personal dignity: the union bosses as well as the company bosses have been shown their place. At the same time, of course, the very affront to routine that can be pleasurable in a strike can also cause anxiety, and if the strike lasts too long, fear: the whole economic routine of households may be threatened. If you were standing off looking with some sense of history at a country like Australia, the routine character of the strike would be one of its distinctive characteristics.

Although Australia was early in becoming one of the most unionized of countries it took time for strikes to fit naturally into the Australian way of things. In 1840 the *Sydney Gazette* said, 'The striking menace seems to have gained ground in Australia', as if it were a new disease; for the rest of the century it still seemed a disturbing new development that might, nevertheless, be expected, later, to go away. A special sense of threat came with the Hunter Valley coal-miners' strike of 1888: the newspapers played it up as a national crisis; the government sent an artillery unit to the coalfields, with seventy men, seven officers and a field gun; sixteen strike leaders were arrested. This new treatment of strikes became normal with the big strikes of the 1890s, which were presented as the work of 'a closely knit band of criminals', 'a force of armed bandits': special constables took arms; troops intervened. In the most sensational 1890s strike, that of the Queensland shearers, when unionists set up military camps and did their drill with rival camps of police and military nearby, there were reminders of the shocks of the Paris Commune and talk of revolution and civil war. However, the 1890s strikes were so successfully smashed that there was confidence that governments and employers could now control the new disease. This confidence continued. For the first two decades of the twentieth century almost all the sensational strikes were lost because governments broke them. Government action suppressed the Victorian rail strike in 1903 and the attempts at a general strike in Queensland in 1912; in the 1909 general coal strike the government passed special laws to gaol the miners and the miners' leader was led off to prison in chains; the 1917 semi-general strike was defeated by a government full of the high spirits that came from fighting a war against the Hun. By this time the fashion for syndicalism in trade unions gave big strikes the air of an international conspiracy. After the Russian revolution, and in particular in the government battles in the 1920s against the wharfies and seamen's unions, the government presented itself as fighting to preserve the British Empire against the onslaughts of Bolshevism. Communist influence in unions later became real instead of existing mainly in politicians' rhetoric and when the communists began an adventurist thrust in 1949 to take over the labour movement from the 'reformist' Labor Party ('just as anti-Labor as Hitler and Mussolini and the Japanese imperialists'), the Labor government raided Communist Party headquarters, froze union funds, jailed seven officials and put the troops in to work the mines.

This was the last time there was such intervention. It is only since then that the normality of the strike has come to be recognized. The participants have all come to accept certain ground rules for running strikes or combating them; these now involve quite a lot of shadow play, including the use of the shadows of television; strikes become part of the personality drama of public entertainment, and the parties to them (especially the politicians) make guesses about the reactions of public opinion. But if the economic crisis continues, if people continue to fear that 'they' don't know how to run the economy any more, or if the political crisis that began in November 1975 reached another climax, the ground rules for using strikes as part of the shadow play of an industrial dispute may disappear.

A lot else may disappear. The power of unions can be questioned not only by the more conservative parties but even by many unionists, if they define themselves as 'consumers' or 'the public' rather than as 'workers'. Surveys in the mid-1970s suggested that while a majority of people accepted unions as, in principle, a good thing (only 28 per cent saw unions as bad), about a third put the main blame for inflation on union demands, something like two thirds thought unions had too much power, even more questioned compulsory unionism and 90 per cent thought there were too many strikes, most people attributing strikes not to the wishes of the workers but to the power of union officials. In Britain by the mid-1970s, left-wingers could see in the 'syndicalism' of the union leaders a threat to their own socialism; in Australia, although leftism can be associated with the unions, or with some of the unions, especially those with communist officials, there is among many Labor Party politicians considerable private distrust, even hatred, for union officials.

The possibility of challenges to the present set-up spreads much wider than discontent towards the blue-collar unions with their working-class legitimacy: it spreads to all of the organized quasi-monopolist economic groups that between them look as if they are pretty well running the place. Closest to traditional unions are the 'white-collar unions', which account for an increasing percentage of total union membership; not only clerks and shop assistants but teachers, nurses, bank clerks, even airline pilots who take home some of the country's largest salaries, use some of the tactics of the Broken Hill workers who were trying to save their comrades from death in the mines; but the secretary of the airline pilots' union is not likely to be led off to gaol in chains. The physicians and surgeons, trained at the taxpayers' expense and receiving fees that would be much less without tax-subsidized health schemes, organize with great efficiency to increase their take from the tax monies. The various farmers' organizations have been a force in politics for generations. The big business companies are in themselves great bureaucracies that make a large number of economic decisions in Australia. And just as the idea of 'the worker' developed, and became associated with the trade unions, the idea of 'the employer' and of a solidarity of employers, legitimized by the faith of 'free enterprise', also developed; federations of employers were formed, to play politics and to resist the unions. Broken Hill has the solidarity of the Mining Managers' Association facing the solidarity of the unions.

The big quasi-monopoly groups – the unions, the white-collar associations, farmers' organizations, the big companies, industry groups and employers' associations have had a great run. The whole show has been working well enough for almost all of their acts to prosper. What will happen if governments no longer feel they know how to regulate the economy? Governments got used to some relatively easy tricks in the 1950s and 1960s. What will happen to the quasi-monopolies if, as began to be feared in the 1970s, these tricks stop working? Economic policies had simplicity: governments had merely to decide overall matters – how to raise revenue, how to spend it, what interest rates and the international price of the currency should be. Apart from the settling of these overall matters the details could be left to the market, which meant, to a large extent, the quasi-monopolies of the unions, white-collar associations, farmers' organizations, big business and combinations of managements all out for their cut. Employment kept up; inflation wasn't much of a problem. What happens to the quasi-monopolies if governments find they can't leave so many matters to them any more? One tip is that we may move from the neo-Keynesian 'fine tuning' stage of the mixed economy, with its relatively easy manipulations of taxes, budgets and credit, to a stage of 'corporatism', with more detailed physical controls fixed by networks of big business, big government and big unions, and even less left to the market.

Religions, growing out of the human imagination, give authority and meaning to existence by inventing ideas about powers, supposedly present in all situations, that explain everything; rules of conduct arise for propitiating these powers, and in some religions there are rules for a more general goodness. Out of all this comes substance for people's consciences. Some people, when they see the comparative godlessness of a country like Australia, worry that the whole place may fall to bits. I don't think places fall apart like this, but for those who do, here is a suggestion: while it can't be said that in a money-and-machine civilization everything social is religious or that God is present in all human relations, there are nevertheless many people who, adopting a similar formula, believe, or want to believe, or sometimes believe, that everything social is economic or that economic factors are present in all human relations. This is equally true of the extreme capitalist and the extreme socialist: for both of them the economic explains just about everything. In Australia, utopian and apocalyptic visions are expressed in economic terms. The mystery of priesthood is attached to economic experts. The sacred texts are economic precepts. Delphic oracles develop in economic prediction; in the government and business bureaucracies there are careers for magicians and sorcerers.

In political life, in one of the biggest stages for community drama, there have been great themes other than the economic – Imperial loyalties, the cravings for Australia to be *there*, fighting wars as if the nation were a sporting team, the democracy of respectability, the aristocracy of ordinariness. But the political contest between different creeds in the general secular faith of *the economic* is one of the great morality plays of Australian life. The question of freedom, for example, for many Australians is an entirely economic debate: the followers of one creed see it as a matter of the right to pursue private profit without state interference; the followers of another creed see it as the right to a certain minimum amount of money, if necessary state-provided, without which freedom cannot exist. Matters of justice, rationality, perfectibility, natural law and others are also given exclusively economic interpretations.

Australia has seven major creeds in its national economic faith. I am not counting the monetization of so many activities and values, and the machine style, or the general faiths in national development, jobs and growth, exports. Such wider faiths are accepted by followers of the different creeds. I am imagining the creeds as forms of divisiveness within these more widely accepted general faiths. Of course the 'creeds', like creeds in orthodox religions, don't exist in individual persons in perfect form; and there can be overlapping between them.

The seven creeds of national economic faith in Australia are *furtive governmentalism*, *flagrant governmentalism*, *welfarism*, *profitism*, *individualism*, *groupism*, *ruralism*.

The essential ideas of governmentalism have already been developed in several places in this book: whatever they might say in matters of economic high faith, just about all Australian politicians and economic groups believe in strong economic support from governments. Some are proud of this faith and profess it openly. These are the *flagrant governmentalists*. *Furtive governmentalists* encourage government assistance but keep quiet about it. You could put up a case that some Country Party politicians are more governmentalist than many Labor Party members, and that anti-Labor leaders like Playford or Bruce forced more government economic initiatives than many of their opposites; there are divisions over which economic group should get the biggest slice of the cake, or whether governments should lead, or merely support, the private sector; but these are divisions within parties as much as between them; the political difference is not in what a party does, but what it says. 'Free enterprise' cultists believe in tariffs, quotas, embargoes, marketing supports, tax incentives, research, government-provided infrastructure or whatever else they might want – in a famous epigram, the Country Party is said to want to 'capitalize its profits and socialize its losses' – but while believing in government aid they also seek the honour due to individualism; they continue to speak as if they go it alone.

In giving honour to governments, the *flagrant governmentalists* can profess a simple faith in the superior goodness and/or efficiency of government that can make governments seem the one true creative source. In some this faith comes from the *élan* of expertness, particularly among government officials who think they run things better than the businessmen they see as somewhat stupid; in some it comes from seeing the government mystically, as an embodiment of the people, as if this belief had an administrative meaning; some see 'the private sector' as necessarily opposed to most Australians' interests and therefore by definition inefficient. Differences between flagrant governmentalists can be differences in loudness of assertion. Whether John Gorton was more governmentalist than his colleagues and predecessors can best be measured in decibels: he spoke more loudly and honestly about what governments do. There are differences, however, between those who believe the government should actually own and run enterprises, those who believe in government initiatives, carried out in detail by private businesses, those who believe in controlling businesses without owning them or offering initiatives, and those who believe in government support for whatever business wants to do. The question of centralism – of how active the central government should be – adds confusion: State governments can be more governmentalist than Federal governments, as South Australia and Tasmania were in the 1930s, and Queensland was before them.

Welfarism is the belief that governments should intervene with help for those whose wants are not served by the economic system. Which wants are acceptable, and which are not, is constantly disputed, but welfarism in one form or another and in varying degrees is accepted, at least publicly, by almost everyone. It is some time since the moral fibre of the nation was said to be threatened by the old age pension, although the Liberal rhetorician Jim Killen warned, in 1975, of the dangers of 'the doctrine of the soft society'. Australia was one of the first nations to introduce non-contributory old age pensions and a few other measures in which governments softened disparities in money incomes; however apart from the introduction of a basic wage adjusted to cost-of-living movements it stopped innovating, or even imitating: it fell behind most other industrialized countries, picking itself up again only with the Labor governments of the 1940s. Some Labor people used to see one of the great purposes of government as the instituting of new pension schemes, or making the existing pensions more generous. When welfare was defined more widely in the late 1960s, as the removal of all inequalities caused by economic circumstance, the idea of equality became a transcendent purpose for Labor, but it was defined so broadly that it looked as if it might burst under the strain. Apart from its scope, and frequent vagueness, there were two contrary pulls: one was from those who wanted welfare programmes for everyone – national superannuation scheme, national compensation scheme, national health scheme – on the Scandinavian pattern and in the manner of some other western European countries, and those who, on the American pattern, wished to eliminate poverty. A whole section of the programme to which Whitlam clung for a while, even when inflation was what people had become more interested in, was not a coherent policy, but a kind of contest; bits and pieces of welfare schemes put together from here and there would have competed with each other for resources if all the policies had been carried out; middle-income earners would probably have benefited most. However, at just about the time a Labor government had again taken office and had set about making Australia up-to-date in welfare programmes, as the Labor government had done in the 1940s, the world economic crisis seemed to question the very basis of the policies Australia was about to imitate.

I have already outlined a position about *profitism,* the belief in the profit motive as the spring of all prosperity: the dynamic of our economic society has not been profit, but an addiction to growth; to this consideration profit has been subsidiary. However in its full flower, profitism, romantically conjuring up an ideal world (that never existed, in Australia anyway) in which a free market acts with an intrinsic rationality, can still give some moral glamour to the rich and it can give the businessman considerable honour, to the detriment of the initiatives of scientists and technologists, inventors and innovators who made the whole show possible. And by confusing the need for revenue to exceed expenditure in business undertakings with high moral principles and exalted theories of human nature, it makes a significant contribution to the muddling of economic debate.

Profitism is usually associated with *individualism*, with the implication that the pursuit of profit and the liberty of the person are essentially linked. Thus Jim Killen in a New Year message in the *Australian:*

Surely the role for the Liberal Party in 1975 is clear. It is to proclaim its basic philosophic conviction that the importance of the individual is not diminished by the power of the State, to assert the essentials of its association – that men and women do have the right to try and fail and the right to try again and to succeed – that free enterprise is still a precious quality, and the profit motive is not something to be hidden by dust and disguise.

By using rhetoric of this kind, Liberal politicians can appear proponents of true liberty. But there is a trick to it, that I have already mentioned in an earlier chapter: initiative is a minority matter. Most Australians work in a factory civilization, and what is required of most of them at work is carefulness, stamina, punctuality, tidiness – but not initiative. If they spent their time exercising 'the right to try and fail' they would get the sack. Jim Killen may proclaim the 'basic philosophic conviction that the importance of the individual is not diminished by the power of the State', but which Liberals proclaim the basic philosophic conviction that the importance of the individual is not diminished by the power of the Factory? Those who speak of individual liberty in the context of profit often show little regard for liberty in matters of sexual morality, censorship, divorce, racism: by restricting their idea of freedom to the economic they restrict it to an area where for most Australians freedom is not possible. Of course the welfarists find counter-uses for individualism: the recent cult of equality, with 'elitist' as its operative term of abuse, was transfused with freedom rhetoric, but at times the freedom could seem a prescription for one single way of life: in schools, for instance, it could sometimes seem that equality would be obtained simply by a new conformity. In the 1940s many welfarists regularly argued that individual liberties were secondary to general economic welfare, the only true freedom. Perhaps one should suspect all freedom rhetoric from profitists or welfarists, especially if it is concerned mainly with the economic.

The secret ideal of the profitist-individualist is an obedient work force whose members speak the language of individualism without practising it; the ideal of some of the new egalitarians is people 'expressing their personality' in 'socially desirable ways'. The creed of *groupism* is practised more often than it is preached (which is unusual for a creed). An exception is what is left of working-class consciousness in the trade union movement: here there is still a professed faith that the group is greater than the individual. (What goes on in a union usually depends on the relationships between various factions of activists, conducted against a background of union apathy, but that is another matter.) Some of this union profession of groupism rubs off on to the Labor Party, at least in precept, along with vestigial memories of a sense of common humanity and some kinds of Australian folkishness. But the party's predicament is that none of this can any longer be expressed in words: 'working class' is too old-fashioned; 'brotherhood' is sexist; 'mateship' is old-fashioned and sexist: in any case since most wage-earners do not identify themselves as 'working class' (and many of those who do may be ambiguous about it), the Labor Party, wishing to appear fit to govern in the name of the majority, cannot appear to represent only a self-identified minority. Menzies, that old flatterer (and partly, also, inventor) of 'the middle class', ('the kind of people I myself represent in Parliament – salary earners, shopkeepers, skilled artisans, professional men and women, farmers, and so on . . . the middle class, more than any other, provides the intelligent ambition which is the motive power of human progress') won a great symbolic victory.

I have separated *ruralism* from groupism, because as a self-identified interest it has survived more successfully than working-class consciousness in public debate and in politics, where, without harm to legitimacy, it can be identified with a particular party; and because, compared with working-class consciousness, most people economically concerned with farming are proud to identify themselves in that way. The self-worship of the farmer and those who associate with him, and the general honour of the countryside in relation to moral virtue, 'development' and the export, have been given plenty of attention earlier in this book. Just one extra point here: ruralism is an almost perfect example of groupism successfully honouring itself in the language of individualism, while encouraging furtive governmentalism.

To list these seven creeds is to itemize some of the important formalized assertions that give much of their shape to moral codes and estimates of human potential in Australia. They give some Australians their main taste of what religious experience might be like. I have summarized them because I think that as things stand now they are all useless, and because (despite this uselessness or perhaps because of it) they are enjoying a revival. In the period of affluence, when fine tuning seemed to work and economic growth seemed a matter of following correct instructions, the various economic creeds tended to give way to the creed of *the mixed economy*. This took a bit from all the creeds. With the decline in the faith in affluence, people began to fall back on old verities. The old creeds have a comfortingly familiar savour – but now they seem mocked even by their own estimates of what is happening.

At the time of more-or-less consensus on the mixed economy, some of the most principled aspirations came together in the new ideas of 'economic rationality'. This was not the old rationality of a market allocating resources appropriate to people's wants because it was in the nature of markets to do so. It accepted that perfect markets didn't exist and assumed intelligent and humane definitions of priorities in government economic initiatives as a necessary part of the process of satisfying human needs. But given certain guidelines it also believed that in many matters the market was more rational than direct controls. In his mood of man of reason Whitlam was an economic rationalist, wishing to set up mechanisms for establishing priorities and to dismantle mechanisms that impeded markets. As man of action, ironist and fatalist, he would also rush into action without thought, confirming action's absurdity, but even if he himself had not been a principal impediment to his own rationality, events would still have led to crisis. 'Economic rationality' represented the most subtle theoretical compromise of the mixed economy era. It came too late. By then economic events had again become mysterious and opaque.

A last image. It is winter in Canberra, 1975. The annual conference of the Australasian Political Studies Association is being held at the Canberra College of Advanced Education, a palace of learning recently set up on a bleak frontier in a suburb named after S. M. Bruce. The conference theme is reform: the first thousand days of the Whitlam government. This theme was set a year before, after Whitlam had marvellously won his election against Snedden; the conference is being held at the end of the week in which parliament has been called from its winter recess to assemble in Canberra and turn back into the ordinary the passions behind the going of Jim Cairns and the fiasco of the executive minute for a four billion petrodollar loan. For a moment, in a discussion on women's rights, on the conference's second day, all still seems hopeful and reasonable. A speaker is demonstrating her argument with some graphs. The graphs don't quite suit the scale of the white screen on to which they are projected, but we see the general movement. She points to the graphs. She has proved her case. The graphs are going up. They will continue to go up.

References

Significant sections of this book are based on research into Australian political rhetoric undertaken when I was a Research Fellow at the University of New South Wales. After some contradictory tugging of consciousnesses, I have decided not to give source references to this material. It would require hundreds of footnotes and for almost all readers, it would add little to the book except cost. If anyone wishes to raise any question with me privately, please write care of the School of Political Science, University of New South Wales.

Other large sections of the book are based on direct notebook-and-pencil observations made on several different journeys to various parts of Australia in the last few years. The reader can assume that almost every description written comes from this source. In some cases, what is said may be out of date – some country-town espresso bar may have whitewashed its clinker brick – but this doesn't matter. The present tense of the descriptive writing could be thought of as extending over the first half of the 1970s.

Having decided not to footnote my own researches, I decided not to put in footnotes referring to secondary sources where they are related to matters of fairly common knowledge. I feel bound, however, to make the following acknowledgements.

CHAPTER TWO
The Looters and 'The Producers'

On the idea of Australia as an export country: J. W. McCarty, 'Australia as a Region of Recent Settlement in the Nineteenth Century', *Australian Economic History Review*, vol. xiii, no. 2, 1973 and 'The Staple Approach in Australian Economic History',

Business Archives and History, vol. iv, no. 1, 1964; J. V. Levin, *The Export Economies,* Harvard University Press, 1960.

On introduced pests: Eric C. Rolls, *They All Ran Wild,* Angus and Robertson, 1969.

Two regional studies: Bobbie Hardie, *West of the Darling,* Jacaranda Press, 1969; and Louise Tiffany Daley, *Men and a River: Richmond River District, 1828-1895,* Melbourne University Press, 1966.

On the trade diversion episode: Herbert Burton, 'The Trade Diversion Episode of the Thirties', *Australian Outlook,* vol. xxii, no. 1, 1968.

On Aborigines: Geoffrey Dutton, *White on Black,* Macmillan, 1974; and C. D. Rowley, *The Destruction of Aboriginal Society,* A.N.U. Press, 1970.

On whaling etc.: Geoffrey Blainey, *The Tyranny of Distance,* Sun Books, 1966.

CHAPTER THREE
Money Made Us

Some of the approach to money is reminiscent of Veblen, Simmel and H. D. Duncan. The relation to Galbraith of the concluding part of the chapter is obvious. Stretton's excellent summary of the G.N.P. obsession is in the first two chapters of his *Housing and Government. 1974 Boyer Lectures,* Australian Broadcasting Commission, 1974.

In references to women, both here and in later chapters, I have especially drawn on Beverley Kingston, *My Wife, My Daughter and Poor Mary Ann,* Nelson, 1975; Jan Mercer (ed.), *The Other Half: Women in Australian Society,* Penguin, 1975; Edna Ryan and Anne Conlon, *Gentle Invaders: Australian Women at Work,* Nelson, 1975; and Anne Summers, *Damned Whores and God's Police: The Colonization of Women in Australia,* Penguin, 1975.

CHAPTER FOUR
The 'New Nationalism' of Minerals

Geoffrey Blainey, *The Rush That Never Ended,* Melbourne University Press, 1969. Also his *The Rise of Broken Hill* (1968), *Mines in the Spinifex* (1960) and *The Peaks of Lyell* (1967).

For local histories: J. Colin Angus and Harley W. Foster, *The Ovens Valley,* Cypress Books, 1970; Jan Neil, *Bendigo,* Mullaya, 1973; Harley W. Foster, *The Central Goldfields,* Cypress Books, 1973; Kay Robertson, *Myrtleford,* Rigby, 1973; Raymond Paull, *Old Walhalla: Portrait of a Gold Town,* Melbourne University Press, 1963.

CHAPTER FIVE
The Fall of the 'Pure Merinos'

Regional histories: Margaret Kiddle, *Men of Yesterday: A Social History of the Western District of Victoria, 1834-1890,* Melbourne University Press, 1961; Ian Wynd, *Geelong the Pivot,* Cypress Books, 1971; G. L. Buxton, *The Riverina, 1861-1891: An Australian Regional Study,* Melbourne University Press, 1967.

CHAPTER SIX
Standards of Civilized Excellence

South Australian expansion: D. W. Meinig, *On the Margins of the Good Earth: The South Australian Wheat Frontier, 1869-1884,* Rigby, 1970.

Agricultural machinery: Frances Wheelhouse, *Digging Stick to Rotary Hoe: Men and Machines in Rural Australia,* Cassell, 1966.

C.S.I.R.O.: George Currie and John Graham, *The Origin of C.S.I.R.O.: Science and the Commonwealth Government, 1901-1926,* C.S.I.R.O., 1966; Rohan Rivett, *David Rivett, Fighter for Australian Science,* Rivett, 1972; D. E. Tribe, 'Rural Science: Achievements, Failures and Future', A. J. McIntyre, 'The Farmers' Dilemma' and G. Garside, 'Energy from Photosynthetic Materials', in Search, vol. vi, no. 6, 1975; S. C. Hill, P. J. Fensham and I. B. Howden, 'The Education of Ph.D. Scientists in Australia and its Implications for their Employment' and D. R. Stranks, 'The University Scene: Views from on Top, from the Side and from Below', in Australian Academy of Science, *Science and Industry Forum,* 1973; Australian Academy of Science, *Science and Industry Forum. Report No. 5: The Influence of Research and Development on Economic Growth,* 1972.

CHAPTER SEVEN
The Disputed Honour of the Farmer

Books by Buxton (see Chapter Five), Meinig and Wheelhouse (see Chapter Six).

B. D. Graham, *The Formation of the Australian Country Parties,* A.N.U. Press, 1966; D. Aitken, *The Country Party in New South Wales: A Study of Organisation and Survival,* A.N.U. Press, 1972; Ulrich Ellis, *A History of the Australian Country Party,* Melbourne University Press, 1963.

On the disputed honour of farmers: A. D. Hope, 'Steele Rudd and Henry Lawson' and A. A. Phillips, 'Barbara Baynton and the Dissidence of the Nineties', in C. Wallace-Crabbe (ed.), *The Australian Nationalists,* Oxford University Press, 1971.

CHAPTER NINE
The Mysteries of Water

B. R. Davidson, *Australia Wet or Dry?,* Melbourne University Press, 1969; Lionel Wigmore, *Struggle for the Snowy: The Background of the Snowy Mountains Scheme,* Oxford University Press, 1968.

CHAPTER ELEVEN
The Civilizing Virtues of Manufacturing

The first of the two paragraphs on Geelong is based on Ian Wynd, *Geelong the Pivot,* Cypress Books, 1971.

For the mysteries of what I have meant by the phrase 'the lucky country', see *The Lucky Country,* Penguin, rev. edn, 1971; *The Next Australia,* Angus and Robertson, 1970; *The Australian People,* Angus and Robertson, 1972; *Death of The Lucky Country,* Penguin, 1976.

CHAPTER TWELVE
The Secular Faith of 'Growth and Jobs'

On the depression: G. D. Cooksey (ed.), *The Great Depression in Australia,* Labour History no. 17, Australian Society for the Study of Labour History, Canberra, 1970; and L. J. Louis and Ian Turner (eds.), *The Depression of the 1930s,* Cassell, 1968.

CHAPTER THIRTEEN
Keeping up with the Machines

On the development of the Victorian brown coal industry: Cecil Edwards, *Brown Power,* State Electricity Commission of Victoria, Melbourne, 1969; and A. D. Spaull, 'The Rise of the Victorian Briquette Industry, 1895-1935', *Australian Economic History,* vol. ix, no. 1, March 1967.

CHAPTER FIFTEEN
Workers and Bosses

On the history of Broken Hill: Geoffrey Blainey, *The Rise of Broken Hill,* Macmillan, 1968. On trades unions generally: Robin Gollan, *The Coalminers of New South Wales,* Melbourne University Press, 1963; and *Radical and Working Class Politics,* Melbourne University Press, 1960; Ross M. Martin, *Trade Unions in Australia,* Penguin, 1975; Ian Turner, *Industrial Labour and Politics,* A.N.U. Press, 1965.

Readers of Simmel's *The Web of Group Affiliations* will see its influence in a couple of paragraphs.

Other references

Other references to books or articles are made directly in the text.

Index